MANIACAL FANATICISM

IMAMU TOMLINSON, MD, MBA

MANIACAL FANATICISM

SUCCESS *SLIGHTLY DIFFERENT*

Advantage | Books

Published by Advantage Books, Charleston, South Carolina.
An imprint of Advantage Media.

Printed in the United States of America.

10 9 8 7 6 5 4 3 2 1

ISBN: 979-8-89188-267-6 (Paperback)
ISBN: 979-8-89188-268-3 (eBook)

First edition independently published in November 2022
under ISBN-13: 9-798-36133-521-3.

Library of Congress Control Number: 2025920597

Cover design by Lance Buckley.
Layout design by Megan Elger.

09-29-2025 1:46

We are who we are, because they were who they were ...

Dedicated to Zenna, Michael Sr., Adriana, and Jasmine.

CONTENTS

FROM WITHIN
ACCELERATORS
HAPPINESS COMES
WHAT DO YOU FEEL
ASSESSMENT
LUCKY
SUPERSTAR
ALTERATION
ACCEPTANCE
MOTIVATION
MANIACAL
FANATICISM
INERTIA
OBSTACLES
INWARD
HIDDEN
SUCCESS
FOUNDATION
VALUES
FLYWHEEL
FOCUS
SUCCESS
BLAME
CAPACIBILITY
PIVOT
OUTCHECK
FUTILITY
THRESHOLD
DON'T SWEAT THE SMALL STUFF
SUPER TRUST
HERO
YOUR
FAULT
CHECKMATE
NO EXCUSES
NO EXPLANATIONS
BETTER LUCKY THAN GOOD
POISE
PAST PERFORMANCE
FUTURE SUCCESS
CIRCUMSTANCE
PERFECT SITUATION
SUCCESSOLOGY
MANIACAL FANATICISM BEST
SUCCESS PERSISTENCE
CONSISTENCY
SYNERGY

PROLOGUE

For better or worse, I have been cursed with a compulsion to seek out what the world would look like if we did things differently. And this predilection laid the foundation for almost everything I do, and especially everything I write. I consider myself an optimist. I don't fundamentally believe that most things in the world are wrong. I simply believe that almost everything in the world could be right—if we stop for a second to rethink what we believe we know.

Maniacal Fanaticism—the hardy seed for my second book, Less Than One Percent—was planted in the chaos of fevered intensity, rather than the calm of careful introspection. *Maniacal Fanaticism* isn't a gentle contemplation. It's a declaration of war—a war on mediocrity, on the things that are easy, and on the perilous comfort of doing "just enough." It's an attempt to unearth those unrelenting and sometimes indescribable forces that drive people to chase something larger than themselves—even if it comes at great cost.

And yet, as I penned its last page, I found myself staring into a more illuminating truth: the margin between those who "almost" and those who "do" is smaller than anyone cares to admit. That difference lives in fractions, in improbable odds, and in moments that are difficult to predict. That margin is less than one percent.

If *Maniacal Fanaticism* is my hypothesis for rejecting complacency, *Less Than One Percent* is the laboratory where the real alchemy begins. Both books sprouted from the same premise: that our capacity for reinvention and breakthrough lies not in our individual architecture, but in the near-obsessive pursuit of better. Together, they challenge us to live with purpose, attempt audacious things, and revel in the sliver of space where the improbable becomes inevitable.

To put it another way, *Maniacal Fanaticism* is about lighting the fire; *Less Than One Percent* is about those who dare to walk through it. And both are about understanding that success isn't achieved by intensity alone, but by mastering the microcosm between triumph and catastrophe.

So read these words as both prologue and confession: the real work is in finding the narrow path through the chaos, where what was otherwise impossible is just the beginning of something infinitely greater. I haven't totally figured it out, but I invite you to go on this uncommon journey with me.

– IMAMU TOMLINSON

FROM WITHIN
ACCELERATOR
WHAT DO YOU FEEL
HAPPINESS
COMES
ASSESSMENT
SUPERSTAR
LUCKY
ALTERATION
ACCEPTANCE
MOTIVATION
MANIACAL
INERTIA
FANATICISM
OBSTACLES
INWARD
HIDDEN
SUCCESS
FOUNDATION
VALUES
FLYWHEEL
FOCUS
SUCCESS
GOALS
EVIDENCE
BLAME
GUTCHECK
FUTILITY
THRESHOLD
SWEAT THE SMALL
SUPER TRUST
HERO
PROMISE
YOUR
FAULT
ALWAYS
GAME DAY
DENIAL
CHECKMATE
AXIOM
NO EXCUSES
NO EXPLANATIONS
BETTER LUCKY THAN GOOD
POISE
PAST PERFORMANCE
FUTURE SUCCESS
CIRCUMSTANCE
PERFECT SITUATION
SUCCESSOLOGY
MANIACAL FANATICISM BEST
PIVOT
PERSISTENCE
ACCOUNTABLE

BOOK 1
VIDERE

"SEE ONE"

FROM WITHIN
HUMBLE
ACCELERATORS
HAPPINESS COMES
FEEL
WHAT DO YOU
ASSESSMENT
SUPERSTAR
LUCKY
ALTERATION
ACCEPTANCE
MOTIVATION
MANIACAL
INERTIA
LOFTY
FANATICISM
OBSTACLES
INWARD
HIDDEN
M
SUCCESS
FOUNDATION
R
VALUES
FLYWHEEL
FOCUS
SUCCESS
BLAME
GUTCHECK
FUTILITY
THRESHOLD
SWEAT THE SMALL
SUPER HERO
TRUST
PROMISE
FAULT
YOUR
CHECKMATE
NO EXCUSES
NO EXPLANATIONS
BETTER LUCKY THAN GOOD
POISE
PAST PERFORMANCE
FUTURE SUCCESS
CIRCUMSTANCE
PERFECT SITUATION
SUCCESSOLOGY
MANIACAL FANATICISM BEST
PIVOT
CAPABILITY
MEMORY

CHAPTER I

SUCCESS

"That some achieve great success, is proof to all that others can achieve it as well."

– ABRAHAM LINCOLN

The 1982 NCAA Division 1 College Championship game, between the North Carolina Tar Heels and the Georgetown Hoyas, was an instant classic. The game was high speed, high energy, and vigorously contested. It was the kind of game where neither team was able to get the upper hand for very long. North Carolina was the number one seed in the East Region. Likewise, Georgetown was the number one seed in the West Region. This game had it all: two storied college basketball programs, two veteran and enigmatic coaches, and four of the best college basketball players in history.

The coaches, Georgetown's John Thompson and North Carolina's Dean Smith, were both considered the best of their time and would go on to be coaching legends. Georgetown featured young Jamaican-born defensive powerhouse Patrick Ewing at center and Eric "Sleepy" Floyd at guard. Future National Championship Most Valuable Player James Worthy and a young Michael Jordan led North Carolina's potent offense. This back-and-forth contest had fifteen lead changes. With a minute left, Eric "Sleepy" Floyd hit a jumper to put the Hoyas up by one. North Carolina called a time out. The Tar Heels drove down the court. After several passes, they worked the ball to Michael Jordan on the left side of the court. With seventeen seconds left, Michael Jordan took and made the game-winning shot! His Tar Heels would go on to win by one point and become NCAA basketball champions.

For Michael Jordan, this was his origin story. His game-winning shot was the first of many to come. Not only did he epitomize achievement in moments like this, but he would also end up representing excellence and success on a level never seen before. It didn't stop there. Jordan continued to rise to the occasion, taking and making multiple game-winning shots and leading his team to six National Basketball Association Championships. Scoring prowess aside, his ability to perform when it counted is unlikely to ever be matched.

In basketball history, Michael Jordan is arguably as successful as they come. He is an icon. His basketball prowess astounds us. But that astonishment leads us to an almost uncomfortable question. What made him so successful? What made him so different? What made him take, and, more importantly, make so many game-winning shots? And our curiosity about Jordan and his success pursuit makes us even more curious about our own. We want to know if we can be successful. We want to be "like Mike." We want to find courage to take shots and hope we have the execution necessary to make shots when it counts. We want to know how to uncover the attributes and characteristics necessary to achieve success. Maybe, if we can unearth these characteristics, we can gain insight into our own success pursuits.

This fundamental premise compelled me to write this book and has led to many sleepless nights. Is there a blueprint for success? What makes some people more successful than others? I wanted to know what makes us tick. Better yet, I wanted to know what makes us tick well. What made Michael Jordan the best basketball player in history? How did Jerry Rice become one of the greatest football players of all time? Why was Barry Sanders so great? What made Reggie Miller such a clutch shooter? Why were these people and people like them able to perform at such a high level?

Answering those questions seems impossible. There are so many variables to consider. Is success a result of a specific mix of genes, nurturing, and environment? Is it merely a combination of luck, timing, and circumstance? Society teaches us that each successful person is unique. They are anomalies. They are prodigies. They are outliers. We assume successful people are the product of a particular pedigree and are rarely reproducible. We say to one another, "There will never be another Michael Jordan." We consider them one in a million, and we are entirely comfortable and content with that rationale.

Let's face it. A few people will always outperform others. Some companies thrive, while others fail. Some athletes outclass their competition. Most of us believe that outperformers are successful because they are more talented. Successful people, we assume, have more talent than their unsuccessful counterparts. They are smarter. They are faster. They jump higher. They sing better. They have better business sense. They make better decisions. They are luckier. They had the right parents and went to the right schools. They had the right coaches and teachers. They were in the right place, at the right time, with the right resources. We believe that under the right conditions, success inevitably finds them.

We commonly assume that successful people have benefitted from a specific set of miraculous circumstances that led to their success. You have heard it a million times. "If I were in that situation, I would be successful too." Is that it? Are we stuck? Can we only be as successful as our circumstances dictate? Are the extraordinary and the ordinary locked at polar ends of the success spectrum, without the ability to change their caste? Does fate alone anoint the successful? Does circumstance leave the rest of us to wallow in mediocrity? Well, maybe, the way we are looking at success and those who succeed is entirely wrong.

Successful people do have consistent qualities and characteristics, but there appears to be much more to it. It isn't about who they are. It is about what they do and how they do it. It isn't about where they are from. It is about where they are going. It isn't just about their consistent characteristics. It is about their consistent methods. Their ability to navigate the road of success requires a unique approach. Let's be clear. It would be naive to think that only one path to success exists, but this book will give you a little more insight into an approach that is slightly different.

Successful people are different because of what they do, not just who they are. They are different because of the reproducible behaviors that they exhibit. They aren't born with success. They go out and get it. Of course, reading this book may not transform you into Jerry Rice, Michael Jordan, or Barry Sanders. However, reading this book will help you understand a slightly different way to pursue success. It will help you apply these successful behaviors to all aspects of your life. It will help you begin to develop your road map for success. It will help you understand the relationship between success and failure. Successful people may be from different places and have different experiences, but many pursue success in the same maniacal way.

If it isn't talent, what about hard work? Shouldn't hard work be a prerequisite for success? I often tell this story—we hired a general contractor to build our home. We wanted to make it as nice as possible, but we were building a home with champagne taste on a beer budget. We built the house with views of a lake. As they were framing the house, I noticed that the view wasn't quite right. Instead of looking at the lake head-on, the house was at an angle. I had to fix that. I wanted to have a perfect view of the lake. I couldn't afford to have the house ripped down and rebuilt from scratch, but I was determined to make the change.

What did I do? Well, I pushed it! Yes, you read correctly. I tried to push it! I braced myself, knees slightly bent, muscles rippling, and I pushed. For ten minutes, in the hot sun, I pushed. I pushed and pushed and pushed. And do you know what happened? Absolutely nothing! Despite all that fanatical effort, the house didn't move. OK, I am exaggerating a bit, but you get my point. I was unhappy with the position of the house, and no amount of effort on my part would change that. I could spend all day and night pushing, with absolutely no results and absolutely no success. All that fanatical effort would yield no tangible result. My result didn't correlate with my effort. This happens to a lot of us. We work frenetically, but that work doesn't always yield the result we seek. The Antarctic explorer Ernest Shackleton probably said it best: "Superhuman effort isn't worth a damn unless it achieves results."

In this book, I will share this theory. A theory developed after observing, analyzing, and researching some of the most successful people of our time. After reading this book, you will have a better understanding of how and why successful people can achieve at such a high level. You will find out what they think, what they do, and how they do it. You will gain a new perspective on a slightly different way to view the world. You will learn how ordinary people perform extraordinarily.

As you read this book, try to apply the theory to all aspects of your life. You should be asking yourself these questions: "How can I apply it to my business, my family, or my team? How can I become a better parent, a better athlete, a better executive, a better employee, a better coach, or a better spouse?" This isn't your standard, run of the mill, infomercial structured treatise on success. Maniacal Fanaticism will change the way you perceive success and change the way you perceive your ability to achieve it. Be prepared to think in a slightly different way. Instead of waiting for success to find you, go out and find it. That some achieve great success, should be proof that you can achieve it as well.

CHAPTER II

JERRY RICE: WHAT'S YOUR DRAFT PICK?

"If I have ever made any valuable discoveries, it has been due more to patient attention, than to any other talent."
– ISAAC NEWTON

For me, it all started with Jerry Rice. As far as I am concerned, Jerry Rice is the greatest football player of all time. I grew up watching him make catch after catch and score touchdown after touchdown. He was selected to the Pro Bowl thirteen times and won three Super Bowl rings. Jerry Rice is one of the greatest football talents of all time. Or is he?

Was Jerry Rice indeed a great football *talent*? Let's review the data. Jerry Rice was the sixteenth draft pick in the 1985 National Football League draft. Here is the draft order from the 1985 draft: Bruce Smith, Bill Fralic, Ray Childress, Chris Doleman, Duane Bickett, Lomas Brown, Ken Ruettgers, Ron Holmes, Kevin Allen, Al Toon,

Richard Johnson, Jim Lachey, Eddie Brown, Derrick Burroughs and finally, Jerry Rice. Jerry Rice wasn't the first or even the second wide receiver selected in that draft.

Was this a scouting mistake? At least fifteen teams didn't realize that they were passing on the greatest wide receiver in the history of the game. Fifteen teams identified players with more perceived talent than Jerry Rice. Fifteen teams! How did this happen? What didn't they see? Why was his potential for future success not obvious to them? Obviously, they weren't looking for the right thing. They were looking for the *most* talented player, but they weren't looking for the player *most* likely to succeed. In spite of their inaccurate assessment, Jerry Rice became the most successful player in that 1985 draft. Shame on them!

Clearly, the most talented and the most successful aren't always the same thing. Could fifteen other teams, fifteen other scouts, and fifteen other coaches make the same mistake? It is a little unfair to play the role of Monday night quarterback. It is a heck of a lot easier to judge his draft pick retrospectively. However, they obviously missed something. They weren't able to assess his ridiculous effort, his constant drive to improve his game, and his infatuation with the pursuit of success.

In retrospect, it is obvious that the scouts weren't able to see his maniacal focus, his fanatical dedication, and his unbelievable motivation. They had no idea that Jerry Rice was so pathologically motivated. They didn't know he sprinted two and a half miles uphill every day, a workout that was so fierce it served as inspiration for many of his future teammates. They didn't know he would run his routes with more precision than any wide receiver in history. They didn't know he would catch the ball one thousand and forty-nine times. They didn't know he would end up with twenty thousand, eight hundred, and ninety-five receiving yards. They didn't know that he would score two hundred and eight touchdowns. They couldn't anticipate his work ethic and his dedication to the game. They couldn't anticipate his ability to maximize and exceed his perceived talent. To fifteen teams and coaches and scouts, it is now painfully clear that it isn't always just about talent.

Talent, as an isolated quality, isn't what they should have been looking for at all. Obviously, successful people require some threshold ability. No one would say that Jerry Rice isn't talented, but people tend to assume that the most talented people will be the most successful. Jerry Rice proves that this isn't always the case. With this Jerry Rice contradiction in mind, should we be asking different questions?

What exactly is talent? What is the relationship between talent and success? Jerry Rice is proof that talent is no more than potential. Talent can be a predictor of success, but it isn't the *only* predictor. When we say someone has talent, what we are really saying is that the person has the potential to accomplish great things. The keyword is *potential*. Talent is nothing more than raw untapped ability. It is the likelihood of an anticipated positive probability.

Is this confusing? It should be. Defining talent is confusing and complicated, and no one definition suffices. Talent has as much positive predictive value as it has negative predictive value when it comes to anticipated future success. We assume that this untapped ability can be cultivated, but it isn't always clear how. How do we cultivate that talent? Why do Jerry Rice, and the particular subset of people like him, perform beyond their predicted talent? How did he exceed his pedigree? Better yet, how do we exceed ours?

The Jerry Rice contradiction highlights the difference between success potential and success performance. Success is usually perceived as an end product. It is considered a destination or something that you get. Achieving it isn't always a result of successful attitudes, aptitudes, behaviors, or processes. Sometimes success is independent of effort. In our society, success is often defined by wealth. While wealth is a form of success, it is possible to be wealthy without ever having to exhibit successful behaviors. Having a fortune doesn't mean you have the attributes necessary to succeed.

Jerry Rice and others like him achieved their success through predictable, identifiable, and consistent patterns. Understanding what made Jerry Rice great may articulate why some succeed, and others fail. It should shed some light on the difference between winners and losers. From close observation of these overachievers, you will learn about their success characteristics. It will be clear that they aren't just lucky. If you know *"how"* and *"why"* these people do what they do, you can plug yourself into that success equation.

Successful people *are* different. They have different genes, different experiences, different opportunities, different lives, different parents, different schools, and different teachers. They are different, but those differences don't necessarily explain their exceptional performance. Successful people aren't different because of who they are. They are different because of what they do and how they do it. It is less about pedigree and more about the results. Their success is less about form and more about function. It is less about draft pick and more about performance.

After his game-winning shot against the Georgetown Hoyas, Michael Jordan entered the 1984 National Basketball Association draft. Even though he would go on to become the greatest basketball player of all time, he wasn't considered the best player in that draft. He was the third pick after Hakeem Olajuwon and Sam Bowie. This is considered one of the greatest draft mistakes in sports history. How did Michael Jordan, the third pick in the 1984 draft, become the best basketball player in history?

What made Michael Jordan so different? He refused to accept mediocrity, maintained his fanatical drive to get better, and was able to sustain that maniacal focus and commitment. What separates us, from Michael Jordan and Jerry Rice, may not be so intangible. I am not saying that you will be Michael Jordan or Jerry Rice after reading this. But you will be able to develop a blueprint to maximize and exceed your draft pick.

Although it may be more convoluted than we would like, there is a recipe for success. If we pay close attention to those who have achieved great success, specific themes recur. Can *you* achieve your ultimate success? You can and will. Your success pursuit has begun. The path may not be as clear at the outset, but your success destination is coming. This process will change and challenge you. It will alter the way you pursue success.

If we look closely, we will see that successful people pursue the success action as much as the success outcome. The pursuit of success is just as important as the success itself. The means should be just as fulfilling as the ends. Your skills, ability, or talent shouldn't hinder your success journey. To achieve your ultimate goal, your success pursuit should be unwavering and unrelenting.

Successful individuals pursue success maniacally and fanatically, never losing sight of their goals. They intensely and aggressively adhere to their strategic plan to attain the goals they have developed. They are constantly introspective, never content, and always looking for ways to improve. This is what Maniacal Fanaticism is all about. Making valuable discoveries is due more to patient attention than to any other talent. Are you ready to push past your previously perceived limits? Are you ready to outperform your draft pick? Are you ready to leave ordinary for extraordinary?

FROM WITHIN
ACCELERATORS
WHAT DO YOU FEEL
HAPPINESS COMES
ASSESSMENT
SUPERSTAR
LUCKY
ALTERATION
ACCEPTANCE
MOTIVATION
MANIACAL
INERTIA
FANATICISM
OBSTACLES
INWARD
HIDDEN
M
SUCCESS
FOUNDATION
R
VALUES
FLYWHEEL
FOCUS
BLAME
GUTCHECK
FUTILITY
THRESHOLD
SWEAT THE SMALL
SUPER TRUST
HERO
PROMISE
YOUR
FAULT
CHECKMATE
NO EXCUSES
NO EXPLANATIONS
BETTER LUCKY THAN GOOD
POISE
PAST PERFORMANCE
FUTURE SUCCESS
CIRCUMSTANCE
PERFECT SITUATION
SUCCESSOLOGY
MANIACAL FANATICISM BEST

CHAPTER III

HIDDEN EVIDENCE

"Education is not the piling on of learning, information, data, facts, skills, or abilities—that's training or instruction—but is rather making visible what is hidden as a seed."

– THOMAS MOORE

Sufficient evidence exists to contradict the traditional understanding of success. As evident from the Jerry Rice and Michael Jordan examples, perceived talent isn't the best predictor of success. Yet, in spite of the evidence, we continue this flawed way of thinking. As a society, we are in a constant search for talent prodigies. We are always seeking successful pedigrees. We have been brainwashed to think that success only presents itself in a specific way.

We assume success requires the right height, the right weight, the right look, the right size, the right personality, the right training, the right degree, and the right brain. The right attributes may help, but their presence doesn't necessarily guarantee success. Much of the research and education about success "is not the piling on of learning, information, data, facts, skills, or abilities." Success education "is making visible what is hidden as a seed."

Let's look at some compelling and not- so- hidden evidence. Here is a list of the top twenty-five players in National Football League history and their corresponding draft position.

PLAYER	DRAFT POSITION
Jerry Rice	16
Jim Brown	6
Lawrence Taylor	2
Joe Montana	82
Walter Payton	4
Johnny Unitas	102
Reggie White	4
Peyton Manning	1
Don Huston	not drafted
Dick Butkis	3
Ronny Lott	8
Anthony Munoz	3
Joe Greene	4
Sammy Baugh	6
Deacon Jones	186
Otto Graham	4
Barry Sanders	3
Ray Lewis	26
Bronko Nagurski	not drafted
Gayle Sayers	4

John Elway	1
John Hannah	4
Dan Marino	27
Emmitt Smith	17
Deion Sanders	5

The data suggests that a player's draft pick isn't as important as one would think. Draft picks don't wholly predict the future success of an athlete. They tend to be a measure of promise rather than a predictor of future performance. Tom Brady, the most prolific passer in football history, was selected after one hundred and ninety-eight players. Joe Montana, who won four Super Bowl championship rings, was selected after eighty-one other players. Emmitt Smith, who has the record for the most rushing yards in history, was selected after seventeen other players.

Many of the players on this list weren't even selected in the top ten of their draft class. It would appear that being a high pick in the draft is a good predictor for future success, but it isn't as good as you might think. What is even more shocking is the presence of very low draft picks on this list. Johnny Unitas, Deacon Jones, and Tom Brady were all drafted in the hundreds. Nothing about their draft pick predicted their ability to succeed. What was it about these individuals that made them perform at a higher level than expected? What intangibles were missed? What other factors should have been considered? Was the evidence there? It was there, but it was hidden.

Only two players on this list were selected first in their respective drafts: John Elway and Peyton Manning. What happened to all the other first-round picks? You would expect this list to be composed of mostly—if not all—number one picks. I am not trying to criticize the draft process, nor am I claiming to be a draft aficionado. I am simply arguing that there were factors they didn't consider. This phenomenon isn't limited to sports. Society is riddled with similar draft pick misfires. We pride ourselves on our ability to assess talent, but we really aren't very good at predicting success.

What the scouts and teams and coaches failed to recognize was a player's intent to succeed. They failed to recognize their response to failure. They failed to recognize their ability to overcome obstacles. They failed to recognize their maniacal effort and their fanatical ability to improve. They failed to recognize their motivation, focus, and ability to execute. They failed to recognize their response to adversity and their ability to perform on game day. They also failed to recognize that these players would accept blame for suboptimal results and find multiple opportunities for improvement. Unfortunately, teachers, bosses, counselors, and even parents make the same draft pick mistake.

This might sound crazy. It may be that not being the best in your draft class may actually heighten your success pursuit. If you are already the best, there is nothing left to strive for. Your draft pick reflects what you have done. It doesn't predict, at least accurately, what you will do. Usually, a player's draft position is primarily based on success at the collegiate level. Perform well in college, and you will be well on your way to a successful professional career. However, the data gives us a slightly different picture.

How can we quantify the *other* qualities? Is it heart? Is it work ethic? Is it intensity, fire, or hustle? These arbitrary terms aren't easily defined. How do you teach somebody heart? How do you explain fire or intensity? What do you do to improve work ethic or hustle? Subjectively, we all know what these qualities are. Objectively, these qualities are almost impossible to assess.

In 1996, when the National Basketball Association celebrated fifty years in existence, they selected a team of the all-time fifty best players. Here are the top fifty players and their corresponding draft picks.

PLAYER	DRAFT POSITION
Bill Russell	3
Bill Sharman	17
Bill Walton	1
Billy Cunningham	5
Bob Cousy	3
Bob Petit	2
Charles Barkley	5
Clyde Drexler	14
Dave Bing	2
Dave Cowens	4
Dave DeBusschere	territorial pick
David Robinson	1
Dolph Schayes	4
Earl Munroe	2
Elgin Baylor	1
Elvin Hayes	1
George Gervin	40
George Mikan	territorial pick
Hakeem Olajuwon	1
Hal Greer	14
Isiah Thomas	2
James Worthy	1
Jerry Lucas	territorial pick
Jerry West	2
John Havlicek	7

John Stockton	16
Julius Erving	12
Karl Malone	13
Kareem Abdul Jabbar	1
Kevin McHale	3
Larry Bird	6
Lenny Wilkens	6
Magic Johnson	1
Michael Jordan	3
Moses Malone	3
Nate Archibald	19
Nate Thurmond	3
Oscar Robertson	1
Patrick Ewing	1
Paul Arizin	territorial pick
Pete Maravich	3
Rick Barry	2
Robert Parish	8
Sam Jones	8
Scottie Pippen	5
Shaquille O'Neal	1
Walt Frazier	5
Wes Unseld	2
Willis Reed	10
Wilt Chamberlin	territorial pick

The data suggests that a high draft pick doesn't necessarily guarantee success. Most of us would assume that this list would only consist of number one and number two draft picks. There are indeed eleven number one draft picks, but the other thirty-nine picks aren't number one picks.

George Gervin was one of those other thirty-nine. Gervin is best known for inventing a shot called "the finger roll." This was a shot where he rolled the ball off the tips of his fingers into the basket, dropping it in with a feather-like touch. He was also nicknamed "The Iceman" because of his cool demeanor on the court. He won several scoring titles, was a nine-time all-star and even scored sixty-three points in one game. He led professional basketball in scoring from 1978 to 1980. This impressive future wasn't predicted by his unimpressive fortieth draft pick.

In the 1974 National Basketball Association draft, thirty-nine other players were selected before Gervin. The players selected before him were as follows: Bill Walton, Marvin Barnes, Tommy Burleson, John Shumate, Bobby Jones, Scott Wedman, Tom Henderson, Campy Russell, Tome McMillen, Mike Sojourner, Jamaal Wilkes, Brian Winters, Len Elmore, Maurice Lucas, Al Eberhard, Cliff Pondexter, Glenn McDonald, Gary Brokaw, Don Smith, Jan van Breda Kolff, Billy Knight, Truck Robinson, Gus Bailey, Len Kosmalski, John Drew, Leonard Gray, Leon Benbow, Aaron James, Phil Smith, Dennis DuVal, Fred Saunders, Jesse Dark, Eric Money, Phil Lumpkin, Kevin Stacom, Rubin Collins, Coniel Norman, Foots Walker, and Kevin Restani. Bill Walton was the only other top fifty player selected before Gervin in that draft.

A consistent theme recurs. The selection of players, based on past performance and perceived talent, doesn't always predict future success. First-round draft picks only make up twenty-five percent of this top fifty list. If it were just about talent and previous success, we would expect a much higher percentage of first picks than that.

Unfortunately, draft picks don't tell the whole story. Talent doesn't tell the whole tale.

The data muddies the water. It reveals that success education isn't about piling on the data. Rather, it is making visible what is hidden. The data challenges our previously conceived notions of success. It forces us to look for hidden information. It forces us to look for the underlying success trends that aren't entirely evident at first glance.

Society is riddled with merit badges that are primarily based on perception and potential. We trust our flawed predictive method so much that we give millions of dollars to people without knowing a thing about their success ability. We place children in advanced classes based on what they did a semester ago. We give raises based on last year's performance. We are a retrospective society that uses retrograde performance to identify anterograde success.

Draft picks fall short because they are a snapshot. They are an assessment based on a discrete moment in time. They focus on what players were, not what they are or what they will become. They focus on where players have been, not on where they are going. We do the same in other areas of society. We focus on the success people have had, rather than how much future success they will have. It is the same in business. Companies miss the mark because they focus on today's market climate and not the demands of tomorrow. We choose our stocks based on their historical performance, and we assume future performance will be similar.

We live in a world of prototypes and pedigrees. If someone doesn't fit the mold, they don't make the cut. This is how most of us think, but the data doesn't support that mindset. Thinking this way doesn't consider how certain people pursue success, in spite of their caste. Thinking this way doesn't consider how determined some people are to improve. It doesn't account for a subset of people who can be greater than their pedigree. The traditional model doesn't account for people that can push past their preconceived limits and become more than the sum of their parts.

Maniacal Fanaticism describes how people can become more than what they are. It describes the particular process employed by a subset of successful people. Despite their draft pick, they pursue success maniacally and fanatically. They strive to exceed their potential through continual improvement. No one has a stranglehold on success. We all can attain it with the right motivation, focus, and execution. Your draft pick is irrelevant. Success is always possible. You just have to know what to do and how to do it.

FROM WITHIN
HUMBLE
ACCELERATORS
WHAT DO YOU FEEL
HAPPINESS COMES
ASSESSMENT
SUPERSTAR
LUCKY
ALTERATION
ACCEPTANCE
MOTIVATION
MANIACAL
LOFTY
INERTIA
FANATICISM
OBSTACLES
INWARD
HIDDEN
M
SUCCESS
R
FOUNDATION
VALUES
FLYWHEEL
FOCUS
BLAME
GUTCHECK
FUTILITY
THRESHOLD
SWEAT THE SMALL
SUPER TRUST
HERO
PROMISE
YOUR
FAULT
CHECKMATE
WORK
BE CALLED
NO EXCUSES
NO EXPLANATIONS
BETTER LUCKY THAN GOOD
POISE
FUTURE SUCCES
PAST PERFORMANCE
CIRCUMSTANCE
PERFECT SITUATION
SUCCESSOLOGY
MANIACAL FANATICISM BEST
PIVOT
PERSISTENCE
DISCIPLINE
GAME DAY
DENIAL
CONSISTENCY
GOALS

CHAPTER IV

MANIACAL FANATICISM

"It had long since come to my attention that people of accomplishment rarely sat back and let things happen to them. They went out and happened to things."

– LEONARDO DA VINCI

Maniacal Fanaticism is a process used by a particular group of people who pursue success without wavering. This process values the success pursuit just as much as the result of it. It describes a perpetual cycle of goal-orientated behavior necessary to achieve ultimate success. It doesn't guarantee success, but it does force constant individual improvement. This theory contradicts many of the past operant behavior models. Traditional positive reinforcement is often a typical way to encourage behaviors. In other words, a behavior that has a successful result is reinforced and perpetuated.

Maniacal Fanaticism differs in this way. It doesn't require positive reinforcement for every action. It also gives insight into how success can sometimes be the positive result of a negative stimulus.

The title of the theory has significance too. Maniacal, as defined by Merriam-Webster, means ungovernable excitement or frenzy. One who is maniacal is suggestive of or afflicted with insanity. They are characterized by excessive enthusiasm. Why start with the word maniacal? How can insanity, frenzy, excitement, and excessive enthusiasm help to navigate the road to success? Maniacal people believe that their sheer force of will leads to results. Although the word maniacal doesn't typically conjure images of success, it will make more sense as you begin to understand the theory. It simply describes the energy. Frenetic excitement and enthusiasm are the substrates of success. It is the fuel used during the long, arduous road to success.

Energy is important, but it isn't nearly enough. Here is an example. Let's assume you want to drive from New York to Los Angeles. Being maniacal would give you the fuel and the energy to drive the entire way, but how would you know where to go? How would you direct that energy? Without knowing what direction to drive or using a map to plan your route, that frenetic excitement and enthusiasm burn without direction. You would be driving very fast, in nothing but circles!

A maniac is someone with unbridled passion and energy. This unbridled energy lacks focus, or at least enough focus necessary to achieve an outcome. That is why we consider maniacs—well—maniacs! Typically, a maniac is wild and out of control. Although unfocused, being maniacal is the crazy first step. It provides the energy necessary for the long road to success. That inertia, which we will discuss in-depth later, is what starts the Maniacal Fanaticism Flywheel spinning.

The second word in the name of this theory is fanaticism. The term "fan" comes from the word fanatic. If you are a fan of the Chicago Bulls, it means you are fanatic about that team. It describes your passion or love for that team. As a result, all your energy is focused on that team. Linguistically, fanaticism describes the obsessive enthusiasm for a pastime or hobby or religion or government. It is a belief or behavior consumed by uncritical zeal. Fanaticism speaks to the passion and direction of success. Athletes often talk about the love of the game. That "love" is fanaticism.

To be successful, you must dive in headfirst. You can't just put your toes in and test the water. Success requires your full commitment. Fanaticism is the unrelenting and undeniable focus that an individual has for something. We are fanatical about sports teams or fanatical about relationships. Fanaticism describes an intense connection to something. For Maniacal Fanaticism, the fanatical relationship is with success. "Maniacal" is the energy, and "fanaticism" is the direction. "Maniacal" is the spark, and "fanaticism" is the fuse it follows. Maniacal Fanaticism literally translates to frenzied passion, excitable zeal, or insane enthusiasm. It is focused energy personified, the unrelenting pursuit of excellence.

Maniacal Fanatics, MFers for short, are those individuals who exhibit these qualities. This book outlines the qualities, techniques, and methods that MFers use in their pursuit of success. Whether you are running a multinational corporation, are attempting to lose weight, or trying to win your conference championship, you too can apply these principles. While some of these views may seem off the beaten path, so too is success. The beaten path isn't exactly littered with hordes of successful people.

Success is rare, abnormal. It is an oddity. It is an outlier. It is a black swan. To be truly successful means being a little different, a little odd, and a little extreme. Like success, Maniacal Fanaticism is a little different, a little odd, and a little extreme. For MFers, success is always attainable. Goals are always accomplishable. Results are always possible. MFers rarely sit back and let things happen to them. They don't let success find them. They actively seek it out. Things don't happen to them. They go out and happen to things. They pursue perfection with frenzied passion. They execute with excitable zeal. They exhibit effort with insane enthusiasm. For Maniacal Fanatics, success is an activity, not a reward. It is something they do, not something they get.

CHAPTER V
FOUNDATION VALUES

"Try not to become a man of success but rather try to become a man of value."
– ALBERT EINSTEIN

Before I describe the "how" of Maniacal Fanaticism, I would like to spend a little time describing the "who." Because of their unique characteristics and values, MFers have a slightly different way of looking at the world. These values distinguish them from most of the general population. They give them the fortitude to pursue success, in this not so ordinary way.

The MFer's foundation values aren't exclusive. Everybody has them in varying degrees. Whether innate or learned, they consistently create the foundation for successful people. MFers are acutely aware of these values, and they have spent years honing them. If you don't feel you have them, it doesn't mean you can't develop them. As you read the foundation values, you may realize that you have a lot to work on, but you may also realize that you have a lot more to work with.

MFers are the super doers of society. They are the overachievers. They never stop doing and are always striving for excellence. Even when failure is imminent, they keep moving forward. They are self-critical in a peculiarly positive way, allowing for continual improvement, refinement, and personal growth. While most people alter their goals to achieve success, MFers alter themselves. They believe the laws of nature are static and that the individual is the only malleable variable. Changing yourself is much easier than changing the world around you. The first step in any success pursuit is learning to become a person of value and dare success to follow.

Foundation Values

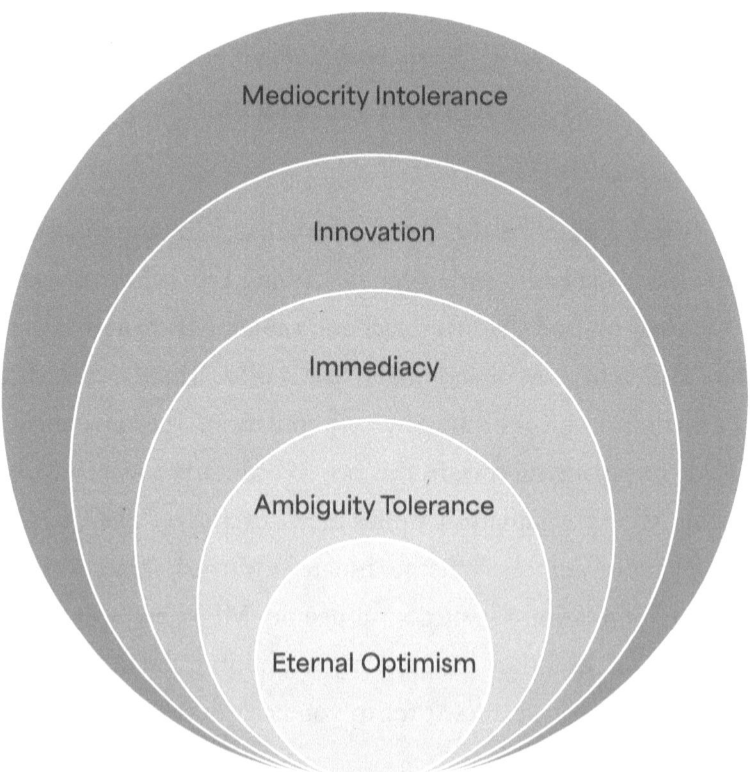

ETERNAL OPTIMISM

MFer core values serve as a foundation for their success. The foundation values are consistent across genres and disciplines. They serve as a base to build success on. The first of these values is eternal optimism. Don't confuse eternal optimism with hope. Hope is wish for a result, without extending any effort to make that result happen. For example, I hope it doesn't rain. But weather, at least for most of us mere mortals, isn't within our sphere of control. Hope implies nothing can be done to change an outcome. Hope assumes the outcome is beyond your control. It is passive and unactionable.

Conversely, eternal optimism is *knowing* that you can achieve the result. No matter what the goal is, eternal optimists believe there is always an action that can get them there. MFers are sure they can get better, work harder, to accomplish their goals. They know it. Eternal optimism is the ability to be self-critical and attack your weaknesses without diminishing your effort, spirit, enthusiasm, or optimism.

To be successful, you must develop an itinerary of success actions. Hoping and wishing aren't actionable behaviors. These inherently passive behaviors conflict with MFers' desire for action. In other words, it is better to do something than do nothing. Eternal optimism doesn't mean that you ignore reality. It merely acknowledges the first step, knowing you can always succeed.

With three seconds left, the Chicago Bulls were down by one point to the Cleveland Cavaliers. It was the first round of the NBA playoffs, and upstart Michael Jordan had yet to see the playoff success he had a North Carolina. Jordan received the inbound pass from Brad Sellers. After catching the ball, he jumped as high as he could. "Air" Jordan, as he was so aptly called, jumped so high and for so long that he appeared to be frozen in—well—air. Craig Ehlo, the unfortunate soul who was tasked with guarding Jordan, also jumped to block the shot. As Craig Ehlo descended, Michael continued to elevate and released his shot. As the buzzer sounded, the ball splashed through the net and Craig Ehlo crumbled to the ground in disbelief. "The shot," as it would later be called, won the game and the series.

Like his shot against Georgetown, this kind of game-day performance would become Michael Jordan's calling card. Did he know he would make it? Yes! Making that shot was within his control. Eternal optimists know they have the motivation, focus, and execution to achieve the desired outcome. Jordan was able to execute one of the most important shots of his life, because he knew he could make it. He knew he could make it because of his preparation. Being "clutch" simply means that in the most critical moments, MFers have prepared to execute. Because of that preparation, they expect a positive result.

AMBIGUITY TOLERANCE

The second foundation value is ambiguity tolerance. Though they are calculated and are careful to develop successful strategies, MFers do take chances. Ambiguity tolerance is the ability to attempt success, even when there is limited evidence to predict an outcome. Because of this tolerance, MFers aren't afraid to try, and they tolerate the ambiguity of an unknown outcome.

If you never take a leap of faith and are always comfortable with the status quo, you may avoid failure. Unfortunately, in your effort to avoid failure, you may also inadvertently avoid success. Tolerating that ambiguity gives MFers a chance at success. They understand that investing effort and time may not always yield the result they desire. Would you invest your efforts, without the guarantee of success?

People who can't tolerate ambiguity are always regretful over missed opportunities. They say, "I wish I would've bought that stock. I wish I would've taken that job. Why didn't I think of that invention? Why didn't I take that shot? Why didn't I write that book? If I would've just...?" As you can see, most people discuss success as a retrospective pivot point. How many times have you heard someone say? "I would've been successful too, if that had happened to me."

Success pursuits often come with inherent unknowns. Quantifying the future result of one's effort is almost impossible. MFers aren't afraid to fail. They play to win instead of playing not to lose. Success pursuit isn't safe, and success isn't guaranteed. Some choices have more risk than others, but all choices have some risk. MFers are neither wholly risk-takers, nor are they wholly risk-averse, but they can accept the unknown consequences of their actions.

In fact, MFers don't just tolerate ambiguity. They accept and embrace it. There isn't always enough data to be methodical, analytical, and introspective. Even when a preponderance of data supports a choice, some information will always be unknown. That unknown information shouldn't dissuade you. Just like Michael Jordan, you have to tolerate the ambiguity of each shot you take. MFers don't always make the shot, but failure is guaranteed if they refuse to take it.

IMMEDIACY

The third MFer foundation value is immediacy. Immediacy is the ability to remain in the moment and make decisions using the information they have at the time. They choose to focus their energy, based on the available information. Contemplating retrospective and prospective decisions detracts from the decision-making process. MFers make the best decision they can without regret. In other words, not making a decision in the moment is worse than making the wrong decision.

Michael Jordan has often said he has no regrets. In other words, the choices he made in the past were made with all the available information. Regret is retrospective. Meaning, you would do things differently, knowing what you know now. Unfortunately, you didn't know then what you know now. The decision you made is the decision you made. This doesn't mean that MFers don't consider future consequences of their actions, nor do they ignore lessons learned in the past. Robbing a bank may not be the best thing to do, unless you are trying to become a world-class criminal.

Immediacy describes intelligent decisions and performances that are rooted in the present. Think of a kicker kicking a game-winning field goal. The field goal kicker's previous percentage is irrelevant. The game against the division rival next week is irrelevant. At that moment, what the kicker has to do is all that is relevant. He has to kick the field goal to win the game *now*. Past failures and successes are irrelevant. Future performance doesn't matter. On game day, the immediate execution is all that counts.

INNOVATION

The fourth foundation value of Maniacal Fanaticism is innovation. This may be the most important of the five foundation values. Obviously, those who innovate and create new products or services can find success rather easily. Steve Jobs, Bill Gates, Michael Jordan, Sergey Brin, Larry Page, Mark Zuckerberg, and Pele are innovators. Their accomplishments are primarily a result of their ability to think differently. Inventing something completely new can redefine an entire industry, but innovation doesn't only refer to invention. It can also describe a new way of thinking. MFers view the world from a different perspective. They find new ways to interpret the stimuli and data around them. They can create innovative solutions to new problems and find new ways to solve old problems.

The innovation of astronomer and mathematician Nicolaus Copernicus changed our understanding of our solar system. It required creativity to develop a theory that placed the sun, not the earth, at the center of the universe. In the Maniacal Fanaticism construct, success is almost impossible without innovation. Michael Jordan's success hinged on his scoring proficiency, but it also hinged on his basketball innovation. Scoring baskets was something old. But, scoring them the way he did—flying through the air and defying the laws of gravity—was indeed something new!

MEDIOCRITY INTOLERANCE

The fifth and final foundation value is mediocrity intolerance. MFers hate the status quo. Something in Jerry Rice made him want more than an average football career. Michael Jordan wasn't happy with only one basketball championship. Undeniably, success satisfies some primal urge, but avoiding average seems to drive MFers even more. In their eyes, being mediocre may be worse than failing. Even after reaching goals others only dream about, they always want more.

MFers are exceedingly uncomfortable with middle of the road results. They often say, "Can I do more? What can I do differently? Where can I improve? What else can I do? What else can I achieve? Am I working hard enough?" These questions are assessing who they are and what they are doing. To the MFer, mediocrity is a gnawing, festering wound that is excruciating when exposed. Even after they succeed, these mediocrity avoidant feelings haunt them.

MFers always want to do more than what is standard. They want to be better than they are. They make no excuses, give no explanations, and have no regrets. They come early and stay late. To add more productive hours to the day, they avoid sleep. They are always pushing. MFers feel they can always give more effort and more energy. They strive for more than the sum of their parts, irrespective of their innate talent. They weren't picked first, but they sure play like it.

These five core foundation values aren't the only values that MFers have, but they are the values that set them apart. The house of success can only be as strong as the foundation it rests on. Eternal optimism means they know it. Ambiguity tolerance means they will try it. Immediacy keeps them in the moment. Innovation allows them to create new things and create new ways to do old things. They won't settle for the status quo. Consistently, repeatedly, and indefatigably, these five foundation values are always present.

Let's revisit the original question. What makes people successful? What makes them pursue excellence? The road to success isn't as tortuous, convoluted, or indistinct as we think. Before we get on that road, we need to choose the vehicle. The foundation values are that vehicle. What values do you possess, to what degree, and in what proportion? Not everyone will be successful, but anyone can be.

Before you read any further, stop and review these core values. Do you have them? Can you attain them? Can you think differently? Know it, with eternal optimism. Try it, with ambiguity tolerance. Stay in the moment, with immediacy. Do it differently, with innovation. Exceed the status quo, with mediocrity intolerance. To become a person of success, you must become a person of value. Our foundation for excellence is laid. Let's start building!

CHAPTER VI
CAPACIBILITY

"If I have the belief that I can do it, I shall surely acquire the capacity to do it even if I may not have it at the beginning."
– GANDHI

Before we move on to the Flywheel, which is the heart and soul of Maniacal Fanaticism, let's examine what is necessary to get there. The foundation principles outline some basic tenets by which MFers live their lives. They serve as a foundation that will support the house of success. What's the next step? The chapter's title isn't a misprint. Capacibility is an analysis of how prepared you are to pursue success.

Capacibility is the pretest for Maniacal Fanaticism. It is an assessment of what you can potentially do, what you want to do and what you need to do to get there. As you can infer from the title of this chapter, capacibility is a measure of how likely you are to be successful at something. It begins with capacity, the amount of work of which you are capable. It ends with ability, the innate and acquired skill necessary to accomplish your goal.

In manufacturing, capacity is the maximum or optimum amount that can be produced. Depending on all the tasks that you have to accomplish, capacity is a measure of how much you can do. It is a summation of how much you are currently doing, and how much you can potentially accomplish. Capacity is the innate potential for growth, development, or accomplishment.

While we may be able to exceed our capacity occasionally, it still ultimately has a limit. It is unlikely that you could become an astronaut, a professional basketball player, and a physician in the same lifetime. Capacity is limited, but it isn't entirely static. We also can increase our capacity through training.

To understand how this works, think of training for a marathon. On the first step of the first day of your training, you would have a limited capacity for distance. At first, it is unlikely that you could run the requisite twenty-six miles. As you train, your capacity to run long distances increases. You should be able to run two miles after the first week, six miles after a month, ten miles after three months, and so on. Simply put, we all have limits, but we can overcome and extend these limits with training.

The second component of capacibility is ability. Ability describes our natural or acquired skill and talent. Ability, in some ways, is less concrete than capacity. Improving ability is a little more complicated. Some abilities can improve through repetition. The more you shoot free throws, the better you will shoot free throws. Areas related to skill can usually improve with repetition. On the other hand, you can't teach height.

Michael Jordan had the ability to play several sports, but only had the capacity for one of them. Capacibility allows you to determine where to direct your energy. If you are blessed with a high capacity and a high ability in a given area, your likelihood of success is significantly higher. Individuals like this are called overachievers. They *can* and *will.*

Conversely, if you have low capacity and low ability, your likelihood of success decreases. These people are called low performers. They *can't* and *won't.* That isn't to say that these people aren't motivated. They just don't have the capacity to do any more than they are doing. They also have low ability because they currently lack the skill or talent necessary to perform.

Differentiating overachievers from low performers is easy because they are at opposite ends of the spectrum. However, most of us reside in categories that aren't as definitive. If you have high ability and low capacity, you are likely to underachieve. These people *can* but *won't.* Their achievements fall below expectations. This type of person is very frustrating to deal with. They disappoint because we expect so much more from them. Their high level of ability makes their lack of success puzzling to us. These are the underachievers.

Underachievers have the ability to succeed and lack the capacity to accomplish it. I can remember one of my very few and utterly painful trips to the mall. As I stood perusing the car-payment-priced shoes, I saw a Nike shirt that perfectly explained this category of people. The shirt read "talented but lazy," high ability and low capacity.

Lastly, low ability and a high capacity would make someone a jack of all trades. They are a jack of all trades and a master of none. Their ability limits them. They can't but will. With high capacity, these individuals can accomplish an exceptional number of tasks. At least at the beginning, they just can't perform at a high level. Sometimes they can perform at a high level in an isolated area, but only with exceptional work ethic.

What category are you? Are you an overachiever, can and will? Are you an underachiever, can and won't? Are you a low performer, can't and won't? Are you a jack of all trades, can't and will? Who is more likely to be successful? Who is more likely to attain excellence? The answer lies in a person's capacity. Remember our draft picks? The reason so many people got those draft picks wrong is that they focused on ability rather than capacity. If they focused on the player's capacity, they could have better predicted a player's likelihood to succeed. There were others with Jerry Rice's and Michael Jordan's ability, but not many who had their capacity.

Capacity, then, is the key to success. Both overachievers and jack of all trades have high capacity. Though jack of all trades need to work harder than overachievers, they can both succeed. Because they have limited capacity, underachievers and low performers have very sparing and limited success. People who *won't* have difficulty doing just about anything. Succeeding is close to impossible if you are talented and lazy.

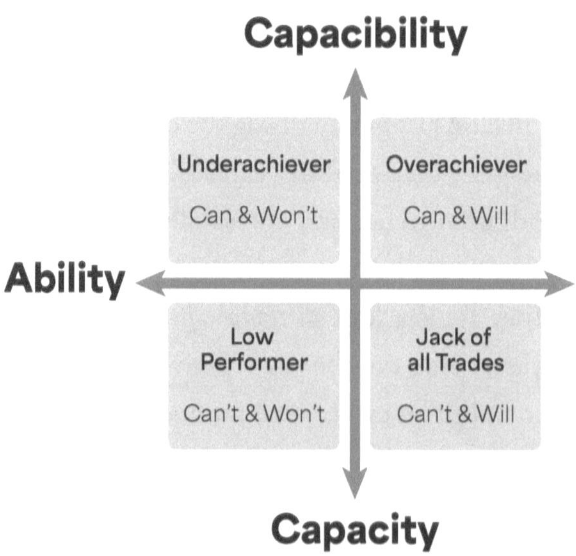

Understanding capacibility is one thing, but it is useless if we can't assess it. Determining capacibility is something that we do all the time instinctively. Doing what we are good at is self-fulfilling. It feels good. Positive outcomes reinforce the theory that we do something well. A good math student prefers to do math homework. A child who excels in soccer and struggles in basketball may consider quitting basketball to focus on soccer.

While capacity seems to be an internal and introspective investigation, ability is usually determined externally. Teachers, coaches, and parents are often the evaluators of our ability. Ability assessment can also come from coworkers, bosses, and even competitors. Ability can sometimes be self-determined, but we are often unrealistic when evaluating our abilities. The following outlines a process that can help you determine your capacibility.

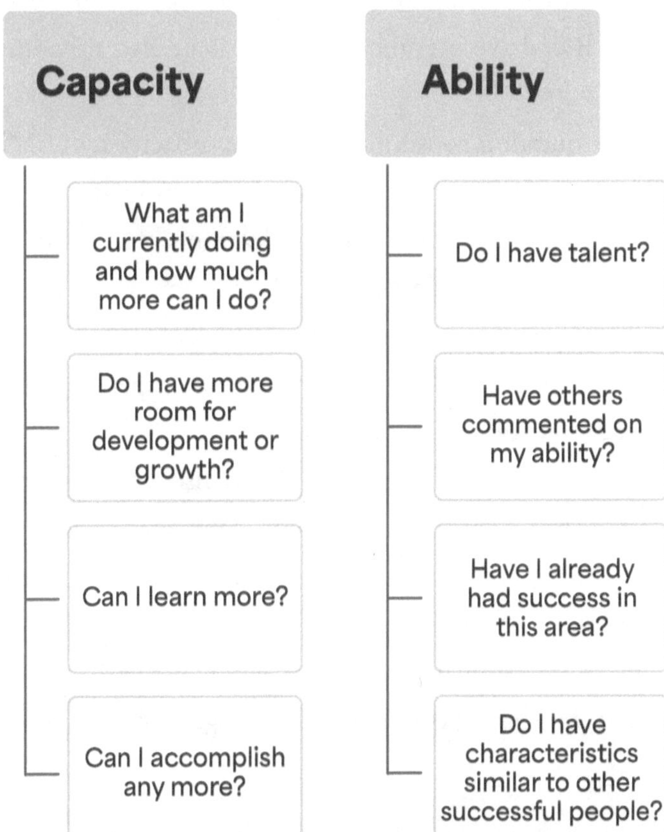

To determine your capacity in an area of pursuit, ask yourself the following questions: "What am I currently doing? How much more can I do? Do I have more room for development or growth? Can I learn more? Can I accomplish anymore?" These questions help you gain insight into your capacity for success. If your plate is already full, trying to accomplish much more isn't very realistic. During medical school, I studied an average of twelve to sixteen hours a day. Obviously, I didn't have the capacity for much else at that time. I managed to squeeze in an occasional round of golf and some basketball, but even that demanded a heroic effort.

To determine capacity, ask yourself, "Do I have more room for development or growth? Undoubtedly, you know a few people who are limited by their unwillingness to learn. If you have no additional room for growth, it is unlikely you have any additional capacity. Would Jerry Rice have become Jerry Rice if he had no additional room for growth?

The next question to ask to determine capacity is this: "What more can I learn?" If you aren't learning, you aren't living. We should spend our entire lives learning. Without learning, it is almost impossible for us to find success in any area. A willingness to learn significantly increases an individual's capacity. This is true even for those near their capacity limit. Though you may be an expert in your field, you still need to retain the ability to learn.

To determine your capacity, you should also ask, "Is there more I can accomplish?" If you are comfortable where you are in life, there isn't going to be much room for improvement. Being content isn't necessarily a bad thing. If you are content, you are probably happy where you are. If you are happy where you are, you won't have any impetus to change. If you have no impetus to change, you will inherently have a low capacity. If Michael Jordan was content with only three championships, would he have come out of retirement?

To determine ability, the first question you should ask is, "Do I have talent? Having the talent to pursue your goals isn't always a necessity, but it makes success a little easier. You have to be honest with yourself. Overestimating or underestimating your talent will only muddy the water. Overestimating your talent may lead to perceived underachievement and unrealistic expectations. Underestimating your talent will create a self-imposed success ceiling.

If you have difficulty acknowledging how talented you are, you may not be as successful as you could be. Have others commented on your ability? People around you may have a better grasp of how talented you actually are. Coaches, teachers, coworkers, supervisors are just a few people, who are constantly exposed to your talent or lack thereof. Presumably, they have an objective view of just how talented you are. As you already know from the data, talent assessments have their limitations. You shouldn't rely totally on these assessments, but they give another data point.

The next question you should ask is this: "Have I already had success in this area?" This question is intuitive. If the answer to this question is yes, then you have a lot of potential for success. You must recognize how great you can become. Lastly, you should ask yourself, "Do I have the characteristics of other successful people?" Evaluate your competition. How are you similar to them? How are you different? Success is easier to attain if you already know what it looks like.

As a writer, I have always studied those successful authors that have come before me. What characteristics did they have? Why reinvent the wheel? We often ignore the information right in front of our eyes. We should seek out successful people, try to determine their methods, and incorporate what they do into our own lives. Doing this won't make success easier, but it will give your success pursuit more clarity.

Determining your capacity and ability will provide insight into how to pursue your success. Capacibility gives you a beginning. It signifies the beginning of your success journey. It is where you determine how fast, how long, and how hard your success journey will be. Your ability may be limited, but your capacity will carry you through. "If you have the belief that you can do it, you shall surely acquire the capacity to do it even if you may not have it at the beginning."

CHAPTER VII

MANIACAL FANATICISM FLYWHEEL

"If you want to succeed you should strike out on new paths, rather than travel the worn paths of accepted success."
– JOHN D. ROCKEFELLER

The heart and soul of Maniacal Fanaticism is the Flywheel. It outlines an alternate path to success, a path that is slightly different. This path is less traveled, less worn, and not as well understood. The Flywheel outlines the process employed by a unique group of individuals. They have a slightly different view of the world and pursue success in unexpected ways.

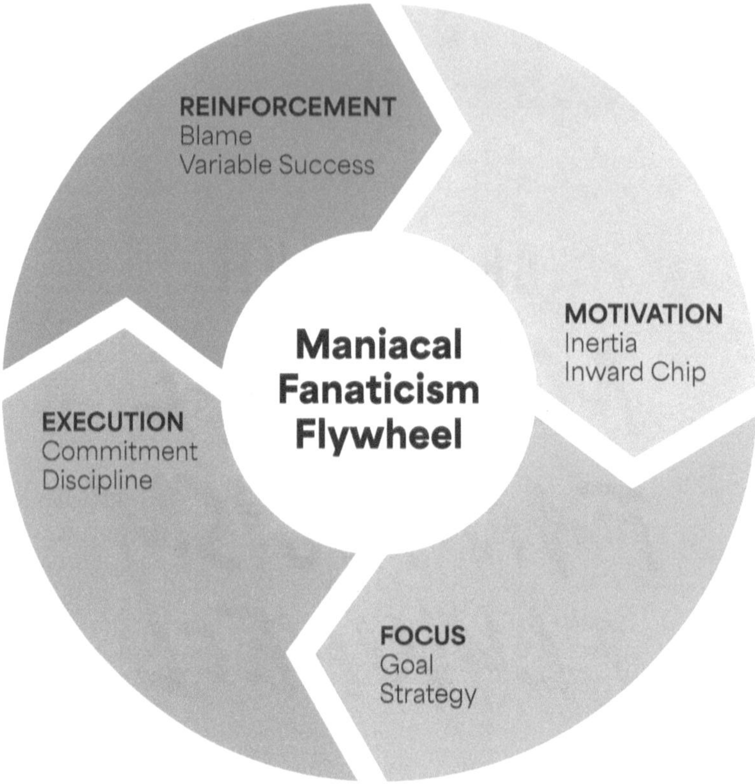

MFers are more than just a quarry of qualities, a vault of virtues, or a pantheon of principles. They aren't successful because of who they are. They are successful because of how they pursue success. The Flywheel isn't a recipe. It isn't a collection of ingredients. It is a manual or a map—it is directional. It describes the "how" of success and gives us insight into a particular subset of successful people. It is the GPS for our success journey. Structurally, the Flywheel is broken down into phases. Each phase builds on the previous phase. Transitions between phases only occur after the previous phase is completed.

These phases outline the major actions necessary for this kind of success. The four phases of the Flywheel are *Motivation*, *Focus*, *Execution*, and *Reinforcement*. The term MFer describes an individual who knowingly or unknowingly makes his or her way through the Flywheel phases. These phases will be easy to remember because MFer is the acronym for the phases of the Maniacal Fanaticism Flywheel. *M* is for *Motivation. F* is for *Focus. e* is for *Execution. r* is for *Reinforcement.*

The Flywheel, like all success pursuits, starts with *Motivation.* Almost everything we do requires motivation. If you don't want to do it, it isn't going to get done. Motivation is the "why" of Maniacal Fanaticism. Exceptional results require exceptional performance. Exceptional performance requires exceptional motivation. The motivation phase is comprised of two thresholds, inertia and the inward chip. Each threshold requires a specific amount of energy to be completed. Meaning, they are either all or none. Partially completing a threshold is typically the reason many are unable to complete the motivation phase, resulting in failure to complete the flywheel.

The next phase of the MF Flywheel is *Focus. Focus* is the refinement of motivation. In this phase, goals and strategies congeal. Having vision is motivation. Having clearer vision is focus. The devil is in the details, and the focus phase is where we develop those devilish details. This is where we develop the "what" of Maniacal Fanaticism.

The focus phase breaks down into two thresholds, goal and strategy development. In this phase, people drill down, determine what they want to accomplish and, develop a plan to accomplish it. For example, I could get very motivated to be a successful golfer in the motivation phase. In the focus phase, I would need to develop a plan to win the United States Open and develop a plan to get there. Motivation is general, and focus is specific. Essentially, focus is the minutia of motivation.

The next phase is *Execution.* Execution is the hardest phase of the Flywheel. It is where most of us falter. It is where great plans fizzle, and the hard work begins. The execution phase is composed of the commitment and discipline thresholds. Commitment is the promise. Discipline is the delivery on that promise. Execution is the "how" of the Maniacal Fanaticism Flywheel.

The last phase of the Flywheel is *Reinforcement*. This phase helps us understand how people achieve success, even when they don't initially accomplish their goals. MFers use this phase to contemplate the possibility of not achieving their goals. The reinforcement phase is responsible for self-analysis and introspection. It allows MFers to self-correct, change their vision, and find opportunities for improvement. The results of this phase create future motivation.

Like all the other phases, the reinforcement phase is composed of two thresholds. They are *variable results* and *blame*. Completion of this phase leads us back to the motivation phase, and the process starts all over again. The faster the Flywheel spins, the more successful the person will be. A faster Flywheel results in more motivation, more focus, more execution, and more reinforcement. A faster Flywheel also creates more opportunities to self-correct, self-analyze, improve, and eventually succeed.

To make more sense of the Flywheel, think of it this way. Motivation is the "why." Why do you want to be successful? Focus is the "what." What are your success goals, and what strategies are necessary to get there? Execution is the "how." How do you implement the strategy? How much work will it take? Reinforcement is the "when." When the goals are achieved, are they consistent with the previously developed goals? If the goals aren't met, why weren't they? Asking "why" the goals were or weren't achieved stimulates renewed motivation. Even when success is attained, we can always find opportunities for improvement.

With that, the cycle starts again. By understanding why, what, how, and when, you can begin your transition to becoming a Maniacal

Fanatic. If you want to succeed, you should strike out on a new path. The Flywheel is that path. It may be slightly different. It may be less accepted and less worn. If you have the motivation, focus, execution, and reinforcement, you can make plausible the previously impossible.

FROM WITHIN
ACCELERATORS
FEEL
SUPERSTAR
LUCKY
ALTERATION
MOTIVATION
MANIACAL
INERTIA
FANATICISM
OBSTACLES
INWARD
HIDDEN
M
SUCCESS
FOUNDATION
R
VALUES
FLYWHEEL
FOCUS
SUCCESS
BLAME
t
GUTCHECK
FUTILITY
THRESHOLD
SWEAT THE SMALL
SUPER TRUST
HERO
YOUR
CHECKMATE
NO EXPLANATIONS
NO EXCUSES
BETTER LUCKY THAN GOOD
PAST PERFORMANCE
CIRCUMSTANCE
SUCCESSOLOGY
MANIACAL FANATICISM BEST

CHAPTER VIII

THE MOTIVATION PHASE

"The will to win, the desire to succeed, the urge to reach your full potential ... these are the keys that will unlock the door to personal excellence."

– CONFUCIUS

The motivation phase starts the Flywheel and is the spark for all action. Motivation is the entry point of the Flywheel. Ultimately, every intended action begins with an initial motivation. Even before a jury can convict someone for murder, they have to establish a motive. Many people confuse the results of success with the motives for success. In our culture, success often means fame and fortune. Because of that, people often assume that these are the best motivators. In our capitalistic society, money can be a great motivator. However, money isn't the only motivator. In most cases, money may not matter at all. When Michael Jordan returned from retirement, he was on top of the world financially. He already had three championships and was one of the greatest players of all time. So why come back?

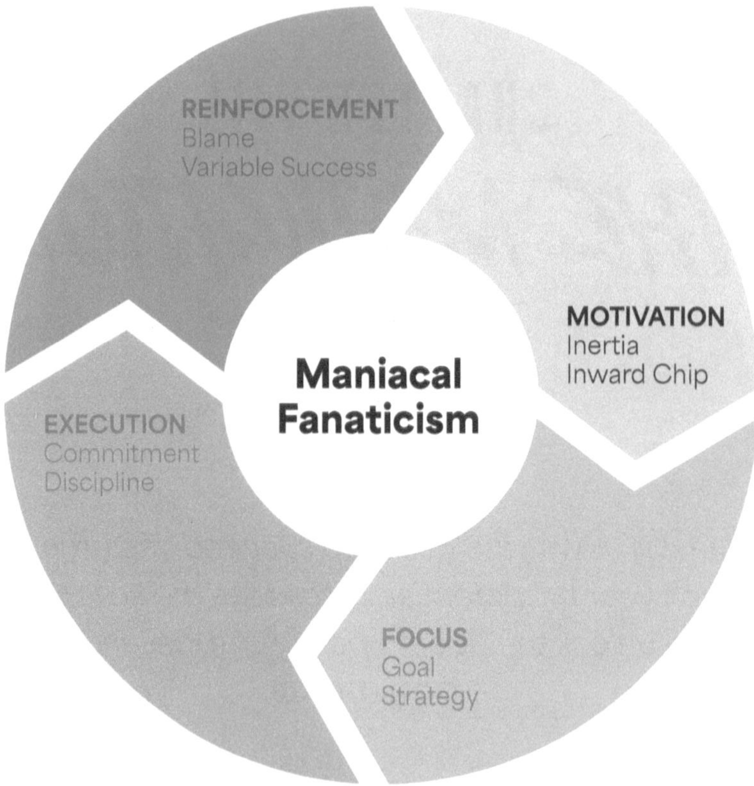

After having so much success with the San Francisco 49ers, why would Jerry Rice move on to play in Oakland? MFers aren't all motivated by the same thing, but their response to motivation is very predictable. To be successful, you have to find your motivation. The more motivation, the faster the Flywheel spins. The quicker the Flywheel spins, the better the chance of success. Motivation is the desire to succeed. It is the will to win. Your task is to find the keys and unlock the doors to success. Before you embark on your success journey, you should ask yourself one question. Why?

INERTIA

"Every body continues in its state of rest, or of uniform motion in a right line, unless it is compelled to change that state by forces impressed upon it."
– ISAAC NEWTON

No motivation can occur without inertia. If that premise is true, inaction should be self-explanatory. The first of two thresholds in the motivation phase is a prerequisite for success. Inertia is necessary to overcome the natural tendency for people to remain at rest. Simply put, it is harder to get going than it is to keep going. Inertia is the fuel that keeps the Maniacal Fanaticism Flywheel energized. Without it, no goal is achievable. It is impossible to finish what you haven't started. Inertia is necessary to take the first step across the starting line of your success journey.

Passion for a particular activity, hobby, or endeavor can supply enough inertia. If you like to play golf, getting off the couch to play a round doesn't require much inertia. However, MFers take this to an entirely different level. For them, the pursuit of success is the most potent form of inertia. Tiger Woods is an excellent example of both kinds of inertia. Encouraged by his father, Tiger Woods inherited his father's passion for golf at a very early age. This early passion was enough inertia to start spinning his golf Flywheel. As Tiger began to compete, he developed his own inertia. His well-known motivation, to surpass Jack Nicklaus' major tournament win record, provided him with the inertia necessary to become the greatest player of all time.

From a physics perspective, inertia is the resistance of any physical object to a change in its state of motion or rest. Also, an object tends to resist any change in motion. In other words, doing something requires overcoming the resistance of doing nothing. Therefore, the first step of Maniacal Fanaticism is to get off the darn couch.

Once you develop enough inertia and overcome the resistance to get started, you will have the momentum to achieve your goal. Inertia is the spark that starts the raging success fire. The entire Maniacal Fanaticism concept hinges on inertia. We all have dreams, hopes, and aspirations. We all really *want* to be successful. When the dream ends, inertia transforms hope into something more actionable. Inertia overcomes the stagnation of wishing, hoping, and praying that an outcome will happen. It is the fuel, energy, and lifeblood of your success pursuit.

Most people tend to think of MFers as self-motivated. Self-motivation simply means that MFers have a low threshold for inertia generation. They understand that without motivation the Flywheel is unable to start spinning at all. Maniacal Fanaticism's version of motivation is different from traditional motivation models. In traditional motivation theory, there is an already established goal. For example, I am motivated to finish writing this book.

Traditional motivation concepts imply that a goal is a destination or the result of a task. In other words, to win the race one is motivated to run fast. Or, to make money one is motivated to get that job. The motivation of Maniacal Fanaticism is slightly different. MFers in the motivation phase are simply gathering energy. They understand that they are preparing for flight and use this phase to start their engines. No goal is required, at least at this point. They are motivated to do something, but they haven't determined what that something is yet. What does this mean? Think about going out to dinner. Hunger is motivating you. Hunger is the inertia. You have enough motivation for you to go to dinner, but it isn't necessary to choose the type of food, the restaurant, or the directions to get there.

Why use the term threshold? Thresholds require a particular amount of effort to accomplish them. Like the action potential of a neuron, Flywheel thresholds require a specific amount of electrical energy to fire. In the human body, each type of nerve has a unique action potential. Energy requirements differ based on the location and the type of nerve. Nerves responsible for sensation have very different action potentials than those responsible for locomotion. The Flywheel works similarly. Each threshold in each phase requires a minimum amount of energy necessary to progress to the next phase. The amount and type of energy are specific to the threshold. The trick is determining the amount and type of energy that is required to complete each of your thresholds.

What is your action potential? Do you have a low or high inertia threshold? How much energy do you need to get your next project started? How much energy is required for your action potential? Do you have the inertia to get off the couch? Does your organization or company have the inertia necessary to spin its Flywheel? If your success pursuit is at rest, change its state with whatever force you can impress upon it. After you have started your uniform motion, no force in the world can stop you.

FROM WITHIN
HUMBLE
ACCELERATORS
WHAT DO YOU FEEL
HAPPINESS COMES
ASSESSMENT
SUPERSTAR
LUCKY
ALTERATION
ACCEPTANCE
MOTIVATION
MANIACAL
INERTIA
FANATICISM
OBSTACLES
INWARD
HIDDEN
M
SUCCESS FOUNDATION
R
VALUES
FLYWHEEL
FOCUS
SUCCESS
STRATEGY
BLAME
E
GUTCHECK
FUTILITY
THRESHOLD
DON'T SWEAT THE SMALL
SUPER TRUST
HERO
PROMISE
YOUR
FAULT
CHECKMATE
NO EXCUSES
NO EXPLANATIONS
BETTER LUCKY THAN GOOD
POISE
PAST PERFORMANCE
FUTURE SUCCESS
CIRCUMSTANCE
PERFECT SITUATION
SUCCESSOLOGY
MANIACAL FANATICISM BEST
PIVOT
CAPABILITY
INTERESTS
MENTALITY
VARIABLE
EXECUTION
CONSISTENCY
PERSISTENCE
DISCIPLINE
DENIAL
GAME DAY
MEMORIES
BELIEF
FAILURE
GOALS
EVIDENCE
TRUST

CHAPTER IX
THE INWARD CHIP

"A fanatic is a man who consciously over-compensates a secret doubt."
– ALDOUS HUXLEY

The second threshold in the motivation phase is the *Inward Chip*. This unique quality of MFers is perhaps the most critical threshold of the Flywheel. The inward chip is what makes this type of success pursuit so unique. The chip originates from a perceived grievance, a sense of inferiority, or doubt. You are probably thinking, successful people are typically confident and self-assured. Why would MFers feel inferior or have any doubt?

Outwardly, a chip on the shoulder is usually a negative quality. These people often exhibit counterproductive behavior. They can be negative and downright angry. People with an outward chip always feel as though life mistreats them. They have an inflated perception of self. They think any criticism is unfounded and external to their action, performance, and results. If they have a poor outcome, they usually attribute it to an external cause. They believe failure is beyond their control.

People with an outward chip often have a victim complex and rarely find fault from within. They rarely identify any opportunities for improvement. They are paralyzed by the following questions: "Is he better than I am? Why can't I ever get a break? Isn't she lucky?" They believe they are always performing at one hundred percent, and they believe that peak performance requires a perfect situation. People with an outward chip believe that external factors are always the cause of their failures.

Conversely, the inward chip describes the positive aspects of the traditional "chip on your shoulder." MFers may be outwardly confident, but they often carry a subterranean feeling of inferiority. This inward inferiority produces a constant compulsion to improve. MFers believe that all outcomes are within their control, and all goals are achievable.

The inward and outward chips both illicit compensatory behaviors, but the behaviors they elicit are what separate them. The outward chip creates negative compensatory behaviors, while the inward chip produces positive compensatory behaviors. Their names describe the direction of their focus. Those who carry an outward chip have a primarily external focus, while those with an inward chip focus internally.

MFers consciously overcompensate for a secret doubt. MFers are outwardly confident, but inwardly they are trying to overcome subterranean doubt. As a result, MFers are perpetually introspective. They constantly ask themselves, "How can I get better? Am I doing enough? What skills am I lacking? Where can I improve? Where are my weaknesses?" MFers believe winning and losing are always the result of internal factors. They believe that all results are within their control. By the sheer force of their will, they always believe they can overcome any circumstance. No matter how successful they become, MFers never believe their performance is adequate. They don't tolerate mediocre performance or effort. They always believe they can do more and work harder. And they always blame themselves, but we'll talk about that a little later.

Many of the people who immigrated to the United States have this mentality. Due to their sense of perceived inequality, they find equality by overcompensation. They don't believe equality is granted. Instead, they work hard to gain it. Because of this mentality, they also encourage their children to be overachievers. Instead of complaining about the five-dollar-an-hour job and asking for fifteen dollars per hour, they work three five-dollar-an-hour jobs to make fifteen dollars per hour. Instead of focusing on the injustice of the system, they overwhelm the unjust system with hard work.

Unlike inertia, the inward chip is more difficult to control. It requires taking an outward chip and turning that chip inward. MFers do this by accepting their doubt. That is half the battle. The more aware you are of your chip, the more likely you are to understand your weaknesses and force your chip inward. Of course, the inward chip isn't an entirely new concept. In sports, the classic example of the inward chip is the underdog.

Underdogs are teams or athletes that are perceived to have less skill or talent than their opposition. When the underdog wins, it is thought to be a result of a gritty virtuoso performance. But, it is more likely that exceptional performance is a result of the underdog's overcompensation. This quality is what makes the inward chip so powerful. Whether it's true or not, MFers believe they aren't good enough, and that is why they are always fighting to get better.

When I wrote this book, my inward chip was rampant. Will I be a good enough writer? Is this book good enough? How can I be better? I would write, edit, and rewrite continuously because I worried that the book wouldn't be good enough. When I asked myself those questions, it didn't discourage me. That subterranean doubt motivated me. As a writer, I am definitely an underdog. Let's face it. I am no Malcolm Gladwell. But I am still writing that story.

Questioning your ability can actually be healthy. If you believe you are perfect, then you really can't get any better. You won't create any opportunities for improvement. The self-doubt of the inward chip is a powerful motivator. A maniacal fanatic is one who consciously over-compensates for that secret doubt. To achieve your ultimate success, find that doubt. Overcompensate and turn your chip inward. Challenge yourself and ask those difficult questions. Your doubt should tell you that you aren't as good as you think, *yet.*

CHAPTER X

BEYOND SELF-INTEREST

"The true value of a human being can be found in the degree to which he has attained liberation from the self."

– ALBERT EINSTEIN

I hate the term self-motivation. It is redundant. At some level, all motivation is self-propagated. Although external factors can have a marginal effect, motivation is and will always be an internal activity. External factors affect us differently because of our *self*-motivations. As a result, the motivation phase of the Flywheel is internal. There is no place on the Flywheel for external motivation. Both inertia and the inward chip can only be satisfied from within. We are all exposed to similar external factors, but MFers respond to them slightly differently.

In 2011, Tim Tebow made an improbable and impressive playoff run. He led his Denver Bronco team from an early-season loser to a playoff winner. When it mattered most, he prevailed. When the game was on the line, he could rise to that occasion. Even though experts doubted his quarterback ability, they underestimated his capacity. His strong spiritual belief allowed him to overachieve and exceed everybody's expectation, maybe even his own.

Motivation, like Tim Tebow's, that goes beyond self-interest, can sustain a Flywheel indefinitely. My obligations as a father and a husband motivate me beyond my self-interest. My obligation to them keeps my Flywheel spinning, even when my intrinsic motivation wanes. Likewise, Tim Tebow's higher calling enabled him to elevate his play when it counted.

In the 1999 hit movie *The Matrix*, the main character Neo was prophesized to be the chosen one. Morpheus, Neo's mentor, believed that Neo was a prophet. Neo was to fulfill a prophecy and free the human slaves from a computer-generated alternative reality. At first, Neo didn't seem to be all that special. That would quickly change.

With Morpheus' training, Neo progressed more rapidly than any previous trainee had. It was clear that he was special. Just when Neo started to believe the prophecy, he went to see the Oracle. The Oracle, a fortuneteller of sorts, was going to tell Neo if he was indeed the chosen one. And after their lukewarm conversation, Neo felt he had definitive confirmation that Morpheus' prophecy wasn't true. He wasn't the one. Dejected, his motivation waned. He thought he didn't have the potential that his mentor Morpheus believed he had. His self-interest wasn't enough.

All that changed when Morpheus was in danger. When Neo believed that he was the only one who could save Morpheus, he achieved a level of performance he previously thought to be impossible.

Once he began to think beyond his self-interest, his potential was limitless. Of course, this is fiction, but it isn't much different in the real world. In 2016, 19-year-old Charlotte Heffelmire lifted one end of a truck to save her trapped father. In 2015, Carlo Pettigrew crawled out of his crashed SUV and ran half a mile to save his kids from a fire. These are the stuff of legends! Or are they?

When we are pushed to our limits, we are capable of unfathomable feats. We just need the right motivation. If we rely only on self-interest, we can self-limit. The lion's share of motivation must come from within, but it shouldn't just be all about you. Although your desires can spark your Flywheel, selfless motives can accelerate the Flywheel even faster. As you move through the motivation phase, don't limit yourself to self-interested motivations. Religion, family, or friends can significantly enhance your motivation.

What is your motivation beyond just what is important only to you? Who is your Morpheus? Who inspires you to be better? Do people rely on you? Can something or someone motivate you to be better than you are? Find this motivation, and you can overshoot your abilities. Like Neo or Charlotte or Carlo, once you believe, your performance may exceed your wildest dreams. Your true value as a human being will be determined by the degree to which you have attained liberation from yourself.

How would you satisfy your inertia and inward chip thresholds? Analyzing how you can improve, by reflecting on your weaknesses, starts the process of fulfilling the inward chip. The motivation phase isn't preoccupied with the "how" of goal-oriented success. We aren't quite there yet. Instead, the motivation phase focuses on the "why." Why am I not better? Why don't I have better results? Why am I not a better athlete? Why am I not a better leader? Why can't I be a better parent, employee, CEO, or coach? Why do I want to be successful?

Completing just one phase doesn't yet yield a result. However, it does allow the necessary motivational energy to continue on the MF pathway. Once you understand the "why," you will have successfully satisfied the motivation phase. Your journey has just begun.

CHAPTER XI
THE FOCUS PHASE

"Concentrate all your thoughts upon the work at hand. The sun's rays do not burn until brought to a focus."
– ALEXANDER GRAHAM BELL

Every New Year's Eve, millions of people make New Year's resolutions. And, every New Year, millions of people fail to achieve the resolutions they set. Why is this? It happens so regularly. They actually expect resolutions to fail. For the past three-hundred-and-sixty-five days, they have been unable to comply with the previous year's resolutions. Yet each year, they continue to make the same fantastical "resolutions."

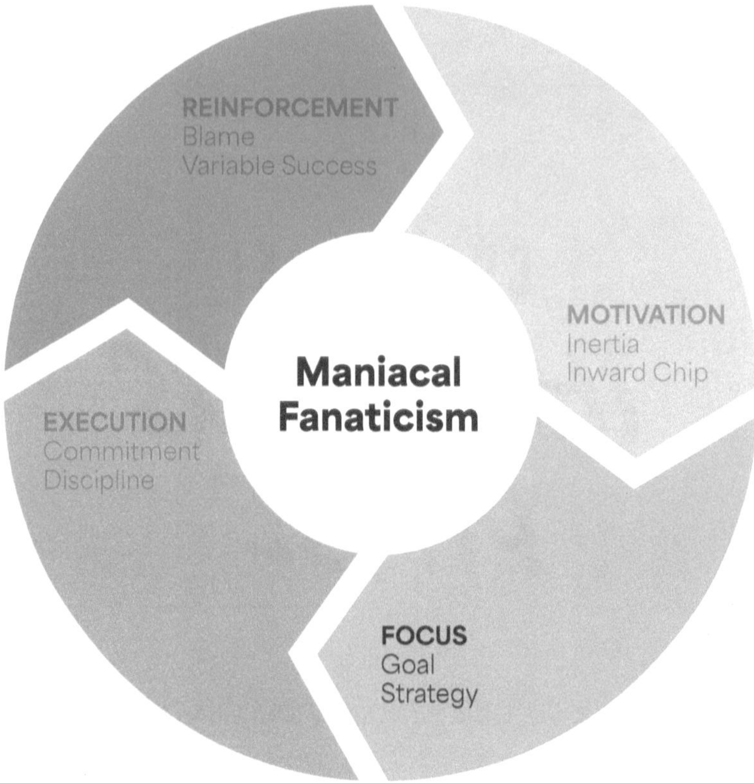

In this chapter, I hope to show how resolutions fail and how you can succeed. To avoid the cycle of broken internal promises, MFers create attainable and accomplishable goals. They do this primarily by using the next phase of the MF Flywheel, the focus phase. The focus phase is the brain of the Flywheel. It focuses on goals and the plans to reach them. Focus is the "what" of Maniacal Fanaticism. Focus helps MFers determine their success goals and the best ways to accomplish them. Like the motivation phase, the focus phase has two thresholds: goals and strategy.

In any successful endeavor, setting goals is imperative. Goal setting enables you to determine the course, direction, and speed of your success journey. It also gives you the ability to plan a strategy. Before you decide which direction to point the ship, you need to know the destination. Setting a single goal isn't nearly enough. As with everything else, MFers do more. They create a spectrum of goals. These goals are divided into requisite, expected, and lofty goals. They are also broken down into short-term, intermediate, and long-term goals. These goals should also be very specific. If goals are general or ill-defined, they could end up becoming another failed New Year's resolution.

Global, broad, or universal goals are virtually worthless. I want to make more money. I want to lose weight. I want a better job. I want to end world hunger. These goals are too indistinct, making them difficult to pursue and even more difficult to know when you've achieved them. Setting goals in this way only leads to more questions. If you want more money, how much money do you want? If you want to lose weight, how much weight do you want to lose? Goals should be as specific as possible. Specificity allows the accomplishment to be more definitive.

Goals should also be measurable. I want to make one million dollars. I want to lose thirty pounds. I want to be the Chief Executive Officer. Why be so specific? The strategy necessary to lose five pounds is markedly different from the strategy needed to lose fifty pounds. We must know the destination before we map the route to get there.

We often hesitate to set specific goals because we are afraid to fail. Specific goals encourage accountability and commitment. It forces us to measure and assess the effectiveness of the plan. By setting goals in this manner, you can create strategies that will stick and allow you to focus on the work you will have to do. The sun's rays don't burn until brought into focus. Likewise, your success pursuit will be ineffective unless your motivation to succeed is also brought into focus.

FROM WITHIN
HUMBLE
ACCELERATORS
HAPPINESS COMES
WHAT DO YOU FEEL
ASSESSMENT
LUCKY
SUPERSTAR
ALTERATION
ACCEPTANCE
MOTIVATION
MANIACAL
INERTIA
FANATICISM
OBSTACLES
INWARD
HIDDEN
SUCCESS
FOUNDATION
VALUES
FLYWHEEL
FOCUS
SUCCESS
STRATEGY
BLAME
GUTCHECK
FUTILITY
THRESHOLD
SWEAT THE SMALL
SUPER TRUST
HERO
PROMISE
YOUR
FAULT
CHECKMATE
NO EXCUSES
NO EXPLANATIONS
BETTER LUCKY THAN GOOD
POISE
PAST PERFORMANCE
FUTURE SUCCESS
CIRCUMSTANCE
PERFECT SITUATION
SUCCESSOLOGY
MANIACAL FANATICISM BEST
PIVOT
PERSISTENCE
PERSUASION
POTENTIATE
SELF DENIAL
GOALS
EVIDENCE
BELIEF
PERSEVERANCE

CHAPTER XII

THE GOALS THRESHOLD

"A goal is not always meant to be reached, it often serves simply as something to aim at."

– BRUCE LEE

Picture a grid with temporal goals defined by length of time on the y-axis. These are the acute goals, sub-acute goals, and ultimate goals. Now, place what we will call the pinnacle goals on the x-axis. These are the requisite goals, expected goals, and lofty goals. This structure gives a spectrum of goal creation. As you already know, MFers don't create singular goals. Singular goals tend to be all or none. They are too limited to be functional. Using only one goal decreases your chance of success.

Conversely, creating a spectrum of goals increases your chance of success. Creating a goal to win a national basketball championship doesn't make any sense unless you also make basketball goals for high school and college. Before you set a goal to become CEO, you may have to become a vice president. Not only do multiple goals give you multiple opportunities to succeed, they are also directional.

Setting specific time limits for each goal is also necessary. Without time limits, goals serve absolutely no purpose. Specifying a time limit for a goal makes that goal more concrete. Setting time limits forces you to create a reasonable strategy in a more accountable way. Time limits may vary from person to person, but there are a few rules of thumb. Typically, acute goals should have a time limit of less than a year. Sub-acute goals should require one to two years. Ultimate goals shouldn't exceed five years.

This is the rule of one-two-five. This goal setting rule is fairly straightforward. It states that for every goal, you should develop one-, two-, and five-year intermediary goals. You can even apply this rule to shorter-term goals, simply exchange years for months. Why be so specific? Why create such an elaborate array of goals? Again, being specific is necessary because specific goals yield specific strategies. You have to know the destination, and the time it will take to get there before you start sailing the ship.

Decoupling time and goals are the reason many of our resolutions fail. Making a goal to lose weight is ridiculously vague. Making a goal to lose ten pounds, without considering how much time is necessary to lose it, is just as ambiguous. Losing ten pounds may take two months or five years. This ambiguity results in lack of commitment, blurs focus, and stops the Flywheel from spinning. It is clear why setting goals and time limits is essential, but why do we create so many goals?

What if we set several weight loss goals? An acute goal of ten pounds in a year, twenty pounds in two years, and fifty pounds in five years is much more specific than saying, "I want to lose weight."

It creates accountability and sets a goal trajectory. Intermediary goals keep the Flywheel spinning and generate more inertia. Achieving the twenty-pound goal creates more inertia to achieve the fifty-pound longer-term goal.

More inertia generates more goals. More goals lead to more strategies, and so on. Success, in this way, becomes infectious. It becomes, well, maniacal! The Flywheel spins faster and faster. The goals get loftier and loftier, until the achievement of your ultimate goal and beyond. If you had a single goal, your entire Flywheel would rely on that goal. If that goal isn't accomplished, your Flywheel grinds to a halt. Multiple goals give you multiple opportunities to succeed and multiple opportunities to keep the Flywheel spinning.

The goal matrix visually represents the spectrum of goals created by MFers. The goal matrix has three temporal goals for each pinnacle goal. This structure gives us three acute goals, three subacute goals, and three ultimate goals. Any given strategy requires at least nine goals. The pinnacle goals break down into three categories. The first category is the requisite goals.

Requisite goals are mandatory to keep the Flywheel spinning. These goals identify the lowest possible level of success necessary to sustain the success pursuit. This lower-level goal signifies that a strategy may be correct but requires significant altering. Requisite goals function as reality checks. A budding undergraduate student, who wants to attend medical school, sets a requisite goal of passing biology. Passing biology is requisite to becoming a physician. Not passing biology may redirect the strategy and allow the student to consider a different field. The student may also develop a different strategy, as the current strategy didn't achieve the basic goals necessary to keep the Flywheel spinning.

You can determine requisite goals, based on the lowest level of goal accomplishment that will enable you to continue on your current path. These goals allow you to be more efficient with your time. If you aren't meeting your requisite goals, you can quickly redirect strategies, or in some cases, adjust your goals.

The next category of pinnacle goals is the expected goals, which represent the anticipated result of a given strategy. The undergraduate, we discussed previously in this chapter, should expect that her current strategy will yield a specific outcome. Her expected acute goal would be achieving better than a B in her medical school prerequisite courses. Her expected sub-acute goal would be graduating in the top twenty percent of her class. Finally, her ultimate goal would be her acceptance to medical school.

Expected goals are steady-state goals or vacuum goals. Their prediction doesn't account for unforeseen obstacles or unexpected boons. When an effective strategy is correctly implemented in a perfect world, these are expected goals. Expected goals have a significant effect on the Flywheel. While requisite goals impart just enough energy to avoid stopping the Flywheel, expected goals allow the Flywheel to spin freely.

The third category of goals is the lofty goals. Lofty goals are just that, lofty. They are the dream result of an implemented strategy. Lofty goals assume near-perfect execution and unexpected boons. Let's go back to our medical student. Her lofty acute goals would be "A" grades in her medical school prerequisites. Her lofty sub-acute goal would be to graduate with summa cum laude distinction. Her lofty ultimate goal would be an acceptance to Harvard medical school. Lofty goal accomplishment has an extremely high-energy effect on the Flywheel. Lofty goals spin the Flywheel faster and longer. Lofty goals attainment can also transfer energy from the Flywheel of one success pursuit to the Flywheel of another.

As you can see, the idea that successful people have a singular focus is a misconception. MFers use a spectrum of goals rather than just a single goal. They also adjust and alter goals based on the situation. Think of a college coach preparing for an upcoming season. Of course, winning the national championship may be the coach's acute lofty goal. But, that is just one goal of many. The acute expected goal may be making the conference playoff. The acute requisite goal may be to have a winning percentage of sixty percent. The ultimate lofty goal may be graduating a certain percentage of players.

Having an array of goals provides flexibility and creates more opportunities to succeed. It also creates more opportunities for improvement, if and when goal achievement falls short. Goals on the goal matrix are sequential and additive. You have to achieve one goal to accomplish the next. They serve as multiple points on the same success trajectory.

Do you remember our college coach? He needs to set three acute goals for wins. The acute requisite goal is the number of wins sufficient to keep his job. The acute expected goal is the number of wins he expects the team can win. The number of expected wins is an educated guess. It is a realistic expectation based on assessing the players and the competition. Next, his acute lofty goal is a result based on a near-perfect strategy. It assumes the right strategy, no obstacles, no Flywheel decelerators, and a little bit of luck. Yes, luck! We will talk about luck a little later. The coach's acute lofty goal may be to win the national championship.

For each revolution of the Flywheel, you should develop at least nine goals. You should follow the one-two-five rule for your requisite, expected, and lofty goals. A journey doesn't make sense without a destination, and your success journey functions in the same way. Creating a goal matrix is necessary to keep you on course. It allows you to plot trajectory, time, and destination. Motivation, inertia, and the inward chip are useless, without focus. Without focus, you have activity but no productivity. Without focus, goals are like the unfocused rays of the sun. Goals may not always be reachable, but they can often serve simply as something to aim at.

CHAPTER XIII

STRATEGY THRESHOLD

*"Vision without action is a daydream.
Action without vision is a nightmare."*
– JAPANESE PROVERB

The next threshold of the Focus phase is the strategy threshold. The goal matrix identifies the destination, and the strategy threshold delineates the path required to get there. Developing a strategy serves as a reality check. It is a way to test the attainability of the previously defined goals. At this point, MFers ask themselves several questions. How realistic are the goals? Is this strategy appropriate?

Strategy development, unlike goal development, must also consider obstacles. Obstacles are difficult to predict and force the redirection of the strategy. Obstacles may delay the strategic implementation, but good strategy development should also consider how to avoid them. It should take into consideration the individual's strengths and weaknesses. Focus, as an acronym, means, "*F*or *o*bstacles, *c*ontinue *u*sing *s*trategy." In other words, focus is the unrelenting and persistent pursuit of a goal.

Obstacles can't and won't get in the way of this pursuit. MFers' eyes are always on the prize. As a result, obstacles have a limited effect on MFers. Focus requires a clear vision of the goals and a detailed strategy to spin the Flywheel to the next phase. When developing your strategy, remember to continue using that strategy for those obstacles you encounter. Develop your goal matrix to generate multiple opportunities for success. Take the time to determine your destination and develop a path to get there. Having adequate motivation and developing the right goals isn't enough.

Vision without action is just a daydream, but action without vision is a nightmare. Before you act and before you embark on your success pursuit, you must have the vision necessary to get there. Your success pursuit vision is a combination of your goals and your strategy. This vision is what separates activity from productivity. It separates your success daydream from the nightmare of failure. Determine where you want to go, develop a plan to get there and clear the runway for your successful take off.

CHAPTER XIV

FOR EVERY ACTION THERE IS A PREACTION

"All men can see these tactics whereby I conquer, but what none can see is the strategy out of which victory is evolved."

– SUN TZU

That was easy enough. Just set the goals and go. Pick the right altitude, direction, and trajectory. Lo and behold, you are ready to take off and fly. Not quite! Goals are important, but goals mean nothing without a way to achieve them. Setting goals takes time and energy. However, developing a strategy may require even more. Strategy development can incorporate a single goal or an entire goal matrix. For example, Jerry Rice's fanatical training strategy allowed him to accomplish an array of goals.

To this point, the Flywheel has yielded no action. Without action, there are no results. Without a strategy, there can be no action. For any action, there must always be a pre-action. A pre-action is the introspection that precedes every action. Pre-actions are needed to avoid the meandering that can occur due to a lack of focus.

We all know people that create lofty goal after lofty goal without really accomplishing anything. Remember our New Year's resolutionists. By January 15, they have abandoned their resolution and are careening toward a new one. To some extent, we are all guilty of this type of incomplete goal pursuit. To be successful, you must develop your strategy in a very structured way. Pre-action is the gap between your goals and your goal actions.

Pre-action breaks down into six separate strategic processes. The P in pre-action represents preparation. Preparation describes the amount of work necessary to achieve a goal. How much training is required? How many shots do you need to take each day to become a great shooter? How much practice do you need? How many hours do you need to study? Whatever goal you happen to be pursuing, you need to know how much preparation is necessary.

A student who is considering medical school should understand that her preparation requires seven years of college. She will also have to identify what preparation is necessary for that kind of commitment. To develop an appropriate preparation plan, she will have to determine her capacibility. What preparation will be required to increase her capacity or develop her ability? How many hours will it take to perfect a skill? When she has answered these questions, she can develop an appropriate preparation plan.

The R in pre-action represents research. Success doesn't happen in a vacuum. Why reinvent the wheel? Successful strategies already exist. Reviewing the successful strategies of other successful people can help you to develop your strategy. Can you commit to Jerry Rice's or Michael Jordan's strategy? Spending a few moments researching what works and what doesn't work can help you save precious time and energy.

Before I started writing this book, I read the works of several authors. I asked questions. I read books on how to write books. I tried to learn from other successful authors. This information was invaluable, and it saved me a considerable amount of work. Why shouldn't you learn from the mistakes and successes of others? Before you start playing chess, you should understand the different abilities of each piece. Researching what you will need to achieve your goal will also help you prepare.

The E represents experience. How much experience do you have? What mistakes have you made in the past? Can those mistakes help your current strategy? Do you already know how to be successful? If you have the experience of a previous successful Flywheel, spinning your current Flywheel is a whole lot easier. A rookie should have a different strategy than a veteran.

The A in pre-action represents anticipation. Anticipation is essential for strategy development. Before Michael Jordan shoots, he anticipates what the outcome will be. MFers don't blindly engage in action after action, continually probing for success. They anticipate the results of their specific strategies. Some people call this instinct. It is a gut feeling. Sometimes you just feel like a given strategy will work.

Unfortunately, gut feelings aren't always correct. They are simply an innate sense of an anticipated result. As we gain experience, we validate our instinct, allowing us to trust our anticipations.

Anticipating isn't a guess. Do you remember the foundation principle of immediacy? Anticipating an outcome is based on the available information at the time. You may not know what the outcome of your strategy will be, but you should anticipate the result to the degree you can.

The C in pre-action stands for creativity. If you aren't successful, repeating the same failing actions won't yield any different results. To perfect my swing, I can hit thousands of golf balls. While practicing the same lousy golf swing will improve my consistency, it won't appreciably improve my results. My swing will just be more consistently lousy. Creativity doesn't only apply to new ideas. It also applies to new and innovative strategies.

Creative strategies can help us achieve previously unfathomable results. The true genius of creativity may not be in finding what is unknown. The genius of creativity may lie in developing new, previously unknown ways to get to what is already known. You don't always have to make something new. It is just as creative to make something old in a new and innovative way. To find new things you explore. To find new ways, you innovate.

Finally, T stands for tactics. Tactics describe the particulars of a success strategy. They outline the minutia and granular detail of the execution phase. This process takes all the available strategic information gathered to this point and creates an implementation itinerary. This itinerary helps to execute the plan. It creates an execution "to do" list for us to follow. Tactics are a documented list of directions that lead to the goal destination. Turn left here. Turn right here. Stop. Go back. Move forward. A tactic is a procedure or set of maneuvers engaged in to achieve an end, aim, or goal. This is the last step of the pre-action.

Setting an executable plan will be one of the most difficult things you do. Maniacal motivation and an ideal goal matrix can't overcome inferior strategy. Do you remember when I tried to push my house? No motivation, effort, or vision in the world can make up for poor strategy. Before blindly applying energy, take the time to introspect. Prepare for success. Find out what it takes to succeed. Don't discount your experience. Anticipate your results and the strategy necessary to get there. Be creative. Document your tactical plan, create your strategy, and execute it. For every action, there is a pre-action. It is easy for us to see the results of successful people. It is more difficult to see the strategy out of which victory has evolved.

FROM WITHIN
ACCELERATORS
WHAT DO YOU FEEL
HAPPINESS COMES
ASSESSMENT
SUPERSTAR
LUCKY
ALTERATION
ACCEPTANCE
MOTIVATION
MANIACAL
FANATICISM
INERTIA
OBSTACLES
INWARD
HIDDEN
M
SUCCESS
FOUNDATION
VALUES
FLYWHEEL
R
FOCUS
SUCCESS
STRATEGY
BLAME
PIVOT
GUTCHECK
FUTILITY
THRESHOLD
SWEAT THE SMALL
SUPER TRUST
HERO
PROMISE
YOUR
FAULT
CHECKMATE
NO EXCUSES
NO EXPLANATIONS
BETTER LUCKY THAN GOOD
POISE
PAST PERFORMANCE
FUTURE SUCCESS
CIRCUMSTANCE
PERFECT SITUATION
SUCCESSOLOGY
MANIACAL FANATICISM BEST

CHAPTER XV

DON'T SWEAT THE SMALL STUFF

"Start by doing what is necessary, then what is possible, and suddenly you are doing the impossible."
– ST. FRANCIS OF ASSISI

I wish I had a dollar for every time I heard someone say, "Don't sweat the small stuff." When people say this, they are trying to be helpful. They are attempting to encourage you to focus on the larger goal. Missing one shot may seem like a big deal until you consider the thousands of shots you may take in your career. One bad day at work may seem like the end of the world until you consider the twelve thousand workdays in your career. They are trying to tell you that the small wins and losses may not be as important as you think.

In the bigger scheme of accomplishment, the smaller things shouldn't affect your ability to pursue a larger goal. People who warn you about sweating the small stuff don't want you to get sidetracked.

They don't want the microscopic detail to bog down your macroscopic goal pursuit. People stuck in the granular detail usually can't see the forest because of the trees. People typically don't think they should be stuck managing the day-to-day minutia. Somehow, the belief is that micro-focus limits macro accomplishment. This mindset is sensible advice and a common way of looking at the world, but MFers are far from common.

Maniacal Fanatics see the world in a very different way. They can focus on micro and macro goals. It isn't necessary to sacrifice one for the other because they are not mutually exclusive. MFers can drill down and get granular when needed, but they also can zoom out to see the entire picture. They see the forest *and* the trees. MFers can see the minutia of short-term goals while maintaining a long-term vision.

In the second phase of the Flywheel, we discussed goal development. Those who can't see the forest for the trees didn't spend the appropriate time developing all of their goals. Multiple goals allow us to meet those acute day-to-day goals and still pay attention to the larger ultimate ones. The goal trajectory allows the opportunity to pay attention to all of our actions. In other words, we don't have to choose between the forest and the trees.

In golf, we have a saying: "You can't birdie all of the holes if you don't birdie the first one." On the second hole, we say, "You can't birdie all of the holes if you don't birdie the first two." For you non-golfers, a birdie is one less shot than par. It is an excellent score on any hole. The "forest" goal is scoring a birdie on all of the holes. The "trees" goal is executing each shot on each hole to achieve a birdie.

The one-two-five rule generates nine goals for each Flywheel. These are the acute requisite goal, the sub-acute requisite goal, the ultimate requisite goal, the acute expected goal, the sub-acute expected goal, the ultimate expected goal, the acute lofty goal, the sub-acute lofty goal, and the ultimate lofty goal. Creating nine goals for every Flywheel provides MFers the opportunity to account for the forest *and* the trees. They can zoom in and zoom out as they need to.

MFers can fly down to a thousand feet and see the trees, but they also can soar to thirty-thousand feet and see the entire forest. They are both nearsighted and farsighted. For highly successful people, every free throw, every putt, every test, every hour of work, every moment is important. They *always* sweat the small stuff! Goals should encompass your entire life. They should be set for each year, each month, each week, and each day. Multiple goals lead to more focus and more reinforcement. I set goals for each day of work. One of those goals is to make everybody's day better. That is my acute requisite goal for each day of work. We should sweat the small stuff because the small stuff becomes bigger stuff.

Accomplishing the necessary and the possible ultimately results in accomplishing the impossible. A successful career is made up of many successful years, which in turn are made up of many successful months, which in turn are made up of many successful days, which are each made up of a simple daily goal: "What can I do to make everybody's day better?" Paying attention to that simple goal helps me to manage every day of each month of each year of my career.

Indeed, the small stuff is important. Every tree is necessary to complete the forest. When people tell you not to sweat the small stuff. Tell them "No!" Sweating the small stuff is essential for achieving your success. Each free throw, each grade, each meeting, each hour of each day should count. Living this way may be intense, but it is a non-negotiable requirement for MFer's.

Even in losing seasons, Michael Jordan tried to dominate every single game. Jerry Rice didn't slow down when he was losing. They always sweated the small stuff. Every task is important. Every small goal is a step closer to a bigger goal. Each micro success contributes to macro success. You can't have a healthy forest without tending to each and every single tree. No matter what they tell you, you should always sweat the small stuff.

CHAPTER XVI
OBSTACLES

"Obstacles cannot crush me. Every obstacle yields to stern resolve. He who is fixed to a star does not change his mind."
– LEONARDO DA VINCI

No goal pursuit is devoid of obstacles. There isn't a successful person who hasn't faced obstacles. My father used to tell me, "If it doesn't kill you, it will make you stronger." He was talking about obstacles. Obstacles slow the rate at which the Flywheel spins. When the Flywheel slows down, it takes more time and more effort to achieve a goal. Obstacles in the focus phase have the most significant effect on the Flywheel.

As we discussed in the previous chapter, focus shows us how to deal with obstacles. For Obstacles Create Unrelenting Strategy, this acronym explains how MFers minimize the effect of obstacles on their goal pursuit. They attack obstacles head-on. They don't change their strategy every time an obstacle is in their way. Why?

Changing the strategy would require cycling through the Flywheel all over again. Obstacles prevent the completion of the execution phase, causing the stagnation of the Flywheel. Obstacles will always exist. They are an inevitable and unavoidable part of goal pursuit. In many cases, success may occur because of obstacles and not in spite of them. Yes! Success may occur because of obstacles! And those obstacles often make success that much sweeter. When we have something to overcome, goal achievement is that much more satisfying. And oddly enough, obstacles may actually heighten our performance.

How do MFers circumnavigate obstacles? Think about a time in your life when you were attempting to achieve a goal. Based on your knowledge of the Flywheel, try to recall a time when you were in the execution phase. What obstacle got in your way? What did you do to overcome it? Did you perceive that obstacle as insurmountable? Were you able to achieve that goal?

There is no Flywheel phase, threshold, or component for overcoming obstacles. Why? MFers anticipate obstacles, but they don't dwell on them. When the going gets tough, MFers get tougher. When times are hard, they get harder. Without extreme heat and pressure, a diamond is just an ugly lump of coal. Great sailors don't become great by only navigating smooth seas.

When it comes to obstacles, MFers go harder. They go around them, through them, over them or under them. They create an unrelenting strategy to overcome them. MFers do whatever it takes to minimize obstacles and their effect on their goal pursuit. They know that obstacles will yield to their stern resolve.

Unfortunately, most people don't deal with obstacles in the same manner that MFers do. We tend to dwell on the obstacle, spending an excessive amount of energy determining how to overcome it. Therefore, altering our focus. Non-MFers inadvertently begin to focus on the obstacle instead of the goal. Focusing on overcoming the obstacle changes your perspective. It obstructs your ability to see your ultimate goal or any goal for that matter. You lose the ability to remain fixed to the star. MFers avoid dwelling in the negativity of the obstruction. They maintain their stern resolve. Michael Jordan said it best: "Obstacles don't have to stop you. If you run into a wall, don't turn around and give up. Figure out how to climb it, go through it, or work around it."

In 2011, LeBron James and the Miami Heat made their way to the National Basketball Association Championship series. This was the first year that the trio of LeBron James, Dwayne Wade, and Chris Bosh played together. Even though they were heavily favored, they lost the championship series to the Dallas Mavericks. Miami was supposed to win. After all, they were the overwhelming favorites. Most people thought LeBron didn't deliver his best. The Miami Heat and LeBron failed to achieve their goal.

What did LeBron James do? He started a new Flywheel. The experience from his failed attempt ignited his new success pursuit. He returned with more inertia and more inward chip. Most of all, LeBron returned with more focus. He knew that for obstacles, he had to create an unrelenting strategy. He knew that obstacles would yield to his stern resolve. Instead of focusing on the obstacle, LeBron focused on the goal. He didn't dwell on the loss. He created a new goal. He was maniacally motivated and fanatically focused to achieve his goal. He knew he had to stay fixed to a star. That star was a championship. The result of LeBron James' renewed focus was a National Basketball Association Championship, and a Finals Most Valuable Player award.

This is the hallmark of Maniacal Fanaticism. If you have difficulty overcoming obstacles, you will have difficulty keeping the goal in view. What obstacles do you have? How are they hindering your success?

Learn from LeBron. Don't dwell on your obstacles. Keep your goals in sight and remain fixed to the star. Obstacles are there to distract you, but they will yield to your stern resolve. They are there to force you off course. They are there to knock you off your path. When you encounter obstacles, create an unrelenting strategy to decrease their effect on your pursuit. Go over, around, under, or through it, but don't you dare dwell on it. Ignore the obstacle. Focus on the goal.

CHAPTER XVII
PIVOT POINT

"In any moment of decision, the best thing you can do is the right thing, the next best thing is the wrong thing, and the worst thing you can do is nothing."
– THEODORE ROOSEVELT

Can you remember the last big decision you had to make? Do you take that new job? Do you accept that promotion? Do you move to that different neighborhood? Should you spend the rest of your life with this person? Should we go through with the merger? Is this the best school for my child? These are life-changing decisions. They are decisions that usually require hours and even days of reflection. These are pivot points.

In sports, a pivot is a move that results in a change of direction. In life, a pivot point is a point in time when an individual changes direction. Not every change in direction is life-altering. We face less challenging pivot points every day. Where should we eat dinner? What should I wear today? What time do I want to play golf?

Our principles, tendencies and values guide the decisions we make at each pivot point. We use our intuition, acquired knowledge, and experience to make the best decision possible with the available information at the time. Unfortunately, we can't accurately predict the consequences of all of our actions. We have to tolerate some outcome ambiguity. Most pivot points aren't black and white. Most of our decision-making outcomes are varying shades of gray. No matter how painstakingly thorough we are, no matter how we deliberate, no matter how many people we ask to assist us, we aren't guaranteed clarity. There isn't a decision where every variable can be accounted for.

Success requires continuous decision-making. Our evaluation of successful people usually focuses on the decisions they have made. We typically analyze their efforts retrospectively. We assume that they make their brilliant decisions, because of their ability to see into the future. This is flawed logic. Their success makes us assume that every decision they have made was the right one.

MFers aren't clairvoyant. Their ability to make the "right" decision stems primarily from the fact that they force themselves to make one. It isn't rocket science. MFers make decisions. Immediacy and ambiguity tolerance, two of the foundation principles, enhance their decision-making ability. If we knew all the possible outcomes and had unlimited time to consider each one, making decisions would be easy.

Decisions are easier to make when looking through the retrospectoscope. Unfortunately, most of the time, decision making isn't that cut and dried. We usually have a limited time to pivot into the right decision. Even the simplest decisions come with some ambiguity. Not every outcome can be anticipated. Not every factor can be calculated. Not every variable can be predicted. All of the information isn't always available. The decision must be made with only the information available at the time.

MFers tolerate this ambiguity. They don't require a guaranteed outcome to make a decision. They tolerate this ambiguity because they can accept the consequences of their actions. If you already have a contingency plan, decisions are a little less daunting. MFers create contingencies for the consequences of those decisions, both desirable and undesirable. This is how they tolerate ambiguity. They can mitigate poorer decision outcomes and anticipate successful ones. This is the source of their perceived clairvoyance. This isn't to say that they predict all the possible outcomes. They do occasionally make the wrong decision, but they focus on contingencies for the most likely outcomes. They anticipate.

To make this a little clearer, think of how a football quarterback decides to throw the ball. On every pass attempt, the quarterback has several pivot points to consider before the defense closes in on him. Every passing attempt is a pivot point. In each moment of decision, he has to consider all the possible variables. Where is the receiver? Where is the defender? How far away is the receiver? How many yards does he need for a first down? How much time does he have to throw the ball? After he throws the ball, how will the receiver respond?

In an instant, the quarterback must consider all of these variables. Every throw has a degree of ambiguity. If he only passes the ball when he is certain of success, how successful would he be? If he only passes the ball when he is certain the receiver would catch it, he wouldn't throw the ball very often. A quarterback like that wouldn't be much of a quarterback at all.

This is precisely what most of us do. We hold the ball. We receive the snap. We take a step back and look at the receivers. We get to the point where we are about to throw the ball. And, we freeze. Due to the uncertainty of the outcome, we fail to throw the ball. We live most of our lives in this indecisive purgatory. Without the guarantee of success, we refuse to pass the ball. We get to our pivot point, and we freeze. After a while, no receivers are open. We either throw the ball away, or we are sacked.

The inability to tolerate ambiguity limits our success. Instead of touchdowns, we hold the ball. Instead of first downs, we get sacked. No pass. No touchdown. No first down. No completion. No incompletion. No interception. No action. No success. We explain away these opportunities. The receivers weren't open. The wind was too strong. The defense was too good. These are excuses and explanations. We use them to make us feel better about our inability to make a decision. To be successful, you must make pivot point decisions in the moment and throw the ball.

At your pivot point, remain in the moment and use all the information available to you. That is worth reiterating. You must use all the available information at the time a decision is necessary. It doesn't have to be the right decision, but you have to make one. Without immediacy, the opportunity is gone. That pivot point will never return. That specific decision, at that particular moment in time, with those particular variables, is gone. The success moment has passed. The opportunity to pass to that receiver, in that game, on that day, will never again present itself in that way.

The same is true for pivot points in your life. They are as unique as snowflakes. You must attack your pivot points. You must consider the options and all the likely consequences. You must tolerate the ambiguity of not knowing the outcome. You must use immediacy and make decisions with only the available information. Most of all, you should understand that not making a decision is indeed a decision. Not making a decision is a decision to deny success. Without making a decision, you will be sacked.

You can't throw a touchdown without first releasing the ball. You may throw an interception, but you have anticipated that. When you get to your pivot point, take in all the information. Don't let the ambiguity paralyze you. Consider your contingency for all the foreseeable outcomes. I think Gandhi said it best: "You may never know what results come from your action. But if you do nothing, there will be no result." You may not make the right decision, but you have to make one. Throw the ball!

FROM WITHIN
ACCELERATORS
WHAT DO YOU FEEL
HAPPINESS COMES
ASSESSMENT
SUPERSTAR
LUCKY
ALTERATION
ACCEPTANCE
MOTIVATION
MANIACAL
FANATICISM
INERTIA
OBSTACLES
LOFTY
HIDDEN
INWARD
SUCCESS
FOUNDATION
VALUES
FLYWHEEL
FOCUS
SUCCESS STRATEGY
BLAME
GUTCHECK
FUTILITY
THRESHOLD
DON'T SWEAT THE SMALL STUFF
SUPER TRUST
HERO
PROMISE
YOUR FAULT
CHECKMATE
NO EXPLANATIONS
NO EXCUSES
BETTER LUCKY THAN GOOD
POISE
PAST PERFORMANCE
FUTURE SUCCESS
CIRCUMSTANCE
PERFECT SITUATION
SUCCESSOLOGY
MANIACAL FANATICISM BEST
PIVOT
PERSISTENCE
SELF DENIAL
DISCIPLINE
GAME DAY
BELIEF
CONSISTENCY
SYNERGY
GOALS
EVIDENCE

BOOK 2
UNUM

"DO ONE"

FROM WITHIN
HUMBLE
ACCELERATORS
LUCKY
ASSESSMENT
SUPERSTAR
ALTERATION
MOTIVATION
MANIACAL
INERTIA
FANATICISM
OBSTACLES
INWARD
HIDDEN
SUCCESS
FOUNDATION
VALUES
FLYWHEEL
FOCUS
BLAME
PIVOT
GUTCHECK
FUTILITY
THRESHOLD
SWEAT THE SMALL
SUPER TRUST
HERO
PROMISE
YOUR
FAULT
CHECKMATE
NO EXCUSES
NO EXPLANATIONS
BETTER LUCKY THAN GOOD
POISE
PAST PERFORMANCE
FUTURE SUCCESS
CIRCUMSTANCE
PERFECT SITUATION
SUCCESSOLOGY
MANIACAL FANATICISM BEST

CHAPTER XVIII
MIDWAY REFLECTION

"Take up one idea. Make that one idea your life—think of it, dream of it, live on that idea. Let the brain, muscles, nerves, every part of your body, be full of that idea, and just leave every other idea alone. This is the way to success, that is the way great spiritual giants are produced."

– SWAMI VIVEKANANDA

Let's review what we have learned about the Flywheel so far. Your path to success should start with inertia. You have to get excited about something to generate momentum. My inertia for writing this book was to find an answer to a question. How do people pursue success? This question started my Flywheel. I had to generate enough energy to overcome the stagnation of mediocrity. I had to gather enough energy to go from non-author to author.

Unfortunately, my inertia wasn't enough. I had to ask more questions. Could I write this book? Was it possible? Was I good enough? Would anybody want to read this book? Was I a good enough writer? This was my inward chip. The doubt from my inward chip wasn't all negative. The inward chip increased my motivation.

How should you use your inward chip? Understanding that you aren't the best or the most talented makes you work harder to improve. It increases your motivation. Your inward chip should make you better. It acknowledges where you need improvement. At this point, you aren't required to act on your inward chip. All you have to do is understand it, use it for introspection and allow it to identify areas for improvement.

Having satisfied the inertia threshold and the inward chip, we now move on to the focus phase. The focus phase develops goals and strategies. I will again use this book as an example. My requisite goals focused on the completion time for the book. My expected goals were to find an agent and get the book published. My lofty goals focused on the validity, acceptance, and adoption of the Maniacal Fanaticism Theory. It wouldn't make sense for me to develop a theory without using it myself.

So now that you have the inertia and introspection from the inward chip, what goals are you going to develop? What goals are you going to create for your life, your job, or your company? Remember, a goal isn't a hope. Hope isn't actionable. Hope requires faith, and faith is supposed to be blind. To attain your goals, you need the vision to see them, not just blindly expect them to materialize. Goal and strategy development set the trajectory for your entire goal pursuit. There isn't enough inertia and self-introspection in the world to overcome poor goal development and poor strategy.

Developing workable goals and strategies requires tons of energy. This is where it is easy to lose interest. Procrastination occurs when we don't create effective strategies and goals. Making goals and strategy isn't enough. You should continually reassess them. As long as the Flywheel doesn't stop, slowing down may be necessary to correct the strategy.

No matter what your level of talent or degree of luck, following the Flywheel will give you the structure to maximize your potential. The inward chip, inertia, goals, and strategy should be second nature. You have to dream it. You have to live it. You have to eat it, drink it and sleep it. Executing your success strategy should permeate everything you do. Every fiber of your being should be *motivated* and *focused* to achieve success. This is the way to success. Now that we have seen it, let's do it.

FROM WITHIN
ACCELERATORS
WHAT DO YOU FEEL
HAPPINESS COMES
ASSESSMENT
SUPERSTAR
LUCKY
ALTERATION
MOTIVATION
MANIACAL
INERTIA
FANATICISM
OBSTACLES
INWARD
HIDDEN
M
SUCCESS FOUNDATION
R
VALUES FLYWHEEL
FOCUS
SUCCESS
BLAME
E
GUTCHECK
FUTILITY
THRESHOLD
SWEAT THE SMALL STUFF
SUPER TRUST
HERO
YOUR
CHECKMATE
NO EXCUSES
NO EXPLANATIONS
BETTER LUCKY THAN GOOD
PAST PERFORMANCE
CIRCUMSTANCE
SUCCESSOLOGY
MANIACAL FANATICISM BEST

CHAPTER XIX
EXECUTION PHASE

"We all have dreams. But in order to make dreams come into reality, it takes an awful lot of determination, dedication, self-discipline, and effort."
– JESSE OWENS

Congratulations, you have made it halfway through the MF Flywheel. You now have a better understanding of the "why" and the "what" of Maniacal Fanaticism. You understand that Motivation is the "why" and is composed of inertia and the inward chip. You understand that Focus is the "what." It is composed of goal and strategy development. You also understand that a completed motivation phase leads to the focus phase. Once the focus phase is completed, we are ready to execute.

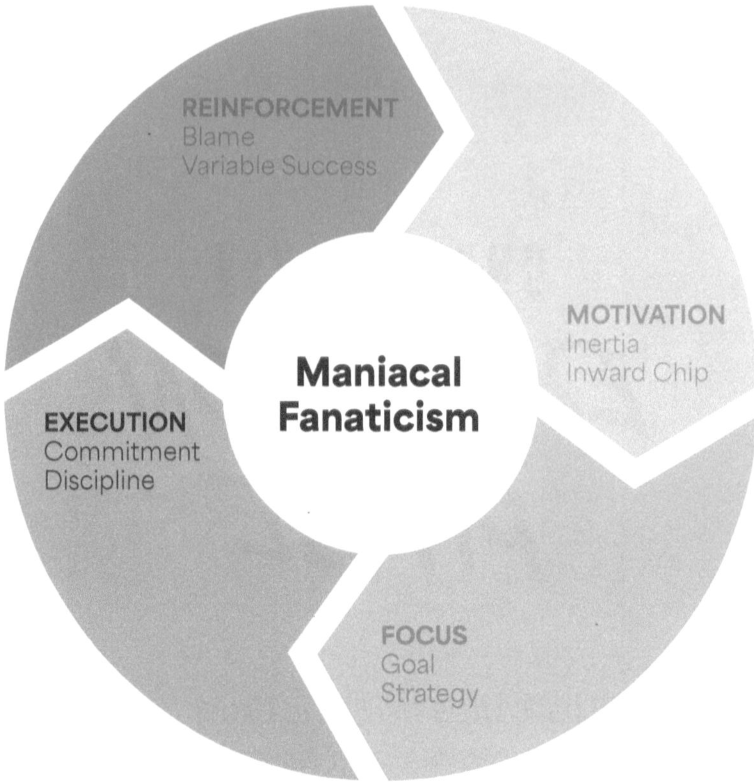

Appropriately, the next phase is the execution phase. The execution phase is the workhorse of the Flywheel. It is the "how" of Maniacal Fanaticism. How are you going to achieve your goals? How are you going to implement your strategy? Motivation and focus occur on the macroscopic level, while execution requires a microscopic view. Successful execution requires attention to the minutia. Execution can't start in January and fizzle out by March. It is time to sweat the small stuff.

Just like the first two phases, execution is composed of two thresholds. Those thresholds are commitment and discipline. As the names imply, this phase is responsible for the fulfillment of the strategy. Commitment describes the buy-in. It is a promise. Discipline is the fulfillment of the promise.

MFers attempt to integrate their strategies into all aspects of their lives. In this way, Maniacal Fanaticism is invasive and unyielding. It isn't a part-time endeavor. MFers eat, drink, sleep, and breathe their strategy. Are you ready to commit? Do you have the discipline to follow through? Most of us are New Year's resolutionists. We start projects with good intentions, only to lose interest a short while later.

The Maniacal Fanaticism Flywheel is a life cycle. It isn't short-lived. Short-term goals and strategies can yield some transient success, but lasting success occurs over a much longer period. Execution is demanding. It requires you to ask yourself some tough questions. What are you willing to give up to initiate your strategy? How much would your life have to change? What other commitments do you have? Are these competing commitments? Are they mutually exclusive?

Lastly, you have to ask yourself, "Are the goals important enough for you to commit to your strategy?" These profound questions are difficult to answer, but they shouldn't scare you. They should help you openly commit to the execution strategy. You should know what you are getting into before you walk down the aisle.

Like individuals, organizations can also follow the Flywheel. Organizations are usually motivated to succeed. As a result, they can generate lots of inertia. They also have relatively minor difficulty determining goals and developing strategy, but getting the commitment from stakeholders is an entirely different challenge. Large organizations need all the individuals involved in the strategy implementation to buy-in. Because of this, organizations and individuals alike have difficulty with execution.

The poet Robert Burns wrote, "The best laid schemes of mice and men oft go awry." He was ahead of his time. He was referring to how difficult execution can be. Execution often fails because of the inability to commit. Without commitment, execution is impossible. In our society, the word commitment is overused. Most people use it without knowing exactly what it means. Successful execution requires specific detail about what commitment really means. The execution phase bridges the gap between dreams and success. Dreams only become a reality with extraordinary determination, dedication, self-discipline, effort, and commitment.

CHAPTER XX
COMMITMENT

"Desire is the key to motivation, but it's determination and commitment to an unrelenting pursuit of your goal–a commitment to excellence–that will enable you to attain the success you seek."

– MARIO ANDRETTI

Essentially, a commitment is a pledge to do something in the future. It is the state or an instance of being obligated or emotionally impelled. To be fully committed, you need to trust. In this phase, you need to trust your strategy and trust that your goals are achievable. Most of all, you have to trust yourself. You develop trust by believing in your strategy and goals. Like an engagement, commitment obligates you to continue the process. Your success is dependent on your ability to fulfill that promise. Commitment serves as the transition point between intangible strategy and an executed plan. It is composed of three elements: belief, promise, and trust.

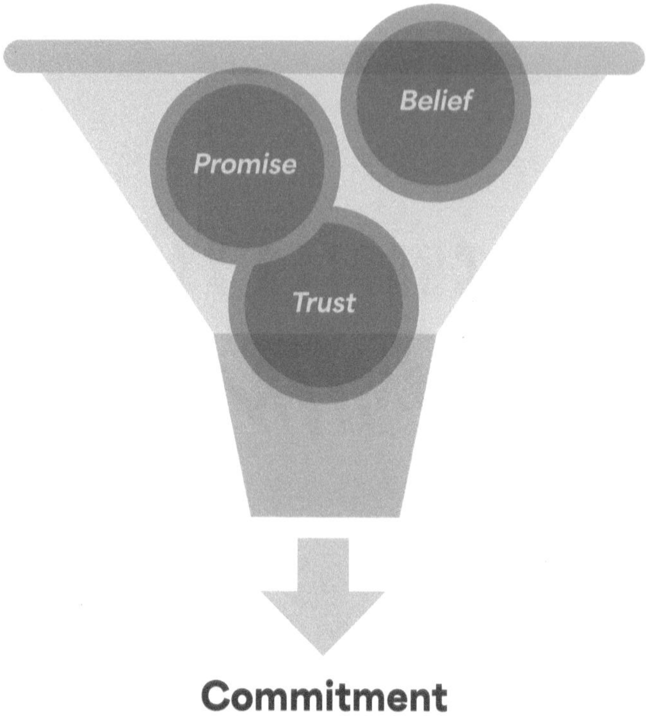

Wholehearted commitment to anything requires that you believe in it. Committing to something you don't believe in is almost impossible. Without a belief that he could be successful at football, Jerry Rice couldn't have committed to his fanatical training regimen. Therefore, it should be no surprise that belief is the first component of commitment. Belief is then broken down even further into three more parts: belief in the strategy, belief in the process, and belief in oneself.

Before we go any further, I want to make a clear distinction. Belief isn't faith. Faith requires no evidence or justification. Don't get me wrong. There is nothing wrong with having a little faith, but belief is very different. For Maniacal Fanatics, belief has a huge role in completing the commitment threshold. Belief has its foundation in logic and requires evidence. Faith, on the other hand, requires no such evidence. For MFers, the evidence is in the process.

The Flywheel, to this point, gives the MFer the supporting evidence to solidify their belief. MFers believe that the process of developing appropriate goals and strategies will result in success. They believe their commitment and discipline will allow them to achieve those goals. MFers also believe in the strategy. If you have developed a strategy, it makes sense that you believe in it. Lastly, MFers must believe in themselves. They have to believe that they can accomplish their goals.

This idea often confuses people because of the inward chip. Does this mean belief and trust are in direct opposition to the inward chip? Not exactly. The inward chip serves a particular purpose at a particular time. It forces introspection. Determining where you aren't very good should compel you to improve. Self-doubt is necessary to satisfy the inward chip threshold, but it serves no purpose in the focus and execution phases.

By the execution phase, the desire to improve replaces inferiority and doubt. The inward chip makes you ask the question: "Can I get better?" The execution phase makes the statement: "I will get better, and this is how." Think of something you would like to improve. Think about a skill you would like to acquire. Think about something you would like to do better. Determining what you need to improve requires introspection and the inward chip. After identifying where you need to improve, you can develop a plan and commit to a strategy to improve it. Remaining doubtful during execution limits your ability to achieve your goals and your ability to succeed.

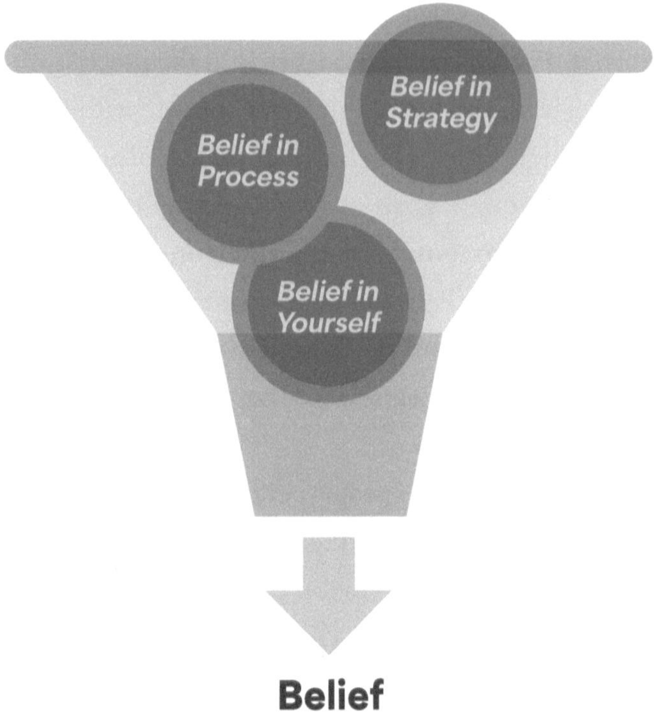

Promise is the next component of commitment. Committing to something or someone is essentially a promise. When MFers commit to executing their strategy, they are making a promise to themselves to follow the process and strategy. Making a declaration about what you want to do isn't as powerful as promising to do it. A promise necessitates a future secondary action. It implies that something else needs to happen. This is why promises are so powerful. Promises are dynamic, engaging, and come with a subsequent action of delivery.

The most obvious example of this is a couple who is engaged to be married. Engagement is a promise to get married. An engagement is more than just saying, "One day we will get married." The ritual of giving an engagement ring signifies something more powerful than just a simple statement. The percentage of couples that get married after an engagement is higher than those who merely state marriage is one of their goals. The promise of engagement results in many future secondary actions. After the engagement, the couple plans the wedding and honeymoon. Without secondary actions, promises are useless.

The last component of the commitment threshold is trust. Commitment can't occur without trust. Trust is necessary for strategy fulfillment. MFers develop an unwavering trust in themselves, their strategy, and their ability to accomplish their goals. Don't confuse trust with confidence. Confidence is an aloof assurance that an outcome will be positive. Confidence doesn't require that you have put the work in. Tiger Woods believed he could win golf tournaments because he trusted his preparation strategy. He trusted he could win those tournaments because he trusted himself to make winning putts.

Trust doesn't always mean that you will have a favorable outcome, but it does mean you have little doubt that you have prepared the right way. When the putt goes in, people perceive this trust as confidence. When the putt doesn't go in, people perceive it as overconfidence. No matter the outcome, Tiger Wood's trust in his ability was unfettered. Confidence and overconfidence are merely how other people perceive him based on the outcome.

Are you ready to commit? Are you ready to make the promise to achieve your goals? Can you commit to implementing your strategy? Can you purge the inward chip and remove all self-doubt? Do you believe in your goals? Do you believe in the strategy? Most of all, do you believe in yourself?

In the execution phase, you are making a promise to yourself. Your success pursuit is what is at stake. Because of its ability to motivate, self-doubt can be a powerful tool. At this point, however, self-doubt is counterproductive. Your trust must be unwavering. You have developed a great strategy, and now you have to commit to it.

Through adversity, pain, hunger, thirst, fatigue, and illness, you won't yield. Commit. Promise. Trust. Believe. Execute!

CHAPTER XXI

DISCIPLINE

"I fear not the man who has practiced 10,000 kicks once, but I fear the man who has practiced one kick 10,000 times."

– BRUCE LEE

Discipline is the intense compulsion for doing tasks we would rather not do, with the same vigor as those tasks we prefer to do. Discipline is the second threshold in the execution phase. If you consider that commitment is a promise, discipline is the delivery on that promise. When people say, "They lack commitment," they really mean they lack discipline. Commitment is simple. It is easy to make a promise. However, delivering on that promise is an entirely different ball game!

The discipline threshold is where the strategy gains some traction. It is where the rubber meets the road. Discipline breaks down into four components: strategy fulfillment, regimen, sacrifice, and self-denial. Strategy fulfillment is self-explanatory. It is the fruit produced from the strategy development seed. Strategy fulfillment is the engine necessary for the heavy lifting of the Flywheel.

Discipline is how the medical school student implements her study strategy, where the Olympic athlete sets his training schedule and where the operations team implements the strategy outlined by the CEO. Strategy can be tweaked a little, but implementation should be fixed for the most part. Changes in strategy force you back to the focus phase to develop a new approach. This can cost time and effort. Staying on task and effectively implementing a strategy is extremely important.

The next component of discipline is regimen. Regimen is exactly what it sounds like. Success requires structure, and regimen is that structure. Regimen is the consistent application of the plan. It is the fanatical adherence to the strategy. It is the obsessive compulsion of Maniacal Fanaticism. MFers are consistent about how much they train, how many hours they study, or how many days a week they work. MFers won't deviate from their regimen.

Why was Jerry Rice so successful? It was partly because of his ability to excel in this phase. His maniacal discipline, ability to fulfill his strategy, and fanatical adherence to his training regimen were unmatched. His Maniacal Fanaticism was a result of his discipline. His adherence to his regimen enhanced his execution.

That brings us to the next two components of discipline. Self-denial and sacrifice may be the most critical components of the discipline threshold. Adherence to the strategy is mandatory. Personal needs and desires are secondary. There is no hunger. There is no thirst. There is no sleep. MFers deny themselves whatever it takes to stick to their regimen. They reject any self-interest that may derail their pursuit. Self-denial and sacrifice may seem to be the same principles, but they are slightly different. Self-denial refers to those things in our lives that we assume are necessities. Sacrifice refers to the loss of those things we hold dear.

To achieve my goal of attending medical school, I had to sacrifice my senior year of college basketball. To achieve my goal of completing medical school, I had to deny myself sleep. Do you see the difference? I didn't need basketball, but I probably required sleep. What are you willing to deny yourself? What are you ready to sacrifice? Can you tolerate the pain? Can you handle the work? Can you be a Maniacal Fanatic?

FROM WITHIN HUMBLE
ACCELERATORS
WHAT DO YOU FEEL
HAPPINESS COMES
ASSESSMENT
LUCKY
SUPERSTAR
ALTERATION
ACCEPTANCE
MOTIVATION
MANIACAL
INERTIA
LOFTY
FANATICISM
OBSTACLES
INWARD
HIDDEN
M
SUCCESS
FOUNDATION
VALUES
FLYWHEEL
R
FOCUS
GOALS
EVIDENCE
BLAME
SUCCESS
STRATEGY
GUTCHECK
FUTILITY
THRESHOLD
SWEAT THE SMALL
SUPER
TRUST
HERO
PROMISE
YOUR
FAULT
CHECKMATE
NO EXCUSES
NO EXPLANATIONS
BETTER LUCKY THAN GOOD
POISE
FUTURE SUCCESS
PAST PERFORMANCE
CIRCUMSTANCE
PERFECT SITUATION
SUCCESSOLOGY
MANIACAL FANATICISM BEST
PIVOT
DON'T
DISCIPLINE
DENIAL
MEMORY
STARTER
FAILURE
EXECUTION
VARIABLE
SELF
INTEREST
CAPACIBILITY
BEYOND
PERSISTENCE
ACCOUNTABLE

CHAPTER XXII

ALWAYS GIVE UP

"One half of knowing what you want is knowing what you must give up before you get it."

– SIDNEY HOWARD

We would be naive to think there is only one road to success. Many roads to success exist, but none of them is easy. Unfortunately, that isn't what we want to hear. Deep down inside, or maybe not so deep for some of us, we would rather take the easy road to success. We would rather take a short cut, one that wasn't so darn difficult. After reading about commitment and discipline, you probably realized you should have bought a book titled "*The Ten Simple Steps to Success!*"

Regrettably, there is no magic pill. There is no quick or easy way to succeed. The work of the Flywheel isn't easy. Although we can stretch the amount of effort and energy we can generate, we do have an effort ceiling. We only have so many hours in the day, and the energy available for the Flywheel isn't limitless. To maintain that maniacal motivation, focus, and effort, something has to give.

Most of us end up being jacks-of-all-trades and masters of none. Mastery requires inordinate effort. By vesting ourselves in multiple areas, mastery becomes increasingly difficult. Because energy is limited, each Flywheel has a speed limit. We also have a limit on the number of Flywheels we can spin at the same time. What do we do? How do we find enough energy to pursue excellence in multiple areas? We have to give up.

I don't mean we should give up in the traditional sense of the phrase. In this case, giving up means we have to recover the energy from somewhere. Something has to be cut out or given up. The fact that many of the most successful people in our history didn't sleep has been well documented. The exact physiological requirement for sleep has never really been determined. Sleep can be invigorating, energizing, and necessary, but it also is an unbelievably catastrophic waste of time.

How much more productive would the human race be without the need for sleep? If the average person sleeps about eight hours a day, not sleeping would make us about thirty percent more productive. What would happen if the most intelligent of us didn't waste precious analytic time in a mind-numbing stupor? What would happen if the most creative of us didn't have to waste precious hours of creative genius in a semi-conscious purgatory?

Spending more time than is required in other non-Flywheel areas lowers the probability of success. It is almost a no-brainer. The less time we spend pursuing success, the less chance we have of succeeding. Somehow, we don't always make that direct correlation. We tend to engage our pursuits occasionally and sporadically. We tend not to acknowledge what we have to exclude, to find time to spin the Flywheel. To be successful, we always have to give up something.

In my last year of college, I began the arduous process of applying for medical school. Applying to medical school requires taking the medical college admission test, multiple interviews, and a myriad of applications. This was one of the most important times of my life. However, I also wanted to continue to play basketball, my first love. I had managed to juggle the two throughout my undergraduate studies, but now I had a conflict. I had to interview at several medical schools, and this process was directly at odds with the demands of college basketball.

Long story short, I had to give up my first love basketball for my second love—medicine. Giving up basketball was devastating. I am not ashamed to say I cried like a baby. In retrospect, this had to happen. To be successful, I had to give up. Giving up basketball enabled me to interview at medical schools around the country and increased my chances of getting in.

My first acceptance was at Michigan State, and I was the first pre-medical student in my class to get in that year. Without giving up basketball, I wasn't going to achieve my goal of becoming a doctor. I had to give up something. My medical school Flywheel required more energy, so my basketball Flywheel had to stop. Devastating as it was, it had to be done.

What will you give up? You can't spin everything at the same time. You shouldn't arbitrarily eliminate anything, but you need to prioritize where you put your energy. You can't simply start and stop Flywheels haphazardly. Unfortunately, you have to give something up and increase your effort efficiency. Giving up may be one of the most important first steps to starting your success journey. Be very careful not to be a jack-of-all-trades and a master of none. To be successful, you have to know what you want. You also have to know what you will give up to get it.

FROM WITHIN
ACCELERATORS
FEEL
SUPERSTAR
ALTERATION
MOTIVATION
MANIACAL
FANATICISM
OBSTACLES
INWARD
HIDDEN
SUCCESS
FOUNDATION
VALUES
FLYWHEEL
FOCUS
BLAME
GUTCHECK
FUTILITY
THRESHOLD
SWEAT THE SMALL
SUPER TRUST
YOUR
CHECKMATE
NO EXCUSES
NO EXPLANATIONS
BETTER LUCKY THAN GOOD
PAST PERFORMANCE
CIRCUMSTANCE
SUCCESSOLOGY
MANIACAL FANATICISM BEST

CHAPTER XXIII

IF IT WAS FUN, IT WOULDN'T BE CALLED WORK

"The happy life is thought to be one of excellence; now an excellent life requires exertion, and does not consist in amusement."

– ARISTOTLE

It should be clear by now; execution is where the work is. Motivation is exhilarating. Goal development is inspiring, and strategy development is exciting. Execution, however, is the place you earn your stripes. This phase is the most difficult to complete and is where most people falter. This is where the heavy lifting is. I would have loved to give a utopian road map to success. Instead of Maniacal Fanaticism, that book would have been called "Effortless Casualism."

This book represents what MFers do and what they do isn't easy. That isn't to say success is impossible. You just have to work at it. As we pursue our goals, we have to be careful not to confuse passion with goal pursuit. Passions are usually enjoyable and something that we want to do. Having a passion for something is markedly different from the work necessary for goal pursuit.

Unfortunately, the work of the execution phase isn't fun. If it were fun, it wouldn't be called work. The error people make is to assume that somehow work should be pleasurable. It is always interesting to me to hear people say that work should be enjoyable. I think most of us truly don't understand what work is. Work is many things, but fun just isn't one of them.

I am sure you are saying to yourself, "I really like my job." I am so glad you like your job. Work, though, is something dramatically different. You can like or dislike a job. You can like or dislike where you work. You can like or dislike the people you work with. You can like or dislike the type of work you do. The work itself isn't likable and isn't particularly fun.

Let's examine the definition of the word work. Work means exerting yourself physically or mentally. Work means making your way slowly and with great difficulty. Work means to move or progress laboriously. Work means fashioning or creating a useful or desired product by expanding labor or exertion. None of these definitions has the word fun in it. None of these definitions has the word pleasure. None of these definitions has the word passion. What words do these definitions include? They include words like exertion, laborious, and difficult. These aren't words we typically associate with fun. If the work of success were fun, we would have many more successful people in the world.

Unless you are a masochist, work isn't fun. We confuse enjoying the type of work we do with enjoying actual work. Not surprisingly, we lose motivation when we find out that work is hard. Jerry Rice's fanatical training regimen was work. If his workout regimen were fun, every player in football would have done it.

Here is another example. I love playing golf. I casually play several pleasurable rounds of golf every month, and I often say to myself, "Wouldn't it be fun to make a living playing golf?" It sounds like fun! However, the fun of golf doesn't change the work of golf. What would it take to become a professional golfer? Even if it were possible, it would require thousands of hours of lessons and practice. It would require—work.

Work is universal. The work needed to improve at golf is the same work necessary for medical school. Jerry Rice used that same work for football. Michael Jordan used the same work for basketball. Work is the labor of the Flywheel. Work is the pain of the pursuit. Work is the exertion of the effort. Work *should* hurt. If it doesn't hurt, it probably isn't work. As you pursue success, and you find yourself in the execution phase, don't expect it to be easy. Understand that this is the work of the Flywheel, and it isn't fun.

The work of execution will test your resolve. You have to set expectations for yourself, and one of those expectations is that you will need to work. It isn't all doom and gloom. Cycling through the Flywheel can be a lot of fun. The success pursuit is what delivers the pleasure, but the work itself will be difficult. Bear down and mentally prepare for it. It isn't good or bad. It just is. Don't get bogged down, expecting the work to be fun because if it were fun, it wouldn't be called work.

FROM WITHIN
ACCELERATORS
WHAT DO YOU FEEL
HAPPINESS COMES
ASSESSMENT
SUPERSTAR
LUCKY
ALTERATION
ACCEPTANCE
MOTIVATION
MANIACAL
INERTIA
FANATICISM
OBSTACLES
INWARD
HIDDEN
M
SUCCESS
FOUNDATION
R
VALUES
FLYWHEEL
FOCUS
SUCCESS
STRATEGY
BLAME
GUTCHECK
FUTILITY
THRESHOLD
SWEAT THE SMALL
SUPER TRUST
HERO
YOUR
FAULT
CHECKMATE
NO EXCUSES
NO EXPLANATIONS
BETTER LUCKY THAN GOOD
POISE
FUTURE SUCCESS
PAST PERFORMANCE
CIRCUMSTANCE
PERFECT SITUATION
SUCCESSOLOGY
MANIACAL FANATICISM
PIVOT
BEYOND
CAPACIBILITY

CHAPTER XXIV
GUT CHECK

"Smooth seas do not make skillful sailors."
– AFRICAN PROVERB

In the winter of 2000, I suffered second- and third-degree burns to twenty percent of my body in a house fire. The burns were so extensive that even walking was challenging. This was one of the worst times of my life. The pain was unbearable. To complicate matters, I was in my last semester of medical school. The doctors recommended admission to the hospital and skin grafts. Grafting would require taking skin from my back and surgically placing it on my legs.

This was my gut check. If I stayed out of school for the required eight weeks, I wouldn't graduate on time. Because the internship starts right after medical school graduation, the timing couldn't have been any worse. Any delay greater than two weeks would mean that my Flywheel would have slowed, or even stopped.

This happens to all of us at some time. We all have those periods in our success pursuit when we face an obstacle so daunting that continuing seems impossible. In Michael Jordan's second season with the

Chicago Bulls, he broke his leg and missed sixty-four games. While the injury wasn't career-threatening, it definitely slowed his Flywheel that season. Winning a championship is hard when you are out for the majority of the season. This was one of Michael Jordan's gut checks.

As much as we try to prepare for these challenges, they are still demoralizing when they occur. Gut checks always seem to come at the most inopportune time. They also seem to follow an accomplishment or occur right before an imminent success. Michael Jordan's gut check came after a stellar Rookie of the Year season. His gut check stalled the anticipation of his upcoming sophomore season. Six months before I was to achieve my eight-year goal of becoming a physician, my Flywheel careened to a halt.

The execution phase of the Flywheel has the greatest chance of not being completed. Can't stop smoking or still unable to lose weight? This is a result of an incomplete execution phase. The gut check is an acute challenge to your commitment and discipline. As the name implies, this is your moment to dig deep. It is often associated with an obstacle that is difficult to overcome. Dictionary.com defines a gut check as a "test of one's nerve, courage, or determination." The burns were my test. Michael Jordan's leg was his test.

A gut check is a finite and singular event where your nerve, courage, and determination are tested. It is the point at which your entire Flywheel is tested. Passing these tests are necessary to keep the Flywheel spinning. For the most part, stopping the Flywheel is a bad thing. In the case of gut checks, briefly stopping the Flywheel may be necessary. Dictionary.com also defines the gut check as a pause to assess the state, progress, or condition of something such as an enterprise or institution. Checking your gut is more than just digging deep. MFers have a particular way they work through them.

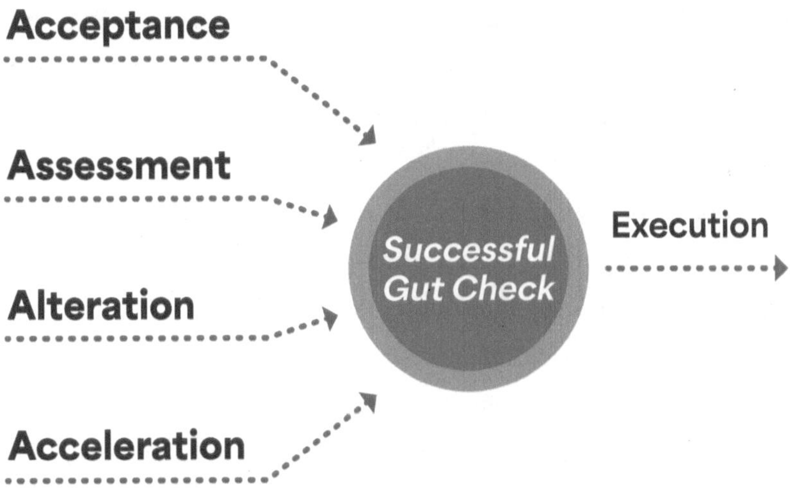

Whether MFers are aware of it or not, they follow a specific gut check process. To be clear, gut checks aren't a part of the Flywheel cycle. This process is necessary to return to the execution phase. These gut check components are additive, but they aren't necessarily sequential. Successful gut checks require the completion of each component. A successful gut check first requires acceptance. Like Elisabeth Kubler-Ross's description of the stages of grief, having the Flywheel stop abruptly is a kind of loss. To get back to execution requires a similar loss progression.

When I was burned, I went through similar stages. Denial, I told myself the burns weren't as bad as they were. Anger, why was I burned? Bargaining, I will do anything to make these burns go away. Depression, I will never get better anyway. Finally, I arrived at acceptance. I accepted the difficult time that lay ahead. Not good, not bad, just is.

Acceptance is the step toward getting past the obstacle. You accept that the Flywheel has slowed or stopped. You accept that work is required to get back to execution. You also must become comfortable with the fact that the gut check will be difficult. My burns were the worst pain I had ever experienced. It was devastating, but I had to accept it. When Michael Jordan broke his leg, he had to accept it.

The next component of the gut check is assessment. Assessment is the evaluation of what must happen next. What impact does the obstacle have on your ability to achieve your goal? The assessment is an appraisal of the situation. It determines what the setback is and what is necessary to get the Flywheel back on track. This component is similar to the strategy threshold. Assess the damage, assess what may be required to get back on track, and assess how much time may be necessary to make it all happen.

Gut check components don't always have to follow each other, but if you don't have acceptance, it is tough to get to assessment. During my gut check assessment, I had to answer several questions. How long will it take me to heal? Will I need burn graft surgery? How long will I need to be out of school? Will I be able to walk? Can I tolerate the pain? These questions don't originate from desperation. They are asked constructively to find a solution.

Highly successful people often try to minimize their obstacles. Having an aggressive outlook is great, but you also have to be realistic. The assessment starts to generate energy. This is the tipping point, the point at which the negativity of the crisis begins to dissipate. It is the point where the thought of finding a solution starts to shine through. The light at the end of the tunnel is now visible. My father would often tell me, "It will be long, but not forever." That is precisely why you find a change in energy here. Assessments provide the opportunity to determine how dark, treacherous, and long the tunnel is. A relative euphoria is associated with envisioning the end of a challenging time, even if that end is a long way away.

Alteration, the next component of the gut check, can be an exciting time. How in the world can a gut check be exciting? If you have been through a tough time, you know exactly what I mean. Alteration is where you get a little of your groove back. You have accepted the gut check. You have assessed the gut check. Now it is time to alter your course. In alteration, you regain a little control.

Assessment exposes the light at the end of the tunnel, and alteration shows you the path to get there. Alteration functions as execution does in the Flywheel. It is the work of recovery. During my gut check, I used alteration to regain control of an awful situation. I refused to let the burns control what I could and couldn't do. I refused to let the pain dictate what I could accomplish. I altered my path. Alteration set the course and enabled me to get back to my Flywheel.

The last component of the gut check is acceleration. Acceleration is just what the name implies. You are accelerating out of the gut check and back into the Flywheel. Obviously, the Flywheel had to slow down to allow a gut check to take place. Now that you are ready to return to the Flywheel, you need to get back up to speed. You are near the end of the gut check, and you know it. The pain of the difficult road is left behind and replaced with the euphoria of finally getting out of the tunnel. Execution is hard, but the gut check is harder. The gut check makes any subsequent execution look like a walk in the park.

The acceleration of the gut check doesn't only accelerate you out of the gut check. It accelerates the entire Flywheel. What doesn't kill you makes you stronger. If the gut check doesn't kill you, your Flywheel will spin faster. If the tough times don't kill your success pursuit, those tough times increase your ability to succeed. Smooth seas don't make skillful sailors and it stands to reason that the best sailors have likely sailed the roughest seas. Your ability to succeed is, in part, dependent on the obstacles you have to overcome. The gut checks train you for the Flywheel. The obstacles train you for success.

I know I left you hanging. You are wondering what happened after I was burned. My goal was too important to let anything get in my way. I refused grafting and was back in school in two weeks. I bandaged my legs and fought through the pain. My wounds healed eventually. More importantly, I graduated on time!

As painful and as difficult as that was, I am glad it happened. That gut check prepared me for future gut checks. That gut check heightened my success pursuit. I used to think that I was able to achieve many of my success goals in spite of my gut check. But the truth is that I was able to achieve many of my success goals because of my gut check. It is difficult to anticipate gut checks, but they are coming. Your gut check will be long, but not forever. You can't be a skillful sailor by only sailing on smooth seas. How deep can you dig? Your gut check is coming. Will you be ready?

CHAPTER XXV
SUPERHERO

"I think a hero is an ordinary individual who finds strength to persevere and endure in spite of overwhelming obstacles."
– CHRISTOPHER REEVE

Like all young kids, the kids in my neighborhood all wanted to be superheroes. It was intense. We would spend all our free time battling evil villains. I remember wearing a makeshift cape and pretending I could fly. I would spend hours thinking about what powers I would have, and what my secret identity would be. At school, we had some passionate seven-year-old debates about who the best superhero was. We would pretend to scale the side of the school building and jump down from the steps in full flight. I can even remember a time where I thought I had x-ray vision. It sounds crazy, but I believed it.

Superpowers are great, but they aren't a prerequisite for superhero status. We know this is true because many of those evil villains had superpowers, and they were far from heroes. Independently, superpowers don't make you a superhero, and being a superhero doesn't require superpowers. Superheroes are superheroes, because of what they chose to do.

In those days, every television show ended with the superhero prevailing. The hero *always* triumphed over evil. The circumstances didn't matter. The obstacles didn't matter. The villain didn't matter. The superhero always found a way to win. Only rarely was this not true, and that was when there was a two-part series. By the end of the second show, though, all was good.

The superheroes on television are fictional characters, but they set a very realistic precedent. Superheroes always win. Always! Superheroes are ordinary people who believe they can always win. They find the strength to fight through insurmountable obstacles. If you want to be a superhero, all you have to do is believe you can win. By the end of the show, you will win. If superpowers don't separate superheroes from ordinary people, what does? Is it honor, valor, courage, or confidence? These traits and others like them allow the ordinary to persevere and endure. They take everyday people and make them superheroes. Success is similar.

The traits that separate MFers from ordinary are eternal optimism, ambiguity tolerance, immediacy, innovation, mediocrity intolerance, inertia, inward chip, developed goals and strategy, commitment, discipline, variable success, and blame, consistency, and synergy. These traits aren't superpowers, but they allow ordinary people to persevere and endure. They make ordinary people extraordinary.

Ultimately, *you* get to decide to be a superhero. *You* get to decide to be a success. You already know this type of person. Look around your office, your organization, your team, your shift, your class, or your family. Who are the superheroes? Who are ordinary people that choose to be extraordinary? Who are the people that always choose to win?

I can remember watching the original Batman series on television. It was the series with the words "Pow" and "Bang" every time Batman punched someone. I will never forget the end of almost every episode. Just before the commercial break, the commentator would ask a question: "Will Batman pull past this precarious predicament premeditated and planned by the pernicious Penguin?"

As we watched, we always knew what the answer would be. The outcome was always the same. We knew good would triumph over evil. We knew that Batman would somehow pull through. We stayed glued to the TV because we wanted to find out how. The "how" is what held our interest. The "how" is the way Batman endured, persevered, and executed. We wanted to find out the "how" of heroism.

Batman is an ordinary person who chose to be extraordinary. He chose to be a superhero. The real world isn't much different. Some people always win. They always find success. They choose to be extraordinary. They choose to be successful. No matter how dire the situation, no matter how great the odds, no matter how powerful the enemy, they persevere. They always win. They are MFers. They are superheroes. They know that if they just wait until the commercial break, they will succeed.

As you matriculate through the Flywheel, remember that you decide your superhero status. Of course, a fifty-inch vertical leap helps. A four-and-a-half-second forty-yard dash time may make it easier. A four-hundred-pound bench press shows your strength. But, becoming a superhero is much more than that. That is why Batman may be the best superhero of all, because he has no superpowers. He doesn't have invincibility, like Superman. He isn't a demigod, like Thor. He doesn't have a power ring, like the Green Lantern.

Batman is a superhero because he chooses to be one. He chooses to succeed. He knows that after the commercial break, he will find a way to endure and persevere, no matter what obstacles are in his way. This is Maniacal Fanaticism. You can endure and persevere, even when the situation is dire.

If you can wait for the next commercial break, you will win. That doesn't mean you won't have to work at it. It doesn't mean it won't be hard. It doesn't mean you won't have gut checks. The journey may be long, but you will find a solution. The answer will present itself through hard work. You will persevere and endure by spinning the Flywheel as fast and as long as you can.

Like success, superhero status is within your grasp. Just decide to be a superhero! I know you are curious. Did Batman pull past the precarious predicament premeditated and planned by the pernicious Penguin? Of course, he perfectly proved he could persevere as a hero possessing a paucity of powers, as he prolifically pummeled the Penguin. "Pow!"

CHAPTER XXVI

REINFORCEMENT PHASE

"Success is stumbling from failure to failure with no loss of enthusiasm."

– WINSTON CHURCHILL

The next phase of the Flywheel is the reinforcement phase. MFers have an alternative view of success. Interestingly enough, their view of failure is even more intriguing. They hold themselves accountable for their failures as well as their successes. When MFers perform poorly, they don't make excuses or give explanations. They attribute all results to their actions, both good and bad. MFers understand that failure is nothing more than a suboptimal result—not good, not bad, just is.

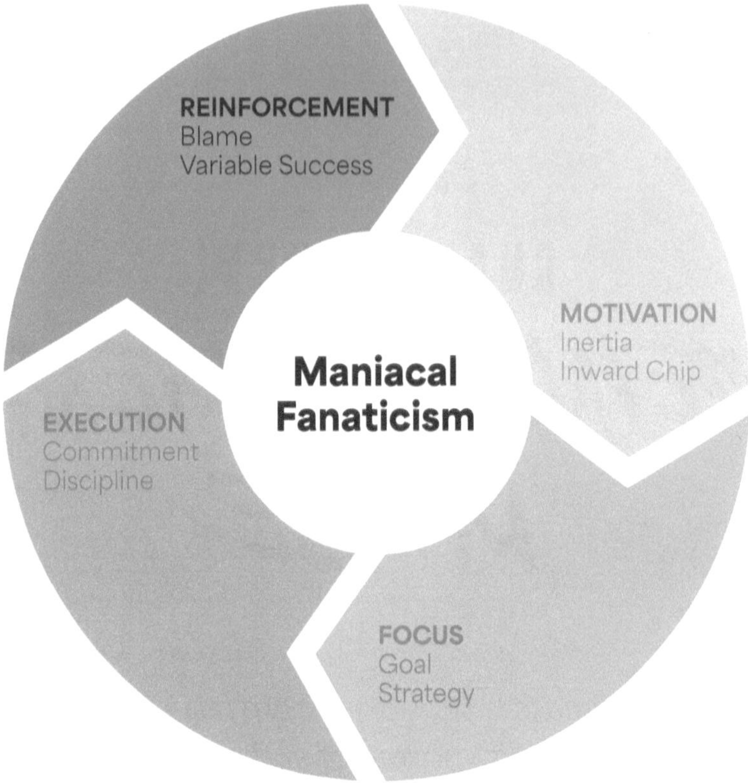

I remember watching an exciting championship basketball game. After the game, a reporter interviewed the star player for the losing team. She scored thirty-eight points and collected twelve rebounds. The reporter asked how she would rate her performance. Her first statement was, "I wish I would have done more." She was very upset about missing a few decisive shots. She described several crucial plays where she thought she could have done things a little differently.

Individually, this superstar player outperformed every player in the gym. She performed at a high level, and her team still lost. She didn't focus on the opposition or how good they were. She didn't focus on the rest of her team, whose contributions were poor. She didn't talk about the biased referees making calls for the home team, which they did. She focused on what *she* could have done differently. Her result was her result, no one else's. She blamed herself.

This mindset is what Maniacal Fanaticism is all about. It isn't just lip service. MFers truly want the blame for the result. They believe that their performance is singularly responsible for the outcome. They believe they could have done more, worked harder, or made better decisions. MFers believe winning is within their control and losing is a direct consequence of their effort.

Having the ability to accept blame gives them motivation and the introspection necessary to improve. It creates opportunities for improvement. It would have been easy for the basketball player to say, "I played my best, but sometimes you don't get the result you anticipated. The team didn't play as well as we were hoping, and I hope we can win next time."

Responses like these are from people who assume results are external to their actions. "That's just the way the ball bounces. It just wasn't my day. That's all I could do. I did my best. There is no way we could beat that team. I couldn't have secured that contract. Who can survive in this market?" These responses assume that outcomes are independent of effort. They believe that the outcomes are a result of fate, a predestined determination over which they have no control.

The reinforcement phase serves two significant purposes. It reinforces the work of the Flywheel and provides positive reinforcement for the success pursuit. It also creates opportunities for introspection. These opportunities, usually sparked by failures, allow individuals to alter strategy. Many success pursuits fail because no accommodation is made for failure.

In most cases, success follows many initial failures. Failures function to correct the course. They are the boundaries of your success pursuit. For MFers, failures may be more important than successes.

Failures refine the pursuit and challenge the individual to change. So long as failures aren't fatal, they may be a required component of success pursuit. A fully functioning Flywheel that fails isn't necessarily a failed success pursuit.

That may be a little confusing, so it is worth repeating. A success pursuit that fails isn't necessarily a failure. Do you remember the first time you tried to ride a bike? Do you remember all the falls you had when you were learning? Those falls were failures. Without those early failures, you wouldn't have learned to ride. As painful as they were, those early failures were required for bike-riding success.

Success isn't measured by the height of our ascents, but by the recovery from the depths of our failures. Churchill asserted, "Success is moving from one failure to another with no loss of enthusiasm." Success pursuit should be like learning to ride a bike. Fall, after fall, after fall, after fall, the child doesn't lose enthusiasm. The child doesn't lose the fanatic desire to ride that bike. Adults are far more risk averse. Unlike children, who pursue their goals with reckless abandon, we tend to be more reserved. When we fall, we are scared to get back on the bike. When we fail, we curtail our success pursuit.

The reinforcement phase outlines MFers' response to success and failures. It allows them to go from failure to failure without losing enthusiasm. Just like learning to ride a bike, falling may be necessary and even required. Success spins the Flywheel, but so does failure. Ironically, some failures spin the Flywheel even faster than some successes.

The reinforcement phase allows for variable outcomes. It provides the introspection necessary to deal with suboptimal outcomes. It reinforces accountability for the result. The name of the phase describes exactly what it does. It reinforces the success pursuit. Completion of the reinforcement phase completes a full revolution of the Flywheel. Its completion transitions you back to the motivation phase.

During the next few chapters, I will outline the thresholds that compose the reinforcement phase. You will gain an understanding of how success pursuits are reinforced. You will understand how variable success and blame interact. You will understand how this phase influences the Flywheel and heightens success pursuit. Finally, you will understand how to define success by stumbling from failure to failure without any loss of enthusiasm.

FROM WITHIN
ACCELERATORS
WHAT DO YOU FEEL
HAPPINESS
COMES
ASSESSMENT
SUPERSTAR
LUCKY
ALTERATION
ACCEPTANCE
MOTIVATION
MANIACAL
INERTIA
FANATICISM
OBSTACLES
INWARD
HIDDEN
SUCCESS
FOUNDATION
VALUES
FLYWHEEL
R
M
FOCUS
SUCCESS
BLAME
PIVOT
GUTCHECK
FUTILITY
THRESHOLD
DON'T SWEAT THE SMALL
SUPER TRUST
HERO
PROMISE
YOUR
FAULT
CHECKMATE
NO EXCUSES
NO EXPLANATIONS
BETTER LUCKY THAN GOOD
PAST PERFORMANCE
CIRCUMSTANCE
PERFECT SITUATION
SUCCESSOLOGY
MANIACAL FANATICISM BEST
POISE
DENIAL
DAYS
FUTURE SUCCESS

CHAPTER XXVII

BLAME THRESHOLD

"If you could kick the person in the pants responsible for most of your trouble, you wouldn't sit for a month."
– THEODORE ROOSEVELT

Blame is one of the two thresholds in the reinforcement phase. When people first learn about the Flywheel, they often question the presence of blame. Traditionally, blame is often associated with negativity. Like the inward chip, it isn't typically associated with the pursuit of success. Blame isn't the first word that comes to mind when describing successful people. But for Maniacal Fanatics, blame actually can be a very positive attribute. It can power change, drive performance, force improvement, encourage accountability, and implore introspection.

Using the same failing strategy repeatedly will result in the same poor outcome. That is Einstein's definition of insanity. While repeating a failing strategy won't yield a successful outcome, working harder and executing better won't always guarantee success either. If that is the case, how do you alter the course? How do you change the strategy? How do you create opportunities to improve? The ability to alter the course, the ability to change your strategy, the ability to create opportunities to improve are all a result of blame. Blaming yourself for your results creates opportunities for improvement. Opportunities for improvement create changes in the strategy.

Blame exists to remind us that our results are our own. It exists to allow for midcourse correction on our success journey. Blame exists to enable us to improve from A to A+. It is responsible for the change effort. Blame doesn't and shouldn't imply negativity. It allows the person, athlete, organization, leader, parent, or coach to take responsibility for a result. Whether they are negative or positive, you are accountable for your results. Running faster, jumping higher, thinking quicker, and studying harder will only improve your results to a point.

By this point in the book, you know just how mediocre of a golfer I am. Hitting one-thousand balls, every day for a year with the same bad golf swing, will only improve my golf game to a point. I can improve a poor swing only so much. Practice can maximize my B- golf game. Unfortunately, one hundred percent of B- is still B-.

To improve to A or A+, I would have to change my swing. I would have to learn to do things differently. I would have to develop a better golf swing to get a better golf result. The golfers who are reading this know exactly what I mean. Changing your swing is very painful for several reasons. First, you have to acknowledge that your swing is bad, which is difficult enough for the ego. You have to blame yourself for your results, not the golf course or the weather. Second, you have to adopt a new swing that will take months and even years to perfect. The painful process of learning to do something you've always done a certain way in a new way feels absolutely horrible. This is the pain of blame. It is the pain of change. It doesn't feel good, it isn't pleasant, and it requires uncomfortable work.

Plutarch argued, "To find fault is easy; to do better may be difficult." Blame is difficult because we don't always want to hear what we could have done better. We don't ever want to hear that our efforts yielded poor results. Honestly, I don't want to hear that my golf swing sucks. However, the results that are possible with an improved golf swing far surpass the results of the perfected bad swing. Blaming my golf swing hurts my ego, but not fixing it will hurt my long-term results and limit my golf success.

Doing the wrong thing well never yields the right result. Blame gives you the ability to change the wrong thing to the right thing, to get the right result. This is why blame can be very positive. Traditionally, blame is a product and occurs at the end of the process. In Maniacal Fanaticism, blame starts the process of improvement. Blame focuses on "how" rather than "how much."

You may be doing enough, but you may not be doing enough the right way. Should you change the motivation? Should you alter the goals? Should you change the strategy? Did you commit sufficiently? Did you have enough discipline? In this way, blame is tremendously positive. MFers take ownership of the bad pass, the bad shot, or the bad business decision. Blame lies within. It can't be externally assigned. Similar to the inward chip, Blame is introspective, focused inward and deeply personable. Each individual has to find his or her blame.

Organizations must find fault from within, not blame the external markets. Players must be critical of their performance and not blame their teammates. An employee has to take the blame for her productivity and not focus on the faults of her manager. The student must take responsibility for his grade and not criticize the teacher's methods. The point guard can't blame the center. Marketing can't blame operations. The chief operating officer can't blame the chief financial officer. The quarterback can't blame the wide receiver. If a member of a team blames him or herself and finds ways to improve, the whole team will improve as a result.

Blaming yourself will improve your results if you focus on where *you* can improve. Finding ways to improve yourself starts with taking responsibility for your results, not just your actions. That important distinction is worth repeating. Improvement begins by taking responsibility for your actions as well as your results. Meaning, a right action that yields the wrong result still may need to be changed.

How many times have you heard, "It isn't about winning and losing, it's how you play the game?" *Good* parents are supposed to tell kids to "do their best." Without regard to the outcome, your best is very difficult to quantify. Don't worry. You didn't have bad parents. They were just trying to build your self-esteem. They thought they were doing the right thing. Unfortunately, your parents were wrong.

In Maniacal Fanaticism, there is no best. Doing your "best" implies no opportunity for improvement. Doing your best implies that you are without blame. The result of your effort should be the achievement of a goal. If you fail to reach your goal, you should always feel like you can improve your effort and strategy. Blame always exists. This isn't a win at all costs strategy. It isn't about being unethical or immoral. It isn't about crushing your self-esteem.

Blame is simply an acknowledgment that a poor result isn't the right result. Finding blame for a wrong result creates an opportunity to take accountability and improve. Essentially, a poor outcome is a suboptimal success. It leads to blame. Blame leads to opportunities to improve. Opportunities to improve lead to a change in strategy. The more times you go through that cycle, the closer you get to your unachievable "best."

If Maniacal Fanaticism is the mathematics of success, Blame would be considered an asymptote. The definition of an asymptote is a line that continually approaches a given curve but does not meet it at any finite distance. More simply, an asymptote is a line that approaches, but never touches a curve. Through Blame your success trajectory and effort will approach, but never actually get you to their ultimate height. Not because you can't achieve your ultimate goal, but because Blame constantly adjusts your variable outcomes so you can reach higher and achieve more. "Your best" will continually be adjusted, refined, and accelerated by Blame.

No matter how good MFers' results are, they can always do better. Blame makes them feel they can achieve more and always give more effort. The line they are attempting to reach is constantly pushed just outside their reach. And as such, there is no best. Crossing the "line" of best never occurs for an asymptote success trajectory. So, from a practical standpoint, what does that look like? If they don't achieve a goal, they blame themselves and readjust to continue to pursue that goal. If they achieve a goal, they blame themselves because they believe that the goal could have been set higher or achieved sooner.

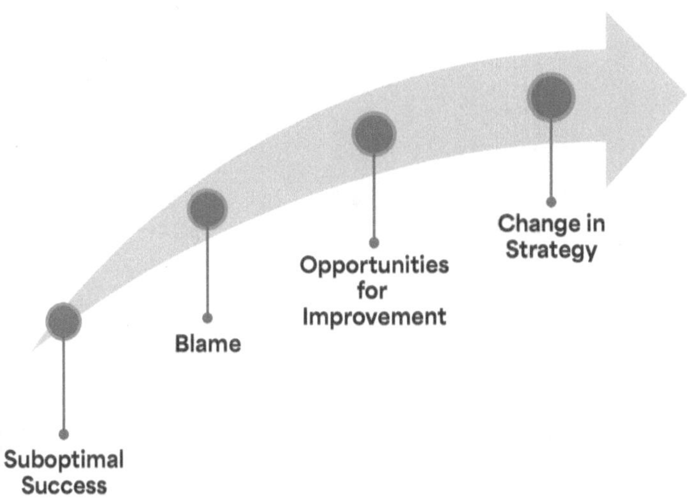

For MFers, this constant Blame grind means there is no best. As a result, trying "your best" truly becomes a nonsensical concept used to avoid ownership of an outcome. This is a simple and very effective way to avoid accountability for suboptimal results. Let's face it. A loss is a loss. You aren't six years old anymore, and your self-esteem can handle it! Trying "your best" implies that the outcome is beyond your control. It means that there is no blame. No blame means no opportunity for improvement and no ability to change.

MFers focus on results. Through blame, they continue to improve and change strategy until they achieve their goals. For them there is no best, just perpetually improving strategy and effort. For them, success trajectory and effort are asymptotes on an infinite course to an achievement they will never actually get to. They are to blame for their success or lack thereof. If you are unable to achieve your goal and you want to get better, start by kicking the person in the pants responsible for most of your trouble. When you are done kicking, it should be very hard to sit down.

CHAPTER XXVIII

IT'S ALWAYS YOUR FAULT

"Criticism may not be agreeable, but it is necessary. It fulfills the same function as pain in the human body. It calls attention to an unhealthy state of things."

– WINSTON CHURCHILL

The inward chip and blame are the thresholds that make Maniacal Fanaticism different from other success theories. We know from these concepts that MFers are self-critical. Because of this, they can be perceived as negative. But that healthy dose of negativity is necessary for both strategy assessment and strategy alteration. Without blame and criticism, opportunities for improvement are harder to identify. Without opportunities for improvement, a strategy is difficult to change.

Self-critiquing is an effective way to ensure the perpetual pursuit of individual excellence. It is how we get from A to A+. As effective as this can be, it is only one perspective. Most of us have an intimate understanding of our strengths and weaknesses, but we all have blind spots. Blind spots are areas that we miss in our self-critique. These areas may be invisible from our perspective, but they are painfully obvious to others. Listening to the counsel, advice, and criticism from a few select individuals can enhance your ability to improve. Coaches, parents, spouses, coworkers, and supervisors can help give you an external perspective.

As I was writing this book, my family and friends would review each draft. Each of them came up with a few pointed critiques of my writing and my theories. I listened to all of them. They were giving me their perspective of the book. When I read my book, I reinforce my perspective. At times, I read what I thought I wrote, rather than what I actually wrote. That was my blind spot. My family and friends, and several very expensive editors, helped me gain an objective perspective on my perspective.

This type of criticism is very helpful and helps to accelerate the Flywheel. These external, open, and honest interpretations of our strengths and weaknesses can change the way we look at the world. It can also reinforce our strengths, thereby validating the path we are on. Of course, you have to consider the source. You must identify any conflicts of interest or any hidden agendas. It wouldn't be prudent for Michael Jordan to enlist the critique of John Starks, one of his fiercest rivals. However, it may make sense for Michael Jordan to listen to his coach and teammates.

Learning should occur over a lifetime. No matter how successful we are, we can always learn. Our ability to tolerate criticism enhances our learning. Even when it is constructive, criticism never feels good. It isn't something that feeds the ego. Our ability to tolerate criticism is truly a skill. Feeling defensive and argumentative after criticism is natural. Criticism is painful, but like pain, criticism is necessary. Pain alerts us to areas of our bodies that are being harmed or need fixing. Criticism functions in the same way. It alerts us to areas in our success pursuit that are being harmed or need fixing.

CIP is a rare condition called congenital insensitivity to pain. As the name implies, these individuals have a genetic mutation that removes their ability to feel pain. At first glance, this would seem as though this shouldn't even be thought of as a disease. The inability to feel pain sounds like a superpower. Unfortunately, it is far from that. Children with CIP are more susceptible to fractures, corneal problems, and infections. They can't participate in sports and have no concept of danger. They rely on their families to give them the external cues about what is and isn't dangerous.

Although not nearly as serious, an inability to deal with criticism works in the same way. "It fulfills the same function as pain in the human body. It calls attention to an unhealthy state of things." Without the ability to appropriately deal with criticism, we are susceptible to illness. That illness is an inability to improve.

How do MFers do it? How do they let their guard down and accept both internal and external criticism? It is easy. They believe it is always their fault. While they take ownership of their successes and failures, they also take ownership of the process. Their drive to succeed is so powerful that they always attribute accountability to themselves. Success is their fault. MFers believe it is their responsibility to improve. Odds and circumstances are irrelevant. The external obstacles are irrelevant. All that is relevant is the unwavering pursuit of success.

As you pursue success, be humble. Understand that learning occurs over a lifetime. To create opportunities for improvement, be inwardly critical and open to external criticism. Remember, criticism is like pain. It hurts, but it is very necessary. Without it, we lose the ability to improve. We lose the ability to avoid the fractures of failure. We lose the ability to identify our injuries. We lose the ability to determine what is dangerous. We lose perspective on our success pursuit. Be humble enough to accept responsibility for your strengths and your weaknesses. Don't be defensive. Take ownership of your wins *and* losses. "Criticism may not be agreeable, but it's necessary." You will get better, and you will achieve your goal. Just remember, it is always your fault.

CHAPTER XXIX
VARIABLE SUCCESS THRESHOLD

"When it is obvious that the goals cannot be reached, don't adjust the goals, adjust the action steps."
– CONFUCIUS

The second threshold in the reinforcement phase is variable success. Before we look more closely at variable success, I want to reinforce that the Flywheel is a cycle. If all the thresholds are met, the Flywheel keeps spinning. Many people view success as linear. Develop a goal and then accomplish that goal. Accomplishing the goal is important for MFers, but it is more important to keep the Flywheel spinning even if the goal isn't achieved.

In Maniacal Fanaticism, there is no failure. There are only variable successes. Achievement of any goal above the requisite goal still propagates the Flywheel. This is fundamentally different from the typical operant Pavlovian theories of success. In those theories, positive behaviors are reinforced by positive stimuli. It seems intuitive enough, but those theories fall short when describing highly successful individuals. Many highly successful people have had catastrophic failures in their lives before their successes. Based on reinforcement theory, where good outcomes are necessary to reinforce success behaviors, failure should inhibit success pursuit.

Think of a team that only practices after a win. Would this be a good way to improve as a team? Can you think of a musician who practices only if the piece is played perfectly? What about a student who only studies after an A, would that be an effective strategy? For MFers, wins spin the Flywheel, but so do the losses. Successful people may even be more motivated to improve with a poorer outcome. Blame and variable success increase the inward chip, forcing the individual to change their strategy, alter their goals, implement more discipline and commitment, and so on.

Variable success and blame work together to complete the Reinforcement Phase of the Flywheel. The Flywheel has now spun a full revolution. The Motivation Phase, inertia, and the inward chip have sufficiently addressed the "why" of success. The Focus Phase, goal, and strategy development have identified the "what" of success. The Execution Phase, commitment, and discipline have delineated the "how." The Reinforcement Phase, blame, and variable success give a blueprint for the "when" of success.

All outcomes accelerate the Flywheel, and the cycle moves on to motivation again. Remember, there is no failure, only variable success. When a suboptimal success is achieved, blame allows the transition to the motivation phase. How can both success and failure result in motivation? Success is an anomaly. It is a rarity, an outlier. Only a small percentage of us will manage to achieve it.

The mathematics of success calculates that you will fail many more times than you will succeed. The pursuit of success may be more appropriately defined by our response to failure. Failure doesn't mean that you can't reach your goal. It simply tells you that the current strategy will need to change to achieve it. The reinforcement phase allows you to adjust the action steps instead of adjusting the goals.

FROM WITHIN
ACCELERATORS
WHAT DO YOU FEEL
LUCKY
SUPERSTAR
ALTERATION
MOTIVATION
MANIACAL
INERTIA
FANATICISM
OBSTACLES
INWARD
HIDDEN
M
SUCCESS
FOUNDATION
R
VALUES
FLYWHEEL
FOCUS
SUCCESS
BLAME
PIVOT
GUTCHECK
FUTILITY
THRESHOLD
SWEAT THE
SMALL
SUPER
TRUST
HERO
YOUR
CHECKMATE
NO EXPLANATIONS
NO EXCUSES
BETTER LUCKY THAN GOOD
PAST PERFORMANCE
CIRCUMSTANCE
SUCCESSOLOGY
MANIACAL FANATICISM BEST

CHAPTER XXX
RUNNING THE FLYWHEEL

"I always loved running ... it was something you could do by yourself, and under your own power. You could go in any direction, fast or slow as you wanted, fighting the wind if you felt like it, seeking out new sights just on the strength of your feet and the courage of your lungs."

– JESSE OWENS

Several years ago, I decided to start running. Before this, I had never run long distances in my life. I had never run a marathon, a half marathon, or even a short five-kilometer run. I didn't have an appreciation or understanding of how far these distances were. However, I am a decent athlete and played soccer and basketball in the past. I was also a decent short distance sprinter and long jumper. Although I knew I didn't have much long-distance running ability, I was sure that I could increase my capacity.

Why was I motivated to run? What made me decide to do something I had never done before? Why did I want to start doing something that I wasn't very good at? Thinking back, I had several different reasons for my initial motivation. Truthfully, I was angry because other people were able to complete half marathons, and I hadn't. If they could do it, so could I. Although I had played college basketball, I had recently given up on playing recreationally to avoid injury. I missed competing and being an athlete. The fact that I couldn't do it motivated me.

This self-inflicted challenge completed my inertia threshold. Then there was my inward chip. Why can't I run a marathon? Why are they better than I am? I am not sure I can run that far. So many people had already done something that I had yet to do. That bothered me. I wasn't sure I could do it. I had a chip on my shoulder, and it was running rampant.

Instead of focusing on other people, I had to turn that chip inward and focus on myself. If they could do it, so could I. I had to show them. Better yet, I had to show myself. I turned my chip inward. My inertia and inward chip were satisfied. After completing the motivation phase, it was time to focus.

During the focus phase, I developed my strategy to become a runner. Many people advised me to follow a marathon plan or get a trainer, but that isn't my style. My strategy was just to run. I decided to run as often and as far as I could. I started with short distances. Over time I would increase both my speed and distance. My strategy threshold was met.

What about my goals? I focused primarily on three goals. My requisite goal was to complete a half-marathon, no matter how long that took. My expected goal was to run the entire race without walking. My ultimate goal was to break the two-hour time mark. To keep my goal in sight, I entered myself in several races. We will talk later about whether I achieved those goals and my lack of acute, subacute, and ultimate goals.

As I have said repeatedly in this book, the execution phase is where the work is. Executing my strategic plan was particularly difficult. I ran four or five times a week. I was hilariously slow. I was so slow that people would stop their cars and ask me if I needed help. I kept running. I remained disciplined and committed. Executing my strategy was all that mattered. That season I ran two half marathons, six 5Ks, and two 10K runs. Surprisingly, it wasn't as hard as I thought. I met two of my goals, but I didn't achieve my lofty goal.

In the blame threshold, I analyzed my run. I realized that I could've run faster, and my training could have been better. What if I lost weight? What if I changed my diet? Could I have trained harder? Was I committed enough? Was I disciplined enough? I blamed myself. I blamed myself for my suboptimal result. I took ownership of my performance. Not bad, not good, just is. It wasn't the course. It wasn't the weather. It wasn't my non-runner body type. I was responsible for my variable success.

Even though I was proud of myself for accomplishing a few of my goals, I knew that I could do better. I knew that I had opportunities to improve. Getting relatively close to my lofty goal increased my motivation, and the process started all over again. The blame from the reinforcement phase fed the inward chip and so on. To be critical, I didn't set any temporal goals. I didn't spend any time defining my subacute and ultimate goals. As a result, my ability to maintain my running performance dwindled. I have continued to run, but never as fast and as long as I did that season.

FROM WITHIN HUMBLE
ACCELERATORS
WHAT DO YOU FEEL
SUPERSTAR
ALTERATION
MOTIVATION
MANIACAL
INERTIA
FANATICISM
OBSTACLES
INWARD
HIDDEN
M
SUCCESS
R
FOUNDATION
VALUES
FLYWHEEL
FOCUS
SUCCESS
BLAME
GUTCHECK
FUTILITY
THRESHOLD
SWEAT THE SMALL
SUPER TRUST
HERO
YOUR
CHECKMATE
NO EXCUSES
NO EXPLANATIONS
BETTER LUCKY THAN GOOD
PAST PERFORMANCE
CIRCUMSTANCE
SUCCESSOLOGY
MANIACAL FANATICISM BEST
LUCKY
PIVOT
CAPACIBILITY
SELF DENIAL
GAME DAY
GOALS
EVIDENCE
POISE

CHAPTER XXXI
BE CRAZY

"Insanity: doing the same thing over and over again and expecting different results."
– ALBERT EINSTEIN

As you probably have already determined from the title of this book, success requires a reasonable amount of crazy. Craziness isn't typically associated with success, but nothing about Maniacal Fanaticism is typical. By definition, successful people are different. They stand out. They aren't normal. They are a little crazy. They are different because success isn't normal.

Success is rare, an outlier. To be successful, you have to think, act, and be different. You need to have crazy performance and crazy results. Like success, craziness isn't normal. Normal is mediocre. Normal leads to standard results, standard performance, and standard behavior. Being normal is a result of a standard effort. Success is crazy, crazy motivation, crazy focus, and crazy execution. To be successful, you must challenge what is standard.

What exactly does it mean to be crazy? Being crazy means you have to depart from standard. You have to be a little abnormal. You have to depart from personal moderation. Most of us moderate our behavior and effort. We hold back, and we don't push ourselves past our previously perceived limits. When you are crazy, moderation is inhibited. Jerry Rice's fanatical training regimen was absolutely crazy. Michael Jordan's maniacal competitiveness was definitely crazy. Neither of those men moderated or proportioned their efforts. Being crazy means that you are possessed by enthusiasm or excitement. It describes a preoccupation and an intensity that goes beyond what is expected.

What will it take to pursue your goals maniacally and fanatically? Have you limited your success by moderating or proportioning your effort? Have you limited your success by doing things the same way and expecting different results? How does being crazy influence the Flywheel?

The motivation phase requires a little craziness. Being infatuated, immoderately fond, and possessed with excitement and enthusiasm are necessary for motivation. Being crazy is necessary to complete the motivation phase. As crazy as it sounds, pun intended, craziness also has a role in the execution phase. If you are crazy, you are considered intensely involved or preoccupied. Fortunately, intensity and preoccupation are helpful with commitment and discipline. Being a little crazy helps you push past your physical, mental, and emotional norm.

Craziness isn't insanity. Insanity is doing the same thing repeatedly and expecting different results. Insanity is thinking that insane effort alone will yield successful results. If you are crazy, you understand that if you want abnormal results, you have to exhibit abnormal behaviors. Don't be complacent with normal or standard. Stand out. Think differently. Be crazy!

CHAPTER XXXII

NO EXCUSES AND NO EXPLANATIONS

"Ninety-nine percent of the failures come from people who have the habit of making excuses."

– GEORGE WASHINGTON CARVER

Most of us hold ourselves accountable for our actions, but we rarely hold ourselves accountable for our results. Remember your mother's tender advice? "It isn't whether you win or lose. It's how you play the game." Of course, she only told you that when you lost. When you won, she was uncontrollably shouting in the stands. We expect that our efforts should be rewarded, irrespective of our results.

Most of us feel that a good result should follow a good effort. This is how we believe the world should work. It is the classic American Dream. Work hard, and the goal should follow. We assume that the inability to achieve a goal follows a relatively poor effort. We have no sympathy for those who don't achieve, primarily because we assume they didn't put forth enough effort.

Most success theories are founded on these relationships. They assume that the relationship between success and success pursuit should be linear. Work hard and achieve success. However, that isn't always the case. When a minimal effort leads to a maximal result, we call that person lucky. This is why we buy lottery tickets and go to casinos. The allure of a life-changing result from minimal effort is downright addicting.

Inappropriately, many of us diffusely attribute all success to this category. We assume all successful people attain their success through luck. Because of the lack of effort, it is assumed that a lucky result isn't deserved. The opposite is also true. Some people put forth a maniacal effort and only manage to generate a poor result. Futility is the term that describes this group of people.

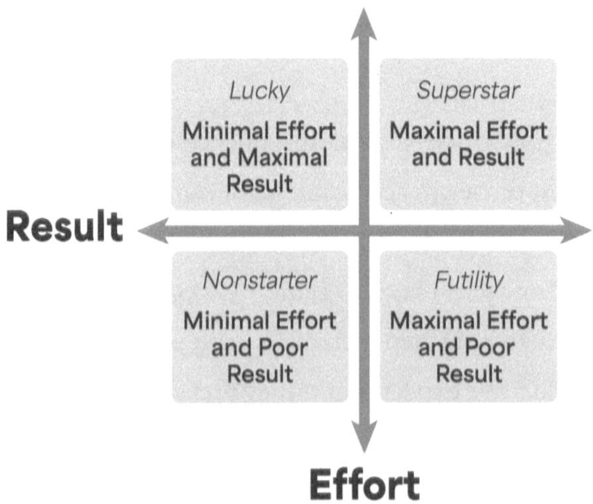

If we graph the correlation between success and effort, we end up with four different quadrants. Each quadrant defines a specific group of individuals, by their effort and results. If you achieve a maximal result with minimal effort, you are lucky. You are a superstar if your maximal effort results in a maximal result. In both of these cases, the result is positive.

What happens when there is a negative result? A maximal effort that yields a poor result, like an unpublished author working on a constantly evolving manuscript, is futility. The last category is nonstarters. This is the place where most people reside. Nonstarters receive a poor result following a minimal effort. I am sure if you asked them, they wouldn't think so. Most people don't usually put forth enough effort to be successful. People don't always realize that their effort isn't commensurate to the result they seek.

When you ask people, "Why haven't you achieved your goal?" you will rarely hear the answer, "I didn't give enough effort." Human beings have an uncanny knack for supporting their self-esteem. People rarely identify themselves as nonstarters, even though that is exactly what they are. It isn't that they don't want to succeed. They just are unrealistic about the effort necessary to do so. Nonstarters knowingly or unknowingly give reasons for their minimal effort or their poor result. They give excuses, justifications for underperformance. Or they give explanations, rationalizations for poor results.

As you can see from our study of the Flywheel, MFers make no allowances for excuses. Their focus is always inward. MFers introspect to determine what they can do better. They use blame to identify areas that require improvement. If you blame yourself, you naturally will want to improve. If you blame external factors, then you will seek to improve your external environment, instead of focusing on your personal improvement. MFers always believe they alone are responsible for their results. And if the goal isn't achieved, they blame themselves for the lack of effort even if they have given tremendous effort. They believe they can always give more.

Nonstarters give excuses for their results and explanations for their lack of effort. Explanations are slightly different from excuses. Explanations are external factors that mute the nonstarter's effort. They are "if-then" statements. If the other team hadn't been so good, we would have won. If the test weren't so hard, I would have done better. If circumstances were different, I would have achieved my goal. These explanations are used to mitigate blame. Nonstarters focus on changing their circumstances instead of improving their effort. They perpetually wait for that unlikely perfect situation, before exerting their effort.

This defense mechanism may be briefly self-fulfilling, but it ultimately leads to poorer results. The Flywheel stops spinning because the blame threshold is never completed. It isn't surprising then that MFers make no excuses and give no explanations. To them, effort is limitless. Results are only limited by their effort. In their world, results are proportional to the effort. When it is clear that no additional effort will yield a better result, they still attempt to dig deeper. They still try to give more. MFers believe they can always affect a result outcome, by the sheer force of their will.

Although rare, sometimes nonstarters get lucky. Lottery winners are the most obvious example of this category. A minimal effort of a few dollars can yield millions in return. This can be very alluring and likely is the motivation to go to your nearest casino. Unfortunately, the odds of success in this category are extremely low. The odds of winning the average lottery are about one in fifteen million.

In many ways, our society reinforces this category. Las Vegas generates billions of dollars on this very premise. Preoccupation with encountering a low-probability luck event often distracts people and limits their ability and productivity. This mindset finds its way into other aspects of their lives, which is what makes it so dangerous. Nonstarters expect lottery-winning results at work, home, and school. They hope for lofty results, with no more effort than it takes to roll the dice or buy a ticket.

Futility describes the next grouping of people. These individuals are constantly elevating their effort, with little or no result. Although the result is poor, futility is still considered a productive category. These individuals display all the effort necessary for success but aren't able to garner any tangible results. This is the arduous road to mastery.

In Malcolm Gladwell's book *Outliers*, he makes the point that mastery requires about ten thousand hours of training. Most of the hours necessary for mastery are spent in futility. These hours are spent practicing, editing, refining, honing, and perfecting a success pursuit with little or no result. Futility is markedly different from the nonstarter category because, in futility, people are doing most things the right way. They keep trying, hustling, fighting, and working. They are the straight line that is slowly transitioning to an asymptote.

Despite the lack of results, those in futility keep producing more and more fanatical effort. These individuals have great motivation. They are able to focus. They have very good execution and are able to satisfy the reinforcement phase. For these individuals, the Flywheel is still spinning at a very high rate because even poor results can satisfy the reinforcement phase.

The reinforcement phase doesn't always have a positive result. As we have previously discussed, a negative result can often be a greater Flywheel accelerator than a positive one. Futility is pending success. Unfortunately, individuals stuck in futility may never achieve success. That is the frustrating thing about futility. All successful people experience periods of futility. The results will change eventually, but how long can you tolerate being in the futility phase? How long can you tolerate maximal effort with little or no reward? How long can you tolerate the arduous ten-thousand hours or meaningful work to get to mastery?

Medical school is a great example of futility. Medical training requires at least seven years of maniacal effort with very little financial or professional reward. During that time, many people disengage from what seems to be an endless process. Those who can hang on get the results they desire. And in the medical school case, the period of futility is well defined by a predetermined time in school and training. Futility requires the ability to delay gratification. The difficulty is determining how long you can delay gratification. Futility lacks results, but it isn't failure. When the results finally come, they quickly go from futility to superstar.

In the end, we are all striving to be superstars. This is the Jerry Rice and Michael Jordan category, where maximal effort yields a maximal result. I have always thought that true happiness comes from exerting extreme effort in something you love and achieving maximal results. This is superstar status, and it is the category we all hope to belong to.

Fortunately, our position in these categories isn't static. People can move from one category to another, depending on the circumstances. People also may be in different categories in different aspects of their lives. You could be a superstar as a parent and in futility at work. You may be lucky financially and a nonstarter in your marriage. These titles aren't fixed, and movement through the categories is fluid. Jerry Rice was in the superstar category for his professional football career but could be in the futility category in golf. Many professional athletes are in the superstar category for their sport but are in the nonstarter category for their investments.

What category are you in? Are you a nonstarter? Are you in the futility category? If so, how long will you wait to get your superstar status? Can you delay gratification? Are you waiting to be lucky, buying lottery ticket after lottery ticket? Are you giving minimal effort and expecting maximal results? What effort are you giving? What additional effort can you give?

At the end of the day, it is all about effort. Your effort should be limitless. Your results are an extension of effort. Your results are your results, nobody else's. Take ownership of them. No excuses: you should never attempt to justify your poor results. If you are in the habit of making excuses, you will fail ninety-nine percent of the time. You can always change your strategy. You can always attain better results.

In the end, success is defined by your effort and your results. Be accountable for all your results. You can always give more effort, no excuses. You can always work harder, no explanations. Your effort should never be dependent on your external circumstances. You should never say, "if-then." If you are a nonstarter, that is easy to fix. You just have to exert more effort. You will have to delay gratification to get to mastery, even though it may seem futile. Be patient. Your day is coming. Follow the Flywheel. Keep exerting your maniacal effort. You will get there. Eventually, you *will* be a superstar.

FROM WITHIN
HUMBLE
ACCELERATORS
WHAT DO YOU FEEL
HAPPINESS COMES
ASSESSMENT
SUPERSTAR
LUCKY
ALTERATION
ACCEPTANCE
MOTIVATION
MANIACAL
INERTIA
LOFTY
FANATICISM
OBSTACLES
INWARD
HIDDEN
SUCCESS
FOUNDATION
VALUES
FLYWHEEL
FOCUS
SUCCESS
BLAME
PIVOT
BEYOND
SELF INTEREST
CAPABILITY
GOALS
EVIDENCE
GUTCHECK
FUTILITY
THRESHOLD
SWEAT THE SMALL STUFF
SUPER TRUST
HERO
PROMISE
YOUR FAULT
CHECKMATE
NO EXCUSES
NO EXPLANATIONS
BETTER LUCKY THAN GOOD
POISE
FUTURE SUCCESS
PAST PERFORMANCE
CIRCUMSTANCE
PERFECT SITUATION
SUCCESSOLOGY
MANIACAL FANATICISM BEST
PERSISTENCE
POTENTIAL
CONSISTENCY
MEMORY
DENIAL
GAME DAY
MENTAL
INERTIA
ACCOUNTABLE

CHAPTER XXXIII
BETTER LUCKY THAN GOOD?

"I'm a great believer in luck and I find the harder I work, the more I have of it."
– THOMAS JEFFERSON

If you ask successful people about their success, they will inevitably mention their luck. It is true. We can't deny the role that luck plays in our ability to succeed. Success is a well-balanced combination of preparation, opportunity, and luck. But what is luck exactly? How do we quantify it? Where does it come from? How do you find it? How does it affect success?

If success were a mathematical equation, luck would be a random independent variable, because it has no predictable relationship to anything. Most of us believe that luck meanders from place to place or person to person, transforming unsuccessful people into successful ones. That isn't entirely true. Luck is arbitrary, but it is also ubiquitous.

At some point in our lives, we all will inevitably experience our share of good and bad luck.

At the beginning of this book, we discussed Jerry Rice and his draft position. Think about how many people in that draft class had just as much luck as Jerry Rice. Luck is often used to describe a random event that changes the fortune of an individual. When we mention the word lucky, we usually consider only good luck, but we probably should also consider bad luck.

How do MFers capitalize on good luck? How do they take advantage of it? How do they prepare for it? They work at it. The harder they work, the more luck they experience. MFers are extremely adept at capitalizing on good luck and minimizing bad luck. If you ask them, they acknowledge when they are lucky. However, they don't count on it. MFers don't preoccupy their time avoiding bad luck either. As far as luck goes, they simply adjust for the luck event, good or bad, when it arrives. In other words, MFers are poised. Poise enables them to capitalize on good luck events. When you are poised for success, you are prepared to maximize your luck potential.

Luck potential is the amount of success possible from a particular luck event. Remember all the CEOs and entrepreneurs who capitalized on the dot com era. In the late nineteen nineties, owning an internet startup company almost guaranteed success. Every company during that era experienced luck potential. Unfortunately, not everybody was able to maximize that potential. Not everybody had the same poise. Not everyone had the same preparation.

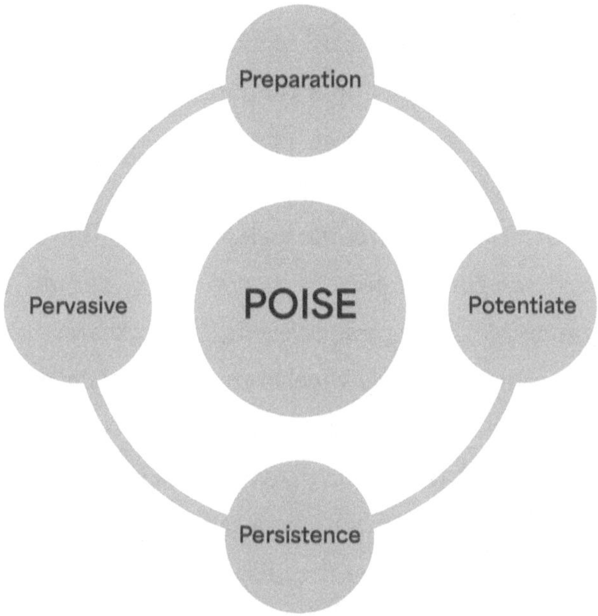

Poise is broken down into four categories. The first is preparation. Being prepared means that you have fine-tuned your training. You have acquired skills and refined them. In essence, you have done whatever it takes to prepare for a luck event—long before you were aware that one was coming.

In 2001, New York Jets linebacker Mo Lewis tackled Drew Bledsoe, the New England Patriots' starting quarterback. At the time, Drew was considered the future of the up-and-coming Patriots. Unfortunately, the tackle was so devastating that Drew suffered a season ending injury. He was taken to the hospital where he was diagnosed with a hemothorax, which is severe bleeding into the chest cavity caused by blunt trauma to the chest. Who replaced him? He was replaced by a sixth-round unproven backup quarterback. His name was Tom Brady.

Yes! This is the same Tom Brady that would go on to win seven National Football League Championships, five Super Bowl MVPs and three National Football League MVPs. Tom Brady was *prepared.* Similar to futility, preparation is the hard work that may not always yield a result. It is the execution without the assurance of reinforcement. It is the hard work of the Flywheel. Preparation requires commitment and discipline. Like Tom Brady's opportunity when Drew Bledsoe was injured, preparation maximizes the luck potential of the event.

The next category of poise is to potentiate. Simply, potentiate means to intensify. During a luck event, the Flywheel starts to spin faster. MFers can spin the Flywheel even faster during this time. The Flywheel is primed, well-oiled, and ready to spin. MFers can potentiate because they understand the Flywheel. They know exactly where they are on the Flywheel, what it will take to get it spinning faster, and understand the lifespan of the luck event.

MFers attempt to capture all the potential energy from a luck event and transfer it to the Flywheel. This leads to more motivation, more focus, better execution, and improved reinforcement. The feeling is intoxicating. At this point, people can't believe their success. It seems to happen so fast. The pain of futility and preparation give way to the rapid euphoria generated during this time.

For athletes, this is often the first championship or a series of big wins. In business, this may be several quarters of growth. In life, this may be a significant promotion. The temptation here is to feel lucky, but it isn't just luck. The arduous hours of preparation have now allowed you to potentiate the positive energy from the luck event.

Next is persistence. Have you ever heard of a one-hit wonder? A one-hit wonder is someone who has prepared for a luck event, experienced a luck event, and potentiated a luck event. That's it. They stop there. That's all they will ever do. All the energy fizzles out, and they achieve only fleeting success. Success is still success, even if it is short-lived. But, that success isn't persistent.

Persistence describes the ability to maintain the luck potential, beyond the actual luck event. Persistence creates sports dynasties, fortune one-hundred companies, and Nobel laureates. It allows successful organizations to endure over time. The Flywheel spins rapidly. It spins without requiring conscious effort. This is the "sweet spot" and where MFers are "dialed in." They understand exactly how to succeed and are able to manifest it over the long term.

Persistence is similar to sky gliding. Imagine a luck event acting like the wind. Even without an engine, the glider can stay in the sky for a long time. A single gust can propel the glider for hundreds of miles. A single luck event can propel someone for a career. MFers know how to maintain their success altitude long after the luck event gust has diminished. In this category, thresholds in the Flywheel are easier to meet, and the transition from phase to phase is seamless.

Sir Isaac Newton's first law of motion reinforces this. Objects in motion tend to remain in motion. Once the boulder gets rolling, it is very hard to stop. People who make it to persistence are resistant to bad luck. A bad luck event can slow the boulder, but it can't completely stop it. One single luck event, like the internet boom of the late nineteen nineties, can create persistent companies such as eBay, Yahoo, and Google.

The last poise category is pervasive. Persistence is specific for a genre or an area of success. When MFers extend their luck event to all areas of their lives, their success pursuit is pervasive. The Merriam-Webster dictionary defines pervasive as "existing in or spreading through every part of something." The pervasive category describes success on a mass scale.

Pervasive people seem to be impervious to bad luck and succeed even in the worst of times. When success is pervasive, multiple Flywheels are spinning wildly. The family Flywheel, the work

Flywheel, the business Flywheel, the student Flywheel, the entrepreneur Flywheel are all rapidly spinning. These individuals and organizations have success, no matter what they do.

Pervasive people aren't jack-of-all-trades. They are masters of all trades. In this category, the Flywheel is spinning so fast that differentiating between the phases is difficult. These people ramp up to elite performance before most of us are in the focus phase. They are the ultimate overachieving superstars.

Luck does exist. A single luck event can provide lasting and even perpetual success. When your luck comes, you will be ready to potentiate it. Take that energy and run with it. Capitalize on its euphoria and take off like a rocket. Start your Flywheel spinning faster than ever before. Be persistent. Don't be a one-hit wonder. Take the luck event energy and glide for as long as you can.

You know how to spin the Flywheel now. Spin it fast and spin it long. Make your success effort pervasive. Extend what you know to all facets of your life. Make your Flywheel blur, and phase transition will become almost imperceptible. Create your success dynasty. You should believe in luck. The harder you work, the more you will have it.

CHAPTER XXXIV
MEMORY

"Do not brood over your past mistakes and failures as this will only fill your mind with grief, regret and depression. Do not repeat them in the future."
– SWAMI SIVANANDA

American Heritage dictionary describes biological memory as the persistent modification of behavior resulting from an animal's experience. Memory allows us to retain expertise and is necessary for us to learn. After all, we are a culmination of our experiences. Our personalities, intelligence, and emotions are all partly rooted in our memory.

Memories from our past successes enhance our ability to succeed in the future. Memories of our past failures can inhibit our future success pursuits. After making it through the maze once, rats find the task fairly simple to repeat. Not only does the rat learn from positive turns, but it also learns from dead ends. It learns by remembering each positive turn, opening, and dead end. Most importantly, the rat remembers the reward at the end of the maze.

It sounds crazy, but the dead ends and the wrong turns may enhance the rat's ability to succeed. When the rat fails to find its way out of the maze, the memory of that failure enhances its ability to succeed in the future. Oddly, the rat's success requires memory of its failures. Your success pursuit is similar. Memories of your failures enhance your future success, because the wrong turns guide your success just as much as the right turns.

In operant conditioning, the memory of a result can enhance or inhibit future behaviors. The Flywheel uses memory in several different ways. It should be obvious that positive memories enhance our ability to succeed in the future, but the response to failure is not always as clear. Like the rat, successful people deal with memory in very specific ways. They understand that memories can accelerate or decelerate the Flywheel.

Fear, for example, is a Flywheel decelerator that has its foundation in memory. The memory of a bad experience or a previous failure can make you fearful in the future. Memories are inert and do not have a specific action associated with them, but the way we react and respond to our memories is what becomes actionable. To this end, MFers compartmentalize memories into short-term, long-term, and functional memory.

Each type of memory serves as an important and unique role. Short-term memory, as the name implies, are those memories that we create based on recent events. Short-term memories are experiences that are retained over days to weeks, while long-term memory is retained over months to years. All long-term memories start as short-term memories, but not all short-term memories become long-term memories. MFers can control how long-term memories stay with them. They also are capable of determining what ways these memories affect them.

Memory	Examples
Short-Term Memory	• Transition Suboptimal Results to Blame • Euphoria from Goal Achievement
Long-Term Memory	• Strategy Know-How • Flywheel Know-How
Functional Memory	• Accelerators and Decelerators • Managing Multiple Flywheels

During Michael Jordan's Hall of Fame induction speech, he spoke of the memories that inspired his basketball success journey. In front of a packed auditorium, he discussed how those memories helped fuel his competitive fire. He talked about his high school sophomore year and his teammate Leroy Smith. Smith received the last spot on the high school varsity team, a spot that the 5'11" Jordan thought belonged to him.

Jordan told the crowd about his fellow North Carolina rookie roommate, Buzz Peterson, who received the prior year's North Carolina High School Player of the Year Award. He talked about how Peterson's accolade, an award Jordan believed was his, motivated him to be better. He reminded the crowd that he was left off of the November 30, 1981 cover of *Sports Illustrated*, that highlighted the best players on that North Carolina team. Ironically, over the next twenty years, he would grace the cover of *Sports Illustrated* almost fifty times. Jordan also mentioned Magic Johnson, George Gervin, and Isiah Thomas trying to stop him from scoring in his first all-star game.

These memories highlight several things. They highlight Michael Jordan's internal motivation and inward chip. Many of us would have lost these events to our short-term memory, but Michael Jordan committed them to his long-term memory. These memories fueled his competitive fire for years. He used them to accelerate his Flywheel, increasing his motivation, inertia, and inward chip. Anyone who snubbed, rejected, doubted, rebuffed, spurned, discredited, slighted, or challenged him unwittingly spun his Flywheel.

Sound familiar? Through his inward chip, Jordan used those memories to dramatically increase his motivation to become the greatest basketball player in history. Like Michael Jordan, your long-term memories can accelerate your Flywheel. Long-term memories are primarily used for strategy and Flywheel know-how. Michael Jordan knew how his Flywheel worked and how to accelerate it. He knew what memories would motivate him because he understood his competitive nature.

Long-term memory can also be used for strategy know-how. Veteran players in most sports have a tactical advantage over their younger, more athletic competition. Some call it guile. Others call it experience. Whatever you call it, this phenomenon is fairly common. Much of this advantage comes from increased strategy know-how. As we learn over time and gain experience, our strategy becomes more refined. Hopefully, this type of memory prevents us from making the same strategic errors over and over again. For long-term memory to give us an advantage, the memories of past mistakes and previously successful strategies are necessary.

Although Michael Jordan's memories accelerated the Flywheel, the memories themselves were far from positive. The effect of memory on a Flywheel is independent of its perceived negativity or positivity. Negative memories can accelerate or decelerate the Flywheel. The same is true for positive memories. The way we process and respond to them varies from individual to individual, but the memories themselves are inert. A memory that decelerates your Flywheel is more likely due to a failure in the Flywheel than a result of the memory. Memories themselves don't necessarily affect the Flywheel, but your reaction to them does.

Your success pursuit shouldn't be dictated by what you remember. Rather, it should be dictated by how you respond to what you remember. For some, being cut from their high school team would decelerate their basketball Flywheel. For others, that same memory would motivate them to work harder. The responses may be different, but the memory itself hasn't changed. We may not always be able to control the content of our memories, but we control how we respond to them. We control how we react to them.

Like Jordan, MFers have an uncanny ability to respond to their memories with improved performance. In this way, long-term memories are an effective means to accelerate the Flywheel. Short-term memory has a very brief and fleeting effect on the Flywheel. Short-term memory is very important during the transition from the reinforcement phase to the motivation phase. The memory of a suboptimal goal and the dysphoria from that experience is necessary to take blame to motivation. This kind of memory must remain short term.

The negative aspects of the inward chip and blame impede the Flywheel if used in other phases. To avoid this, memories of failure should be short-lived. MFers are exceptional at this. They limit the dysphoria of defeat and the euphoria of goal achievement. Doesn't this confuse things? Shouldn't the euphoria from goal achievement be a long-term memory? Absolutely not! If the euphoria from goal achievement and the memory of success lasts too long, the Flywheel will grind to a halt.

Euphoria must be brief to continue the cycle and make new goals. Secondly, if euphoria became long-term, how could we ever satisfy blame and the inward chip again? Euphoric people don't generally blame themselves or focus on their inward chip. Repeated achievement requires a perpetual feeling of underachievement. What if the euphoria from Michael Jordan's first championship never receded? If that euphoria never faded, he wouldn't have generated the motivation necessary for any other championships.

Long-term memories are more focused on strategy know-how and motivation. Having the right strategy may require years of modification, and that requires long term memory. Strategy and strategy adjustment should last through several cycles of the Flywheel. To be successful, you need to control the way your memories affect you. You need to control your reaction to them. You can't necessarily control your memories, but you can control what you do with them and how long those memories last.

Memories that hamper your success pursuit should be purged. Retaining the memory of a particularly stinging failure may cause the Flywheel to stagnate. We all know people like this; people who just can't let things go and travel through life saddled with debilitating bags of memories. They dwell on past experiences. They dwell on their choices. They dwell on their luck. They spend their lives lamenting their memories, debating their decisions, and regretting their actions. They don't control their memories. Their memories control them.

Instead of acting, people stuck in regret spend most of their time reminiscing. They say, "I should've. I could've. I wish I would've." They spend their whole lives thinking about what has happened, instead of what will happen. They preoccupy themselves with what they have done, rather than what they will do. Their inability to let go of the past hinders their ability to capitalize on new opportunities.

Their success journey is slowed by the weight of the luggage they must carry. They go through life wearing cement shoes. Each step forward is slow, heavy, and agonizing.

The opposite is also true. Holding on to euphoric memories of previous goal accomplishments can lead to apathy. These are the one-hit wonders. Early on, these people quickly succeed, but they find it difficult to get there again. They don't have enough motivation to accelerate the Flywheel again. These individuals focus primarily on remote positive memories. They can't improve because most of their energy is directed toward the past. They are completely comfortable with who they are and what they have achieved. In other words, they have arrived. No inward chip. No inertia. No motivation. No future success.

MFers use short-term and long-term memories to manage their success pursuit, but those aren't the only kinds of memories they use. Functional memory is also necessary to manage the Flywheel. Functional memory is necessary for MFers to move from threshold to threshold and from phase to phase. This kind of memory carries phase completion strategies from the past. If you were able to complete the focus phase in the past, that knowledge will help you complete it in the future. Functional memory also allows you to spin multiple simultaneous Flywheels.

As we maneuver our everyday lives, we never use just one Flywheel. At any point in time, we are often in different phases on multiple Flywheels. While attempting to satisfy the blame threshold in one Flywheel, we are developing goals in another. While working on the inward chip in one Flywheel, we are struggling with commitment in another. This juggling of Flywheels requires functional memory. These ultimate multitaskers achieve by successfully spinning multiple Flywheels. Do you know people who find success in all aspects of their lives? Their success is no accident because they use functional memory to create synergy and consistency in all their success pursuits.

How does memory apply to your success pursuit? What can we learn from MFers use of memory? Results, no matter how lofty or dismal, should have only a short-term effect on the Flywheel. You should purge these memories as soon as possible. If you want to continue to achieve, you can't commit your euphoria or dysphoria to long-term memory.

Performance is in the present. If you don't sequester your results to short-term memory, it can cause future poor performance. Dwelling on early success could make you a one-hit wonder. Memorializing the negative feelings from early failure could devastate your Flywheel. Whatever your early results, keep them in your short-term memory. Commit your Flywheel know-how, and your strategy refinements to your long-term memory. Understand what memories to commit to long-term and how they can affect your Flywheel.

Michael Jordan understood his Flywheel and how to sustain his motivation. He realized that his competitive nature exponentially increased his motivation. Leroy Smith made the varsity team instead of him. His roommate Buzz Peterson was the North Carolina high school player of the year. These long-term memories fueled a career-long fire.

Don't dwell on your results. "Do not brood over your past mistakes and failures as this will only fill your mind with grief, regret and depression." Commit your successful strategies to your long-term memory. Retain those long-term memories that accelerate your Flywheel. Know where you are on all of your Flywheels. Use your functional memory to achieve success in multiple areas. Use it to simultaneously succeed on your spouse Flywheel, your career Flywheel, and your parent Flywheel.

Memory is the persistent modification of behavior resulting from your experience. You will make mistakes, but don't brood on them and don't repeat them in the future. Use your memory to modify behavior, enhance your experience, and pursue your success. Your past is only as important as you make it. Use it to your advantage. Succeed because of your past, not in spite of it.

FROM WITHIN
HUMBLE
ACCELERATORS
WHAT DO YOU FEEL
HAPPINESS COMES
ASSESSMENT
SUPERSTAR
LUCKY
ALTERATION
ACCEPTANCE
MOTIVATION
MANIACAL
INERTIA
FANATICISM
OBSTACLES
LOFTY
INWARD
HIDDEN
GRIP
M
SUCCESS
FOUNDATION
R
VALUES
FLYWHEEL
FOCUS
GOALS
EVIDENCE
SUCCESS
STRATEGY
BLAME
t
CAPABILITY
BEYOND
SELF
INTERESTS
PIVOT
GUTCHECK
FUTILITY
PHASES
THRESHOLD
DON'T SWEAT THE SMALL STUFF
SUPER TRUST
HERO
PROMISE
YOUR
FAULT
BELIEF
CONSISTENCY
CHECKMATE
NO EXCUSES
NO EXPLANATIONS
DISCIPLINE
DENIAL
GAME DAY
ALWAYS
PERSISTENCE
STRENGTH
POTENTIAL
BETTER LUCKY THAN GOOD
POISE
PAST PERFORMANCE
FUTURE SUCCESS
CIRCUMSTANCE
PERFECT SITUATION
SERIOUS SUCCESSOLOGY
MANIACAL FANATICISM BEST
ACCOUNTABLE
FAILURE

CHAPTER XXXV

CAN PAST PERFORMANCE PREDICT FUTURE SUCCESS?

"Yesterday is gone. Tomorrow has not yet come. We have only today. Let us begin."

– MOTHER TERESA

As we discussed in the opening chapters, our society tends to assign success potential to those who have had success in the past. Most of what we know about people is based on what they have done. Understandably, this appears to be the most logical and intuitive way to analyze, interpret, and predict successful behaviors. Much of the way we interpret success is based on this mindset. If you were successful in the past, you should theoretically be successful in the future.

This model is reinforced throughout our culture. In school, the children who do well in elementary school are expected to perform well in high school. Those who perform well in high school are expected to be successful college students. The workplace is similar. We promote those who have excelled in the past, and we assume that they will have similar performances in different roles. Multimillion-dollar firms choose their executives based on their previous performances in other roles.

Although success is rare, we assume that those who have had past success will repeat it. We even assume that individuals can transfer their success across disciplines. Physicians often translate their mastery of medicine into losses in the stock market, because they incorrectly assume their mastery of medicine translates to mastery of money. Using past performance to predict future success is our default. It is our comfort zone. Frankly, it feels good. The logic isn't unreasonable, but we adopt this model mostly because it is expedient. This model is intuitive, convenient, and doesn't require much effort.

Imagine a group of ten-year-old children playing football at recess? A team captain is chosen for each team, and those captains pick players for each team. How do they know which players to choose? Of course, captains usually choose players based on their past performance. Bobby scored three touchdowns yesterday, so he gets chosen first. Johnny has never caught the ball and can barely run without falling. Naturally, he is chosen last.

Athletes are awarded gigantic contracts based on their past career performances. Franchises pay large sums of money for players who have a history of high-level performance. Sports teams assume that a player's future performance will mimic his or her past performance. But, is this the best way to identify people who will be successful in the future?

How many times has a sports team been disappointed by its hundred-million-dollar flop? This same disappointment happens at work, with our kids, with our spouses, with our friends, and with our employers. When new performance doesn't match previous performance, we feel let down. It isn't entirely the performer's fault. We feel let down because we inappropriately assess the ability to perform based on past performance.

Every year, the *Heisman Trophy* is awarded to the most valuable college football player. First presented in 1935, it is the most prestigious individual award in college sports. Sports journalists, previous *Heisman Trophy* winners, and fans all vote for who they think is the best collegiate football player in the nation. But how do they quantify "best"? It is usually based on results. Like most awards, the *Heisman Trophy* is awarded for an athlete's past performance.

As expected, our society hoists individuals like these on the past performance pedestal. This award is an accolade, a reward, and an acknowledgment of the player's exceptional individual performance. Although the trophy is a reward for the previous year's play, people assume that it will predict future performance. Is this a correct assumption to make? Is it feasible to assume that performance at one level will become exceptional results at another? What evidence do we use to make that assumption? Is that assumption made with any evidence at all? And by now, you should know the answer to that question.

Here are the Heisman Trophy winners for the twenty years ending in 2011.

HEISMAN TROPHY RECIPIENT	YEAR
Robert Griffin III	2011
Cam Newton	2010
Mark Ingram	2009
Sam Bradford	2008
Tim Tebow	2007
Troy Smith	2006
Reggie Bush	2005
Matt Leinhart	2004
Jason White	2003
Carson Palmer	2002
Eric Couch	2001
Chris Weinke	2000
Ron Dayne	1999
Ricky Williams	1998
Charles Woodson	1997
Danny Wuerffel	1996
Eddie George	1995
Rashaan Salaam	1994
Charlie Ward	1993
Gino Torretta	1992
Desmond Howard	1991
Ty Detmer	1990
Andre Ware	1989

The players on this list had tremendous college football success. As a result of that success, they were awarded the most prestigious individual honor in collegiate football, the Heisman Trophy. The overwhelming majority of the talent pool for professional football comes from the college ranks. As such, it isn't unreasonable to assume that the best college football players should become the best professional football players. That is a simple prediction that most of us would have bet a lot of money on. Maybe it isn't that simple.

While you may recognize some of the names on the list of Heisman Trophy winners, many of them aren't household names. Although they all achieved tremendous success in college, very few achieved similar professional success. Of the over seventy-five Heisman Trophy winners since 1935, only five were selected to the Professional Football Hall of Fame. Only Doak Walker, Roger Staubach, Tony Dorsett, Marcus Allen and Barry Sanders were able to replicate their dominant college performances at a professional level. If we use the award as a predictor of success on the professional level, it has a predictive value of about seven percent. Simply put, success in college football is a poor predictor of similar success in professional football.

Does this mean that the selection process is flawed? Does it mean that something was missed? No, it simply means that past performance doesn't and can't predict future success. If we dig even deeper into the data, we find that many future professional football superstars were outshined in their college years. Marshall Faulk was elected to the Football Hall of Fame in 2011. He ran for over ten thousand yards and one hundred and thirty-six touchdowns. He lost the Heisman Trophy to Gino Torretta in 1992. He also lost to Charlie Ward, Heath Shuler, and David Palmer in 1993.

In 1984, Doug Flutie was selected as the Heisman Trophy winner. The players that followed Doug Flutie were Keith Byers, Robbie Bosco, Bernie Kosar, Kenneth Davis, Bill Fralic, Chuck Long, Gregg Allen, and Jerry Rice. Yes, you read correctly! Jerry Rice, the most prolific wide receiver in professional football history. *Yeah, the guy with the maniacal work ethic,* was selected ninth! You get the picture. If you analyze the data, it is clear that winning the Heisman Trophy doesn't adequately predict future success in the National Football League.

This phenomenon isn't unique to football or sports. Our society is riddled with merit badges, awards based on what we were or what we did. We select people in this way because we have a limited capacity to identify what they will become or what they will do. We are a society preoccupied with retrospective success. Our traditional way of evaluating who will be successful is significantly flawed. The things we identify as predictive aren't very predictive at all. Many of the traits that we feel guarantee success have little or no effect on future performance.

If we dive deeper into the *Heisman* data, we see that *not* winning the *Heisman Trophy* may be a better predictor of future success. I believe Peyton Manning, Drew Brees, Ladanian Tomlinson, Steve Young, Adrian Peterson, Marshall Faulk, and Jerry Rice would all agree with that. Maybe not winning the *Heisman Trophy* was the catalyst for their future superior performance. Not winning the *Heisman* may have led to blame, created opportunities for improvement, and fostered the inward chip. Not winning the *Heisman* made them question their abilities and created unparalleled motivation to push beyond their limits.

We know from what we have learned from Maniacal Fanaticism that there is no best. Maybe not winning the *Heisman* makes it obvious to athletes that they can do better. Maybe not winning the *Heisman* is what created future football MFers. What do you think goes through a player's mind when they find out they weren't good enough to win the *Heisman*?

"I didn't win the *Heisman*. Why did *he* win it? Am I not good enough? What am I doing wrong? Am I better than him? I will show him. I will show them. I'm better!" This is the inward chip. "I will train harder. Lift more weights. Get better coaching! Work harder! Study playbooks!" This is inertia. "I will lead the league in receptions and touchdowns. I will win rookie of the year. I will win a championship." This is goal development. "I will study the playbook for two hours every day. I will train for three hours every day. I will run perfect routes so I will be open all the time. I will always be a team player." This is strategy development.

"I will promise to work harder than anyone else. I believe in my strategy and my ability. I trust this strategy will be successful." This is commitment. "I know I'm better. I can work harder than anyone else. I will get there early and leave late. I can practice one route ten thousand times. I can sprint uphill for two and a half miles every day. I know what I have to give up. I have to keep to my regimen." This is discipline. "I'm almost there. I was second in the rookie of the year voting. We didn't win a championship but won the conference title. I know if I work harder, we can get there. We get closer each year." This is variable success. "We would've won if I just caught that ball in overtime. I could've jumped higher. I will work to jump higher next year. I wasn't strong enough. I have to get stronger. If I play better, we definitely will win." This is blame.

The lack of merit may be more predictive than the receipt of merit. If you consider yourself the best, how can you possibly get better? If you think you are doing your best, you have no inward chip, no blame, no inertia, no Flywheel, and no future success. If you really want to be successful, we can't look at what you have done. Future success requires that we focus on what you will do. If you do your best and achieve your best, you can't get better. You can never really know what our best is. The performances of your past don't predict your future.

Yesterday is gone. Bask in the glow for a moment and then move on. Park it in short-term memory. Every future endeavor should start from scratch. Play every game as though you are trying to make the team. Go to every meeting with the exuberance you had when you first got the job. Interact with people with the same excitement you did, when you first encountered them. Meet every day as if you can accomplish more. Accept the merit badge humbly and gratefully, but understand that yesterday's performance won't mean success tomorrow. "Tomorrow has not yet come. We only have today. Let us begin."

CHAPTER XXXVI
CHECKMATE

"You have to learn the rules of the game. And then you have to play better than anyone else."
– ALBERT EINSTEIN

Chess is one of the most interesting games on the planet. I have been playing chess as long as I can remember. In my lifetime, I have probably played over two-thousand matches. What intrigues me about chess is how it resembles life. For most people, chess is a scaled-down version of a military strategy game. For me, it is so much more.

Each game of chess develops your ability to handle different strategic situations. It hones your ability to succeed under different circumstances. Chess mimics life because no two games are exactly alike. Some games are ordinary and predictable, while others are bizarre and peculiar. This variability makes chess so intriguing.

When I play chess, I use the same opening moves every time. Through my first several moves, I am painfully predictable. Even though I am predictable, the reactions to my predictability are very different. Sometimes my opponent reacts in a similarly predictable fashion, but those reactions are few and far between. Other times, my predictability is countered by my opponent's erraticism.

Every game takes on a personality and flavor of its own. Success is similar to a chess match. No two success stories are entirely the same. While many success pursuits start with very predictable behaviors, success often has its own personality and flavor. Like chess, success offers thousands of different ways to win.

Let me explain what I mean. Each chess piece has a unique ability and can only move in a very specific way on the board. The bishop only moves diagonally. The rook only moves horizontally and vertically. The king moves in all directions, but only one space at a time. The queen moves in all directions as many spaces as she likes, but she can't jump over any pieces. The pawn only moves forward one space at a time, unless that pawn is taking another piece. If the pawn is taking another piece, it moves forward one space diagonally. The knight moves in an L shape and jumps over both teammates and opposition pieces. Every piece on the table has well-defined abilities and limitations.

As you maneuver your pieces against an opponent, you are always strategizing. What pieces can you lose? What pieces can you take from the opposing player? Inevitably, you develop a style. You become very good at using certain combinations of pieces and not so good at other combinations. No matter what pieces you have, one thing is consistent. You always have the opportunity to win.

Imagine that chess pieces represented all of our skills. Each one of us has different combinations of skills and traits. Some of us have more knights than bishops. Some of us have more rooks than pawns. Whatever the combination of pieces that we bring to the table, we always have an opportunity to win the game.

Just like life, we can't change the chess pieces we are given. The chess pieces that we are required to use are predetermined for us. The type, number, and composition of your pieces are immutable. They can't be changed no matter what you do. Each of us is born with a particular set of skills. While it is possible to hone those skills and even discover some that you thought you didn't have, you are what you are.

You are probably wondering if you should stop reading because your hand is already dealt. Does this mean that success is only for those who are dealt with the proper hand? Is your success potential immutable and unchangeable? On the contrary, that would be true in poker. In poker, you are only as good as the hand you are dealt. If you have a great hand, you are likely to win. If you have a bad hand, the only way to win is to fake it. Chess, though, is profoundly different. Even in the most dire of situations, it is always possible to win. This is exactly what MFers do. They maximize their chances of winning, with whatever chess pieces they have.

Yes, it is true. Some people receive a combination of pieces that give them a greater chance to win. However, even with a combination that isn't so favorable, winning is absolutely possible. If you don't have the best circumstances, you may have to spin the Flywheel faster than someone in a better situation. Don't spend energy trying to change your pieces. Don't spend time complaining about how difficult it is to play with the pieces you have. Don't spend time dreaming about being the other player with better pieces.

How should you spend your time? You should focus your energy on developing the best strategy to win with what you have. Learn the rules of the game and then play better than anybody else. In chess, players are often enamored with the queen. The queen is clearly the most powerful piece on the board. If you have the queen and your opponent doesn't, you are guaranteed to win. Surprisingly, this isn't always the case.

Depending on your strategy, the knight may be the most important piece for you. Sometimes, your knight may be more valuable than the queen. Your pawn may be in a better position to win the game. There is a strategy for every combination of pieces, and it is simply a matter of using the right one. People often defeat themselves before they even start. They usually wait for the right opportunity, the right situation, or the right hand to be dealt. That perfect opportunity may never come. Success requires that we determine the correct strategy for the situation.

As you study the Flywheel and get ready to develop your blueprint for success, quit hoping for a queen. The knight moves two spaces vertically and one space horizontally, and you can still win. You can win with a rook. You can win with a bishop. Yes, you can even win with a pawn. You just have to learn the rules of the game and play better than anyone else. You have been blessed with a certain set of skills that are particular to you. Your combination of skills is like no other individual in the world.

Develop your unique strategy based on your particular set of skills. Don't spend time coveting your opponent's queen, bishops, or rooks. Maximize your pawns and knights. Take full advantage of your particular skill set. Spinning the Flywheel is independent of the number of pieces or the talent you have. You should assume success is possible in all situations. Understand the unique skill set that you have been dealt. Don't hesitate to try, because even without a queen, you just might win.

BOOK 3
DOCENT

"TEACH ONE"

FROM WITHIN
ACCELERATORS
WHAT DO YOU FEEL
HAPPINESS
COMES
ASSESSMENT
LUCKY
SUPERSTAR
ALTERATION
ACCEPTANCE
MOTIVATION
MANIACAL
FANATICISM
INERTIA
OBSTACLES
INWARD
HIDDEN
SUCCESS
FOUNDATION
VALUES
FLYWHEEL
FOCUS
BLAME
CAPABILITY
PIVOT
GUTCHECK
FUTILITY
THRESHOLD
DON'T SWEAT THE SMALL
SUPER TRUST
HERO
PROMISE
YOUR
FAULT
CHECKMATE
NO EXCUSES
NO EXPLANATIONS
BETTER LUCKY THAN GOOD
POISE
PAST PERFORMANCE
FUTURE SUCCESS
CIRCUMSTANCE
PERFECT SITUATION
SUCCESSOLOGY
MANIACAL FANATICISM BEST

CHAPTER XXXVII
GAME DAY

"Success depends upon previous preparation, and without such preparation there is sure to be failure."
– CONFUCIUS

So far, we have seen how motivation leads to focus and how focus leads to execution. Execution is where the rubber meets the road. It is where your plan becomes executable, and the strategy gains traction. The execution phase can be a thankless monotonous grind, marked by futility and delayed gratification. More often, the execution phase is dynamic and punctuated periodically by climaxes. These moments of reckoning are the moments that will define our success pursuit.

Inertia, the inward chip, strategy, goals, commitment, and discipline all culminate in one coordinated action. Although executing a plan can take several years, the pivot points along the way can make or break you. These moments help to define successful people. They are the moments of truth. A single moment in time may be what separates success from failure. This moment, however short or long, is called game-day.

Game-day is a hot spot of execution. The entire work of the success effort consolidates to this single point. Motivation, focus, and execution exist simultaneously. Game day is the final exam, and it determines a significant portion of your grade. It is Michael Jordan's game-winning shot. It is that last pitch in the bottom of the ninth. It is that game-tying field goal. Game days are those defining moments when failure isn't an option, and success means so much more.

What is required to succeed on game day? Let's consider two similar individuals. They have similarly effective strategies. They have similar motivation, skills, and talent. Even with all these similarities, differences in their game-day performance can still exist. Unbelievably, some individuals can have better game-day performance than their more qualified counterparts. How is this possible?

Over the years, my game days haven't changed significantly. As a high school and collegiate basketball player, I prepared for my games in the same way. No matter how I was feeling, I forced myself to maintain the same attitude, intensity, and mental approach for every game. I did this to standardize my performance. I wanted to do what was mentally and physically necessary to peak for each game. I knew that if I approached my preparation routine in the same fanatical way, my performance should follow suit.

I didn't start anything special. For years, athletes have had game-day routines. To maximize and standardize their game-day performance, they standardize the structure of their preparation. They do this to ensure that the principles developed in the strategy threshold remain at the forefront. Game days are the perfect opportunity to reinforce goals, reaffirm strategy, and maximize the work of execution.

At the risk of exposing myself, I will share some of my game-day preparation. Before each game, I would get ready in the same way. I would watch a portion of Michael Jordan's movie, *Come Fly with Me*. I would dress in the same way, putting each item of clothing on in a specific order. When I walked out on the court, I would repeatedly hit myself over my heart with my right hand.

After this odd ritual, I was ready to go. I was primed. I was ready to maximize my performance. Hitting my chest was significant. It reminded me that I had more heart, more fight, and more tenacity than anyone else in the gym. My routine was a little more elaborate than this, but this is all I am willing to divulge. This ritual was more than just an obsessive compulsion. It was more than superstition.

I have often asked myself if these game-day rituals were indeed effective. Were they just self-inflicted psych jobs? Did these game-day rituals serve a purpose? Were they necessary? Yes! These game-day rituals prepared me mentally, physically, and emotionally. Whether the effect was real or imagined, my preparation elevated my performance. My game-day routine made me believe I could accomplish anything.

Extraordinary performance starts with an extraordinary belief that the performance you seek is possible. In execution, the inward chip and blame have no role. To execute, you must convince yourself to commit to the strategy and maintain the discipline to follow through. This is even more true on game day. There is no place here for questioning your goals, strategy, or preparation.

In 1999, Minnesota Viking kicker Gary Anderson had a career-defining game-day moment. He was the leading scorer and placekicker for what most consider the best offensive team in National Football League history. Anderson was known for his game-day preparation, and his results showed it. His stellar performance helped lead his undefeated team to the conference title.

Gary Anderson was as dialed in as he ever was in his career during that 1998-1999 season. He totaled 164 regular-season points. And that is even more impressive when you learn how he did that. Anderson made all fifty-nine of his extra-point attempts. Though more difficult, he also made all thirty-five of his field-goal attempts. Yes, you read correctly. He didn't miss a field goal or extra point during his entire sixteen game football season.

Anderson's playoff performance seemed to follow the same trajectory. Of course, he continued to deliver. Leading up to the conference finals, he made all five of his extra-point attempts and all four of his field-goal attempts. Kicking field goals and shooting free throws and meeting quarterly revenue targets all require the same thing. They require preparation, focus, consistency, and many of the other traits that we have discussed in this book.

The Minnesota Vikings were essentially guaranteed a win in the final moments of the 1999 NFC Championship game. All the Vikings needed to seal the game was a short field goal from old reliable—Gary Anderson. With just over two minutes left in the game, the National Football League's best kicker had the opportunity to win the game and send the Minnesota Vikings to the Superbowl.

This was Anderson's game-day moment. Like Michael Jordan's "shot," Gary Anderson had previously proven that his ability to deliver when it counted was unprecedented. From thirty-eight yards away, a relatively uncomplicated distance, a distance he hit nine consecutive field goals from—Gary Anderson kicked his most important game-day field goal wide left. He missed his first field goal in two years. He choked!

What happens when your game-day preparation fails? In the sports world, we call this failure choking. Choking is the failure that occurs at the pinnacle of the execution phase. It is an outright game-day failure. It occurs when people or teams fail to execute, during moments when their best performance is necessary. Why does this happen?

People choke because they question their motivation, focus, and execution on that crucial game day. Instead of experiencing that beautiful moment when all the stages and thresholds harmoniously coalesce, they are riddled with doubt. This isn't the same doubt from the inward chip. This is a paralyzing doubt. This is a doubt about the ability to reach the goals, and it comes from doubting the strategy.

Those who choke doubt their commitment and discipline. They get cold feet. They don't believe they can win. As a result, they underperform. They choke! Don't you know someone with a history of great performance, great strategy and great preparation who fails to deliver when it matters most? This isn't limited to sports. Choking happens in politics. It happens in the corporate world. It happens in the academic world. Like Gary Anderson, game-day failures have marred otherwise brilliant careers.

In these high-performance situations, MFers always perform at a high level. They always manage to elevate their game. They are clutch performers. They are the people who you know will make that shot, make that sale, close that deal, or make the field goal. Often, they exceed previous performance limits. How do they do this? What do they do differently? How are they always able to perform at their best when it matters most?

Before we answer this question, let's take a closer look at my game-day ritual. My pre-game ritual was more about my mental, emotional, and physical preparation than it was about basketball. It wasn't superstition or a self-inflicted psych job. It was priming my mind, heart, soul, and body to launch into action. It was priming the pump. It was greasing the wheels.

Physically, we stretch to prepare muscles, tendons, and joints for activity. Likewise, we also have to prepare mentally and emotionally. We have to stretch our minds and emotions. When I realized that my ritual was about mental honing, I tried to apply it to other areas of my life. I used the same ritual before my medical school tests. It had the same effect. I used it before I ran my marathon. It had the same effect. I even used it before golf tournaments, and it had the same effect.

To this day, although my routine has changed slightly, I use the ritual before every game-day situation I have. Before I sit down to write each chapter of this book, I go through my ritual. Before I go to work, I go through my ritual. Before I run a half-marathon, I go through my ritual. Before an important meeting, I go through my ritual. When I have to perform my best, I go through my ritual.

I am effectively stretching my mind before the game. I am preparing for success. "Success depends upon previous preparation." I am anticipating my peak performance. I am condensing all my motivation, focus, and execution into one moment in time. I am standardizing and maximizing my game day. I am preparing to push past my previous performance limits.

Do you have a ritual? Do you have a way to prepare for your game days? Do you have a way to prepare your mind, body, and soul for success? Game-day rituals are as unique as fingerprints, but some basic principles are necessary. To develop your game-day ritual, it is necessary to use game-day priming. Game-day priming requires very specific and predictable behaviors. This process should maximize execution and eliminate doubt.

GAME-DAY PRIMING

Motivation Priming	• Purge the inward chip • Maximize inertia
Focus Priming	• Anticipate strategy fulfillment • Anticipate goal achievement
Execution Priming	• Envision successful strategy execution • Maximize belief
Reinforcement Priming	• Anticipate lofty goal accomplishment • Relive past success

During the process of game-day priming, MFers lives flash before their eyes. Well, not literally. They walk themselves through the Flywheel to prime themselves mentally, physically, and spiritually. When I was watching Michael Jordan's, *Come Fly with Me*, I was preparing my mind for success. I was preparing my body for action. I was feeding on the energy from the greatest basketball player in history. I wanted to incorporate his heart, his desire, and his will into my game-day situation.

I also wanted to eliminate doubt, the execution killer. Doubt leads to hesitation. Hesitation, in turn, limits execution. To *make* the game-winning shot, you have to *take* the game-winning shot. To *take* the game-winning shot, you have to *know* you can make it. On game day, you have to trust your preparation, strategy, commitment, and discipline. You have a belief in yourself, a belief in the strategy, and a belief in the process. You aren't simply wishing or hoping you will make the shot. You have to know you can make it, and that is an entirely different thing.

You know what results to expect, because of the hard work you have previously done. "Success depends upon previous preparation, and without such preparation there is sure to be failure." When it is time for that game-winning shot, you know exactly what to do. Know you can make the shot. Take the shot. Make the shot. Know it! Take it! Make it!

Essentially, game-day priming can be broken down into the following. Knowing it, this is the knowledge that you have sufficient preparation. Taking it, this is engaging the task with full confidence that you will be successful. Making it, this is achieving the anticipated result. This doesn't just apply to sports. You should approach all game-day situations in your life the same way. Know you can do it. Do it. Get the result. Know it. Take it. Make it.

Doubt limits your ability to pull the trigger. To effectively prime for your game day, you have to minimize your inward chip. If you recall, the inward chip is a manifestation of doubt. It represents the feeling of inadequacy that you may have. While the inward chip is helpful during the early processes of the Flywheel, it can also be an execution killer. On game day, the inward chip has no place and should be purged or, at the very least, minimized.

Remember Michael Jordan's game-winning shot over Craig Ehlo? That shot would come to define Michael Jordan. It was the beginning of his legendary status. But, what if Michael Jordan hadn't taken that shot? What would have happened if he doubted his ability to make that shot? His legacy would have been far different. Fortunately, Michael Jordan did take that shot. He took that shot because he trusted his preparation. He believed in himself. He believed in his strategy. He believed in the process. He knew he could make it, and because of that knowledge, he dared to take it. The rest is history. He made it.

Game-day priming relies on the ability to relive your Flywheel very rapidly. During game day, you quickly review all your phases: motivation, focus, execution, and reinforcement. Motivation priming begins with generating tons of inertia. For example, team cheers excite a team. They add fuel to the motivation fire. The easiest way to get people to overachieve is to overwhelm them with motivation.

Cheering in the locker room before a game is an attempt to drive motivation through the roof. A motivational cheer reaffirms and primes the team's game-day motivations. Motivation priming is the reason underdogs win. Teams or individuals who expect to win tend not to maximize their inertia. Motivation priming also requires the elimination of the inward chip. It is necessary to purge the inward chip and remove all possible doubt. You can't maximize performance if you are filled with doubt.

Game-day priming is a microcosm of the Flywheel. The stages of game-day priming follow the stages of the Flywheel. Therefore, the next game-day stage is focus priming. Focus priming is the anticipation of climax performance. In this stage, MFers anticipate strategy fulfillment and goal achievement.

Do you recall my half marathon preparation? On the day of my half marathon, I anticipated how I would feel if my strategy was fulfilled. I anticipated what achieving my goal would feel like. Just thinking that all my hard work would indeed pay off filled me with euphoria. Anticipating success is intoxicating and was almost as powerful as the success itself.

On game day, you should anticipate the perfect situation. You should anticipate your perfect strategy and the goal accomplishment that follows. Focus priming is often called visualization. You visualize the ball going through the hoop. You visualize the answers on the test. You visualize the golf ball going into the cup. You are preparing your mind for the anticipated result. Your mind, body, and spirit understand what to expect.

Execution priming is similar to focus priming, but it is subtly different. This stage requires envisioning perfect execution. Before my basketball games, I would envision the perfect strategy and the perfect execution of that perfect strategy. Before my medical school tests, I would imagine that my study strategy was perfect.

Belief is also required for execution. If you don't believe you can execute, you won't. When you prime for game day, you have to believe you can execute. You have to maximize your belief. Coaches, teachers, and parents are often instrumental in maximizing our belief. Religious, spiritual, and emotional support can also maximize belief. Tim Tebow's strong Christian belief enhanced his game-day priming.

The last stage of your game-day preparation is reinforcement priming. Reinforcement priming is the process of anticipating your highest level of success. In other words, it is the process of anticipating what you will feel after you achieve your ultimate lofty goal. Long-term memory of past successes acts as a reinforcement priming catalyst. This historical reflection isn't used to change or enhance strategy. It is used to prime the feeling of success. Previous successes enhance the priming for the current game day. If you know what it felt like to win in the past, why not use that experience to succeed again.

In 1998, Michael Jordan won his sixth National Basketball Championship with a game-winning shot over Bryon Russell. That game-day take and make were primed by his playoff shot over Craig Ehlo and his game-winner in North Carolina. The next time you have a game-day moment, think about your previous successes. This is the reason I apply my game-day priming to most of what I do. The more I game-day prime, the better I get at it. I know what I have to do to be successful during my defining moments. Priming allows you to exceed your performance expectations.

Your game day can be your new job interview, a test, a board meeting, the implementation of a major project, or simply a busy day at work. Whatever your game day is, don't forget to game-day prime. You have to know that you can succeed. You must have the courage to attempt success and maintain the vision to anticipate the result. Know it! Take it! Make it!

FROM WITHIN HUMBLE
FEEL
SUPERSTAR
ALTERATION
MOTIVATION
MANIACAL
FANATICISM
OBSTACLES
INWARD
HIDDEN
M
SUCCESS
FOUNDATION
VALUES
FLYWHEEL
R
FOCUS
SUCCESS
BLAME
CAPABILITY
PIVOT
GUTCHECK
FUTILITY
THRESHOLD
DON'T SWEAT THE SMALL
SUPER TRUST
HERO
YOUR
CHECKMATE
NO EXCUSES
NO EXPLANATIONS
BETTER LUCKY THAN GOOD
POISE
PAST PERFORMANCE
CIRCUMSTANCE
SUCCESSOLOGY
MANIACAL FANATICISM BEST

CHAPTER XXXVIII

"WHAT DO YOU FEEL?"

"A man who is master of himself can end a sorrow as easily as he can invent a pleasure. I don't want to be at the mercy of my emotions. I want to use them, to enjoy them, and to dominate them."

– OSCAR WILDE

Unequivocally, I consider Barry Sanders the best running back of all time. To me, it's no surprise that Barry Sanders is a member of both the college and professional football halls of fame. Sanders' ability to evade tackles was unprecedented. I have never seen anybody avoid tackles the way he did. His level of success, determination, and performance was unprecedented. There is no doubt in my mind that Barry Sanders is an MFer.

Barry Sanders wasn't just a great athlete. His approach to the game of football is unique. When I saw him play in college the first time, I knew something was different. He was an exceptional college football running back, but his exceptional performance isn't necessarily what intrigued me. What he did after his exceptional performance was far more interesting.

As a young player, Barry Sanders developed a very unusual way of celebrating touchdowns. Nowadays, football is infamous for its elaborate, falsely spontaneous and entertaining touchdown celebrations. After all, touchdowns are rare, and rare events should be celebrated. Football players are like most people, after achievement they spend a few moments to celebrate a job well done. Well... most people aren't Barry Sanders.

The most exciting running back in the history of football dazzled on the field, but he didn't dazzle anyone with his celebration of rare events. Barry got the hand off from the quarterback and darted to the outside. He stutter-stepped, leaned right, and cut left. He spun. He was partially tackled and almost fell. Just when you thought the play was over, he sped out of the pack. He turned on the speed, thirty-five more yards to another miraculous and unanticipated touchdown.

Touchdowns are rare, and they should be celebrated. How did Sanders celebrate? He ran directly to the referee at the back of the end zone and started his touchdown celebration. He didn't pull a cell phone from his uniform. He didn't dance. He didn't dunk the ball over the goal post or spike the ball. He simply ran to the ref and handed him the ball. That's it! As dazzling and entertaining and spectacular as he was before the touchdown, he was rather mundane after it.

Success is exciting. When we achieve success, we appropriately want to celebrate. Celebrating allows us to acknowledge the hard work and effort that led to success. That is why most players celebrate touchdowns. They are excited. They are happy they have achieved. What did Barry Sanders feel after each touchdown? What did he do when this team was down by fourteen, and he scored a touchdown? What did he do when they were up by twenty, and he scored a touchdown? What did he do when he scored a touchdown in the regular season? What about the playoffs, what did he do then? He did the same thing every time. He simply handed the ball to the ref.

Understandably, emotions play a role in performance. While emotions can provide us with an immediate boost of inertia, the effect of emotion on the Flywheel is variable. This variability occurs largely because of how labile and volatile emotions can be. Emotions bind us to each other, but they are also what makes us individually distinct.

Emotions in varying proportions can either hinder or enhance our performance. Fear, anger, and love are examples of emotions that can alter our abilities. Fear, as we discussed in an earlier chapter, can enhance or hinder performance. The fight or flight mechanism, which is preprogrammed into us, serves to enhance performance in times of danger.

The fight or flight mechanism is necessary for survival, but survival doesn't always equal success. Fight or flight isn't always the best success strategy, unless passing your genetic material to the next generation is your definition of success. But of course, that would be an entirely different book. The fight or flight mechanism is most useful for short fleeting crises, and it often produces levels of performance that aren't typically sustainable.

Cheetahs can run at blistering speeds when pursuing prey. Without the ability to run at this speed, they would starve to death. Whether successful or not, the cheetah must rest after each chase. During this time, the cheetah is vulnerable to attack. The cheetah's incredible speed during a chase is an extreme example of outstanding performance that isn't sustainable.

Many of us perceive and pursue success in this way. We try to perform in extreme and excessive ways. Unfortunately, we can't sustain this level of performance for very long. This is primarily why we fail. We burn hard and burn out. When we rest, we are vulnerable to losing our Flywheel momentum. Like the cheetah, those moments of exhaustion put our success pursuit at risk.

Every winter, Canadian Geese migrate south in search of food and warmer weather. Cheetahs are much faster than geese, but geese migrate thousands of miles in a relatively short period. If we were to analyze the speed of the geese over a short distance, their performance wouldn't be nearly as fast as the cheetah. But, when you analyze their speed and consider the distance over which that speed has been maintained, the performance is almost impossible to fathom. True success is more like a migration.

Pursuing success, like the cheetah, isn't the ideal way to achieve it. A success pursuit made up of short, swift bursts isn't sustainable and will leave you vulnerable. How effective would a sprinter be at trying to win a marathon? No matter how fast she runs the forty-yard dash, she will only travel forty yards. She will still have twenty-six miles left. Even worse, she will have to rest between each burst of blistering speed. Starting and stopping the Flywheel doesn't allow momentum to build. With each consecutive turn of the Flywheel, it becomes easier to meet thresholds and complete phases. Every time the Flywheel stops, restarting, it becomes increasingly difficult.

All that said, the fight or flight mechanism is part of being the human-animal we are. Fear, anger, sadness, and joy conspire to change our performance and productivity. Fight or anger can make us overly aggressive and temperamental. Flight or fear can make us timid and restrained. These biological responses create short sprints, forcing us into several erratic forty-yard dashes. Even joy betrays us.

Euphoria can be very motivational and adds energy to your effort, but it rarely lasts.

Euphoria is a state defined as being different from normal. After a period of euphoria, your demeanor returns to normal. If work only occurs during euphoria, you will experience the on-again, off-again, spinning of the Flywheel. This staccato style success pursuit staggers, because of fleeting episodes of euphoria sandwiched by periods of non-productive euphoria seeking. Emotion does have a role in success pursuit. However, basing your success solely on the emotion of the moment may not be the most effective long-term plan. To have effective, consistent, and pervasive success, you have to run a marathon, not a sprint. You have to run fast, but not so fast that you can't maintain your speed for the duration. And not so fast that you are forced to interrupt your success pursuit with periods of unproductive rest.

Emotion can affect that consistent performance. It can cause unsustainable speed, but it can also burn you out. This doesn't mean that MFers are emotionless. It is quite the opposite. Successful people can be very emotional. What's the difference? They don't let their emotions control their performance. When the performance is necessary, they are fanatically focused on the task. After all we are human and emotions are a part of who we are, but MFers limit the outward representation of that emotion. They can end sorrow as easily as they can invent pleasure. They don't let their emotions dominate them. They dominate their emotions.

When Michael Jordan won his first championship, he was overwhelmed with emotion. I will never forget the picture of him lying on the floor crying, paralyzed with emotion. That emotion didn't all appear out of thin air. That emotion was present every single day of his goal pursuit. That emotion was present during every game of the long, hard season. Every shot, every pass, every play was loaded with emotion. On the brink of the most significant goal of his young career, I am sure he was filled with all kinds of emotion. However, he didn't let that limit his performance.

Barry Sanders handed the ball to the ref. Michael Jordan executed with cold and calculated efficiency. Jerry Rice prepared and prepared and prepared. These MFers weren't emotionless. They just exhibited less emotion. During execution, they picked their spots. They had an uncanny ability to know where and when to express their emotion. They knew how to dominate their emotions and use them to their advantage. Their performance, their execution, and their motivation weren't at the mercy of how they felt.

Emotion isn't good or bad. It just is. As a young high school basketball player, I remember trying to understand this concept. I used to ride the emotional roller coaster of each game. I was thrilled when we were winning and mortified when we were losing. I was angry when I underperformed. Unfortunately, I was also smug and overconfident when things were going my way. My performance followed my emotions, resulting in very schizophrenic results.

The performance of the entire team fluctuated with my emotionally labile leadership. That worked extremely well when we were on an emotional high. When we were low, we were low. I remember one practice when that all changed. Our coach staged what he called the "practice from hell." We scrimmaged for four straight hours.

Every time anybody would show emotion, the coach would make us run. I hit a shot and smiled. We ran. A teammate complained about a foul. We ran. Two players gave each other a high five as they ran down the court. We ran. One player vomited, and another ran to his aid. We ran. We ran and ran and ran.

As we ran back and forth from baseline to baseline, the coach would ask us the same question: "What do you feel?" When anybody scored, he would ask the question. When anybody missed a shot, he would ask the question. Anytime he sensed the slightest emotion, he asked the question. We ran after almost every play. He kept shouting, "What do you feel? What do you feel? What do you feel?" Just as I was about to collapse, I figured it out. It clicked. I got it. What I should feel after each made basket, what I should feel after each botched play, what I should feel after each missed free throw was absolutely nothing.

Years later, I finally understood what my coach was trying to teach. The ability to execute shouldn't be dependent on emotion. In the heat of battle, you should feel nothing. You should just execute. No wasted energy, no wasted effort, all that is required is pure, unadulterated execution.

Execution shouldn't depend on your current emotions. Performance is expected. It shouldn't be dependent on the short-term fleeting emotions of your success journey. When execution is required, you need to be a maniacal fanatic. When you win your championship, you can let the emotion out. When you achieve your goal, you can let the emotion out. When you obtain your variable result, you can let the emotion out. But, when you require execution, you should feel absolutely nothing. You shouldn't be at the mercy of your emotions. You should dominate them. You should run back and play defense. You should simply hand the ball to the ref.

You are at the free-throw line of life. The score is tied, and only two seconds are left in the game. You take a breath and start your pregame routine. You dribble the ball once and spin it in your hands. Half of the crowd is cheering, and the other half is jeering. You focus on the rim and dribble the ball again. You have prepared your whole life for this moment. You exhale. You are motivated. You wipe the sweat from your forehead. You dribble one last time. You are focused. You must now execute. You raise the ball and get ready to release it. Your heart is pounding. You are exhausted. At the time of execution, when your best effort is required, what should you feel? Absolutely nothing!

CHAPTER XXXIX

HAPPINESS COMES FROM WITHIN

"People are just about as happy as they make up their minds to be."
– ABRAHAM LINCOLN

Before we go any further, it is important to make a clear distinction between happiness and success. Happiness and success are closely related, but they aren't the same, nor are they mutually exclusive. Most people believe that achieving their ultimate success will make them happy. It seems intuitive. Those who achieve will, in turn, be happy. At least that is the assumption.

At this point, you are sufficiently motivated. You have developed your goal matrix. You have determined a strategy. You have executed your strategy and are waiting for reinforcement. If you achieved your ultimate goal, would you be happy? Of course you would! Happiness and accomplishment should go hand in hand. The relationship between the two should be straightforward, but we all know highly successful people who aren't happy. Let's face it. Some highly successful people are downright miserable. What is the pursuit of happiness? How does the pursuit of happiness relate to the pursuit of success?

The definition of success can differ from person to person. Each of us has our own definition of success. I have a personal definition of success, and so should you. The purpose of this book isn't to define success. The purpose of this book is to outline a specific process necessary to attain it. Maniacal Fanaticism is a process determined by a specific pattern of actions. It describes a consistent and maniacal pursuit of a goal, but it doesn't decide what that goal should be. You do! You determine the goal. You determine the success.

Maniacal Fanaticism is simply a template. It should serve as a guide. It outlines a particular way to achieve your particular success. Will that success make you happy? That is an entirely different and much more complex question. People tend to equate goal fulfillment with happiness. Goal fulfillment can lead to transient euphoria, but happiness is a different matter.

Happiness isn't a threshold or phase on the Flywheel. Happiness does have a marginal effect on inertia, which is easy to understand. When we are happy, we have more energy. We know this because of what we know about depression. Psychiatrists have studied the major signs and symptoms of depression. One of the major symptoms of depression is decreased energy. The decrease in energy results in decreased productivity. Conversely, the increased energy of happiness helps to satisfy the inertia threshold.

Happiness can add motivation, but no portion of the Flywheel generates happiness. Happiness appears to be a rogue variable, independent from the other factors that affect success. Happiness doesn't require success, and success doesn't require happiness. Well, if happiness doesn't come from success, where exactly does happiness come from?

I can remember my father telling me the story of the man with no shoes. "I was sad because I had no shoes until I met the man with no feet." Initially, the man with no shoes was unhappy. He was unhappy until his relative position was changed. When his unhappiness was compared to someone's situation that was worse, the unhappiness became happiness. The man was unhappy and happy at the same time. How can happiness and unhappiness exist simultaneously in the same person?

The story of the man with no shoes teaches a great lesson. It teaches us that our perspective defines our happiness. It teaches us that happiness comes from within. In this story, the man gained absolutely nothing, and his perceived happiness improved. His position didn't change. He never got the shoes he so desired. He never achieved his goal. He went from barefoot and unhappy to barefoot and happy. All that changed was his internal perspective of his external situation.

I would argue that happiness comes from within. Happiness is an intrinsic quality. It isn't something that you attain. It is what you are. I am not saying that external factors can't affect happiness. Devastating external factors can affect your happiness, but some people always have the uncanny ability to find the cup half-full. Some people always see the positive in every situation. Some people always appear to be happy. To a degree, happiness is relative. Its presence is predicated on perspective.

Happiness isn't always linked to success. In fact, they aren't related at all. You can be happy and successful. You can also be unhappy and successful. Likewise, you can be happy and unsuccessful or unhappy and unsuccessful. Success should never be the object of your happiness. Your happiness isn't defined by results or even your external situation. Your perspective defines it.

In the final analysis, you are only as happy as you make up your mind to be. Unhappy with no shoes and happy with feet exist simultaneously. It is simply a matter of perspective. You just need to change the way you look at things. You aren't exclusively defined by your success. At the end of the day, your journey defines you. The way you pursue success says more about you than what you achieve. The destination is important, but who you are is defined by how you get there.

Jerry Rice's happiness wasn't necessarily about what his accomplishments were, but more about *how* he achieved those accomplishments. That's what makes him so intriguing. That's what makes him an MFer. Your happiness is dependent on you. It is dependent on your internal perspective. It's dependent on how happy you make up your mind to be. It is entirely up to you. You can focus on the lack of shoes or the benefit of feet. Your happiness absolutely comes from within. In the end, the process defines you more than the success ever will. Before you complain about having no shoes, think about the man with no feet.

CHAPTER XL
A HELPING HAND

"None of us has gotten where we are solely by pulling ourselves up from our own bootstraps. We got here because somebody bent down and helped us."
– THURGOOD MARSHALL

No matter where you are on the Flywheel, at some point, you will require help. Although it is often difficult for highly successful people to admit it, success rarely occurs without a helping hand. Many of us assume that all we have accomplished in life is of our own doing. After all, we are all self-made, or so we think. Most of us define ourselves in terms of our accomplishments. We measure our worth by wins and losses. Our egos are elevated by our successes and devastated by our failures.

Education is a perfect example of this warped reality. Even though your parents paid the tuition, and your professors filled your head with information, you received the degree. We think our success occurs in a vacuum. We attribute our accomplishments to hard work. And what happens when we fail? We usually ascribe our failures to external factors. This creates an ideal situation. Winning is a result of our greatness and losing is a result of our bad luck. If we are honest with ourselves, we can see how illogical that logic can be.

All successful people have some help along the way. None of us get where we are solely by our individual effort. No matter how successful we are, someone was always there to help us along the way. Maybe it was a teammate, a boss, or a mentor. At some point in your life, somewhere, somehow, someone has helped you.

MFers are no different. They define success not only by the choices and by actions they make, but also by the culmination of experiences that make them who they are. Success isn't an insular process. It doesn't occur in a vacuum. Successful people recognize when they encounter help and take full advantage of it. We all receive help in our success pursuits, but the real skill is maximizing its returns.

Success is a tenuous mixture of preparation and luck. It isn't always easy to identify where and when a helping hand will come. When the opportunity does come, you need to be ready. If you always have an independent and self-sufficient attitude, you may miss the opportunity to get help. Success comes to those that operate from a position of humility. This isn't a position of weakness. Rather, it is an understanding that we aren't fully in control of the external factors surrounding our success or lack thereof.

Operating from a position of humility allows us to learn. It allows the self-correction from the inward chip and blame to occur. It increases the chance of encountering and benefiting from a helping hand. Help can come from the most unexpected places and at the most surprising times. Where and when you will receive help is impossible to predict.

To find your success, you must assume a position of humility. Success isn't always about you. Your results aren't always based solely on your actions. Your ability to succeed is based on more than just *your* ability.

In the 1997 National Basketball Association finals, Michael Jordan was again in familiar territory. He was in position to take and make another game-winning shot. If he could do it again, it would be the Chicago Bulls' fifth championship. With seconds remaining and the score tied, Michael Jordan dribbled toward the paint. Two Utah Jazz players double-teamed Jordan, and he passed the ball to Steve Kerr. With time running out, Steve Kerr took and hit the go-ahead shot and clinched the fifth championship title for the Chicago Bulls. Steve Kerr's clutch shot also clinched a fifth championship for another well-known clutch player—Michael Jeffery Jordan.

Michael Jordan is recognized by most as the best basketball player in history. As great as he was, he still needed help. Would Michael Jordan have all six of his championships without his teammates? How did coach Phil Jackson help Michael become Michael? How much did Scottie Pippen help him? And what about Steve Kerr, the player he trusted to take and make a game-winning shot. Think about that for a moment. The most heralded game-winning shot taker in history passed the ball to a teammate for help.

We will never truly know the answers to these questions. Undoubtedly, these individuals were instrumental in *helping* Jordan succeed. At some point, he had to decide to accept their help. He had to decide to pass the ball to Scottie Pippen. He had to decide to pass the ball to Steve Kerr. He had to decide to listen to Phil Jackson.

Jerry Rice didn't do it alone, either. He had the honor of playing with two of the greatest quarterbacks of all time. Would Jerry Rice have had the success he had without Joe Montana and Steve Young? These questions may never be answered and are the perpetual subject of sports conjecture. How much help Michael and Jerry received is debatable, but there is no question that their winning stories included some help.

As you spin your Flywheel toward your ultimate success, don't forget to pursue it from a position of humility. Find your Joe Montana. Find your Steve Young. And when you get double-teamed, find your Steve Kerr and confidently pass the ball. Don't let your ego allow you to take full responsibility for your successes. Operate your journey from a position of humility and always be willing to accept that helping hand. If we are humble, we can see the truth. "None of us has gotten where we are solely by pulling ourselves up from our bootstraps. We got here because somebody bent down and helped us."

CHAPTER XLI

HUMBLEBEE

"Do you wish to be great? Then begin by being. Do you desire to construct a vast and lofty fabric? Think first about the foundations of humility. The higher your structure is to be, the deeper must be its foundation."

– SAINT AUGUSTINE

What we remember about success is the brash bravado, the convincing confidence, and the unparalleled passion. We remember the trophy hoisting, the tears of victory, and smiles of success. This book isn't about those moments. Because those moments don't tell the entire story. The ends don't yield any information about the means.

The championship parade doesn't reveal the motivation, the focus, or the execution. You can only learn so much about someone's journey by looking at the destination. Where you are isn't as important as how you got there. How you got there isn't as important as where you are going. What you have accomplished isn't as important as what you are going to accomplish. If you feel as if you are at the top of the mountain, where else can you go? What more can you do?

Our pursuit of success will fall short if we believe we are at the top of the mountain. Our arrogance, our bravado, our hubris restricts us from any further success. If you feel you have arrived at the top of the mountain, you have nowhere else to go. You have no other peak to achieve or no other mountain to climb. When we start believing that we have achieved, when we start focusing on the accolades, when we start believing in our own legacy, we lose the ability to succeed. If you truly wish to be great, think first about the foundations of humility. Think first about stepping down from that lofty perch.

Humility is necessary to achieve ultimate success. The pursuit of success starts at the bottom of the mountain. It starts with a vision, and that vision begins by looking up. Success pursuit starts with understanding how small you really are. It starts with the realization that you aren't and likely will never be at the top of the mountain.

If you are at the top of Mount Everest, twenty-nine thousand and twenty-nine feet in the air, you have only one way to look. The only way to look is down. Conversely, if you are at the bottom of the mountain, you have only one way to look. In that case, the only way to look is up. Humility always brings us back to the bottom of the mountain. Humility is necessary to keep us looking up. It keeps us looking at our lofty goals. It keeps us motivated. It keeps us focused. It keeps us executing. The ascent generates energy. The hunt ignites our fire. Without humility, we are stuck at the top of the mountain, unable to ascend any further.

MFers always view the world from the base of the mountain. They never feel as though they have arrived. They never feel as if they have achieved. They are ready to make the ascent. How do they stay grounded? How do they keep looking up? They stay humble by using their inward chip and blame. The inward chip functions as a grounding agent.

"Am I good enough? I should be better. I don't think I can get there. Am I as good as the other people in my field? Am I ready to succeed? Do I have the talent? Do I have what it takes? Will I fail? Can I get to the top of the mountain?" These are grounding questions. They are humbling questions. These questions aren't filled with bravado, pride, or hubris. These introspective questions march you right down to the bottom of the mountain.

The amount of success we achieve is irrelevant. What happened yesterday does not affect tomorrow's success. Every new success pursuit requires that we look up. The inward chip serves as a humility barometer. It keeps us honest and helps us avoid believing in our own legend. Achieving the inward chip threshold brings us back down the mountain. It generates the motivation necessary to climb the next mountain and extending the ascent.

Blame also delivers a healthy dose of humility. In the reinforcement phase, blame counters variable success. Whether you achieve expected goals, requisite goals, or lofty goals, blame keeps you humble. Like the inward chip, blame also walks you down to the bottom of the mountain. "What could I have done better? I could have done better. Could I have executed better? Was that the best strategy? Do I have the right goals? Was my discipline sufficient? Did I convincingly commit? Did I set my goals high enough? Can I try harder? Where can I improve? Why did I fail? Is it my fault? It is my fault. How can I get higher on the mountain?"

Taking credit for success is easy, but it is hard to take the blame for failure. Many success experts tout blame-free analysis. They believe that assigning blame is counterproductive. In Maniacal Fanaticism, blame is good. It shouldn't be negative. It is only negative if you point the finger at the external factors. If you are truly humble, you will never struggle with blaming yourself for your results. Blame only hurts when you are at the top of the mountain. It only hurts when you feel you can do nothing else. It only hurts when your ego gets in the way. Accepting blame requires a healthy dose of humility.

At the top of the mountain, your attitude is entirely different. At the top of the mountain, you are less willing to accept blame. Instead of asking provocative and introspective questions, you are unwilling to accept responsibility. "It isn't my fault. The job is too hard. I did my best. I did all I can do. It's impossible. No one could do this. It's unattainable. It's unachievable. The goal is out of reach. The mountain is too high. It will take too long. The work is too hard. I'm already a peak performer. I don't think I can get better. I've arrived. I'm entitled to success. I don't deserve my failures. I tried my best. It is what it is. I'm not to blame."

Pay attention to the last statement: "I am not to blame." Without blame, there are no opportunities for improvement. That's the problem. Without blame, there is no change in the strategy. Without blame, we have no opportunity for success. Humility is necessary for success, and success should be humbling. Most of us forget or ignore this connection, especially while we are attending our personal success parades.

Our society equates success with money, power, and fame. Humility gets lost in the fray. Without humility, success is almost impossible. Why? If you never blame yourself, then you will never have the ability to improve. You will be stuck. Your success will be capitated. You will be looking down instead of looking up.

Building success requires a strong foundation. That foundation should be based on humility. To construct a vast and lofty fabric, humility is required. The taller the structure of success, the deeper and broader the foundation must be. Barry Sanders understood this.

Instead of preparing an elaborate television-worthy end-zone celebration, he simply gave the referee the ball. Instead of spiking the ball in aggressive adulation, he jogged to the ref and flipped him the ball. Instead of making the touchdown about him, he made the touchdown about the team. He made the touchdown about the fans. Sanders didn't celebrate because the touchdown was expected, and there was much more to do.

Barry Sanders was looking up. Handing the ball to the ref was his way of walking himself down the mountain. It was his way of challenging himself to be better. This was his foundation, constructed of a vast and lofty fabric. His humility created a wide and substantial foundation. He asked questions about his ability to succeed rather than making statements. What he was going to do was much more important than what he had just done. Touchdowns are yesterday's news.

If you wish to be great, begin by being. To build a foundation that enables the highest structure of success, think first about using a foundation of humility. When you feel that you have reached the top, walk yourself back down to the bottom of the mountain and look up.

FROM WITHIN
ACCELERATORS
WHAT DO YOU FEEL
HAPPINESS COMES
ASSESSMENT
SUPERSTAR
LUCKY
ALTERATION
MOTIVATION
MANIACAL
INERTIA
FANATICISM
OBSTACLES
INWARD
HIDDEN
GRIP
M
SUCCESS
FOUNDATION
R
VALUES
FLYWHEEL
FOCUS
BLAME
GOALS
EVIDENCE
PIVOT
CAPACIBILITY
GUTCHECK
FUTILITY
THRESHOLD
SWEAT THE SMALL
SUPER TRUST
HERO
YOUR
CHECKMATE
NO EXPLANATIONS
NO EXCUSES
BETTER LUCKY THAN GOOD
POISE
PAST PERFORMANCE
CIRCUMSTANCE
PERFECT SITUATION
SUCCESSOLOGY
MANIACAL FANATICISM BEST

CHAPTER XLII

FLYWHEEL ACCELERATORS AND DECELERATORS

"Grant me the serenity to accept the things I cannot change; courage to change the things I can; and wisdom to know the difference."

– REINHOLD NIEBUHR

MFers don't operate in a vacuum. The world around them can shape, alter, and even halt their success pursuit. These external factors can accelerate or decelerate their Flywheels. Accelerators don't guarantee success, and decelerators don't guarantee failure. However, they both change the individual's ability to meet the thresholds in each phase. A great example of an accelerator is the internet. The increased use of the internet in the late 1990s accelerated the Flywheels of some very successful companies, such as eBay and Amazon. Those companies' motivation, focus, execution, and reinforcement phases were accelerated by the wide adoption and usage of the internet.

The internet wasn't an accelerator for all companies. It also had a decelerating effect on many primarily bricks-and-mortar businesses. Unfortunately, accelerators and decelerators are unalterable. External factors can't be changed. Would trying to stop the internet be realistic? Could you stop the sun from rising or the rain from falling? You can adjust and react to external factors, but trying to change them is futile.

When people attempt to change things beyond their control, they lose valuable energy. It is important to direct your energy toward things that are within your control and limit the energy you exert on the things beyond your control. Maniacal effort doesn't always yield tangible results. In spite of how hard I pushed my house, it still didn't move. Success is a result of maximizing the advantages, minimizing the disadvantages, and understanding how to identify the difference between the two.

MFers believe winning is always possible, no matter what hand they are dealt. Fundamentally, this is the heart and soul of Maniacal Fanaticism. Remember eternal optimism? Eternal optimism isn't the hope you can win. It's the knowledge that you can win. You have to believe you will succeed against all odds. Eternal optimists know they will win. They know that adherence to the process will eventually yield the results they seek. MFers know it. They take it. And they make it. Knowledge of the external environment improves our ability to succeed, as long as we don't spend too much energy attempting to alter what is unalterable.

One of the most powerful accelerators is competition. Surprisingly, competition is an external factor because it is beyond the control of the individual. You may think competitiveness is an internal quality, but you can't create competition in a vacuum. What we say someone is competitive, we are simply describing their internal response to external competition. This is the reason people always want to compete against the brightest and the best.

Another very powerful accelerator is a higher calling or purpose. Spirituality can also accelerate the Flywheel. MFers don't believe that they are the center of the universe. For most of them, there is something more. Money, fame, and fortune are great motivators, but these are only marginal accelerants. A sense of obligation to something or someone is much more powerful. Self interest decelerates the Flywheel and limits the height of the success. This doesn't mean that success can't be attained through self-interest. It simply means that self-interest limits how fast the Flywheel can spin.

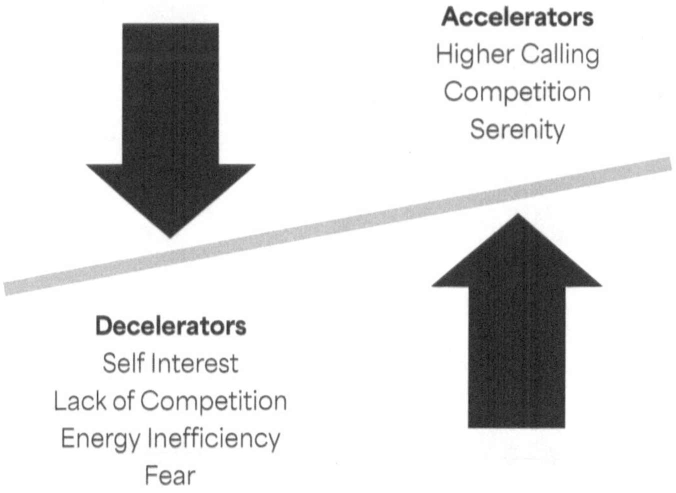

Accelerators speed up the Flywheel, making thresholds and phases easier to accomplish. Decelerators slow and even stop a success Flywheel. You can spend your whole success pursuit trying to move what is unmovable. If you take that road, you will stagnate from frustration and fatigue. You will have worked hard without producing any tangible results. You will have exerted effort without execution. You will have activity without productivity.

Don't waste effort on what is immutable or what you can't change. You can't change your external accelerators and decelerators, but you can change your internal reaction to them. You can alter the speed and direction of your Flywheel. Some factors you can change and others you can't. Your success serenity depends on you understanding the difference.

CHAPTER XLIII

FEAR

"So let me assert my firm belief that the only thing we have to fear is fear itself–nameless, unreasoning, unjustified terror which paralyzes needed efforts to convert retreat into advance."

– FRANKLIN D. ROOSEVELT

Make no mistake. Successful people have been or will be fearful. How can this be? Success and confidence should go hand in hand. Our evaluation of successful people is retrospective. By the time we get around to analyzing successful people, they already have an outward facade of confidence or more accurately overconfidence. Like the inward chip, fear is often imperceptible. It can be both positive and negative.

Although it may sound odd, fear can be protective. Would you pet a lion or swim in open water with a shark? Fear is a necessary part of our evolution as human beings. It helps us to avoid those things that harm us. When avoiding predators, fear is positive.

At the same time, fear can be very negative. It can be a Flywheel decelerator. If you fear water, you will never learn to swim. If you have a fear of heights, learning to fly might be difficult. Likewise, if you have a fear of failure, you will never try to succeed. Fear can be an asset and an ally. Unfortunately, it can also be an on-board terrorist, holding your success pursuit hostage.

As you know, all success starts with inertia. Inertia is the point of entry into the Flywheel. How does fear decelerate the Flywheel? It directly decreases inertia. What are people afraid of? Don't we all want success? Most of us aren't fearful of success. We covet success and seek it out. If success is what we desire, why does fear come into play?

Our fear of succeeding is essentially a fear of failing. To avoid the devastation of failing, many of us don't even try. Not trying decreases the risk of failure. If you never try, you will never fail. If you never try, you will never fear. And, if you never try, the chance of succeeding is zero. For many, the fear of failure overwhelms the urge to succeed.

For this reason, starting a Flywheel requires overcoming fear. Specifically, to generate that initial inertia, you have to overcome the fear of failure. Because of this, MFers are particularly suited to succeed. If you have only one goal and one measure of success, your possibility of failure increases. The purpose of the goal matrix is to make successes and failures not so singular. It makes failure not so fatal. A failure of a single goal is devastating, but a failure among many successes isn't as stinging.

A mixture of failures and successes allows for growth and learning. For most of us, a failed attempt can be devastating, and that devastation limits our future attempts. For MFers, failing actually creates more inertia. In the context of the Flywheel, failure increases inertia and makes the blame threshold easier to achieve. Failure creates the energy to alter the course. After the initial failure, subsequent attempts require less inertia.

Imagine you were a student studying for the Scholastic Aptitude Test, the entry test that all students take before seeking admission to college. You would develop a goal based on a score you would like to achieve. You would then develop a strategy, prepare, and attempt to achieve that goal. If you didn't achieve the goal, then you have failed. Or have you?

Although you "failed" your initial attempt, you still have gained knowledge about the structure of the test. You now know what is necessary to attain your goal. You now know what else you need to study. You understand the format of the test. You have a better idea of what you know and what you don't know.

Repeated failures can lead to lower inertia, but early failures can enhance success pursuit. We see this with toddlers when they are learning to walk. Because they have a limited ability to process failure, they keep trying and trying and trying. If toddlers gave up every time they fell, none of us would have ever learned to walk. The same is also true for kids learning to swim. They have limited fear and jump in the pool with reckless abandon. Teaching an adult to swim is much more difficult because the fear of water is already entrenched in their psyche.

MFers are more like toddlers. They don't process fear the way most of us do. That isn't to say MFers embrace risk with reckless abandon. They simply take calculated risks. They don't avoid trying because of the fear of failure. MFers don't self-limit. Self-limitation is an internal obstacle, founded in the fear of failure. If we are fearful, we fail before we even start. Knowing the different phases, thresholds, and qualities of Maniacal Fanaticism is useless if we decide not to spin the Flywheel. If you self-limit, you guarantee failure. If you never take it, you will never make it.

Fear is paralyzing, non-productive, and problem focused. Success is mobilizing, productive, and solution focused. Success and fear are mutually exclusive. They can't exist together. Because we all will be fearful at some point in our lives, we think we have to learn to overcome them. For MFers, the opposite is true. They don't try to overcome fear at all.

Overcoming fear is the ability to develop the emotional, mental, and physical fortitude to overwhelm it. We are taught that fear can be desensitized or overwhelmed. Immersion into the environment where the fear is present works to desensitize a person to the fearful stimulus. If you fear snakes, exposure to them in a safe environment will theoretically make you less fearful of snakes. This process is called desensitization.

Although desensitization is sometimes successful, MFers deal with fear in a slightly different way. Typical strategies to thwart fear usually fail because the underlying fear still exists. Overcoming fear doesn't erase it. The fear is still intact and is part of the psychological makeup. It lies dormant, ready to rear its ugly head at the most inopportune time.

Think of it like this. A chef who is creating a dish adds a specific combination of flavors. Those flavors have a direct proportion to each other. If the chef adds too much salt, for example, the dish isn't instantly ruined. An expert chef can add other flavors to the dish and compensate for the over-salted food. The dish can still be successful, and most people would never know the difference. However, a few culinary connoisseurs would. The recipe would still be incorrect. It would be a little bit off. No matter how the chef compensated for the wrong ingredients, the extra salt is still there.

Dealing with fear works in the same way. Compensation requires counterbalance and requires other ingredients. To compensate for our fears, we typically offset a lack of something with a large proportion of something else. If that overcompensation doesn't remain in perfect balance, the undesired behavior can resurface. Even worse, the counterbalancing behavior can dominate and create problems of its own. Often, the counterbalance behavior becomes worse than the original fearful behavior. The counterbalance behavior is visible on the surface, but the underlying fear is still present. MFers use a strategy of exclusion, rather than suppression. They remove fear. They erase it. They delete it. They purge it. They remove it from their psychological makeup.

To eliminate fear, you must deal with the underlying issue. You must treat the cause of the fear, however irrational. You don't have to address all your fears, just the few that get in the way. You have to address the fears that decelerate the Flywheel and those that inhibit your success pursuit. How do you purge fear? Is it possible to remove certain fears completely? It sounds easy enough, but is it feasible? The answer is yes.

Think of a sick child with a fever. Most of the time, you can effectively treat the fever. Certain medications, like acetaminophen, will lower the fever and give the appearance that the illness is cured. The child will feel better while the fever is treated. However, after the medicine wears off, the fever returns. The problem with this strategy is that the underlying illness hasn't been treated. Removing the fever doesn't remove the disease. The salt is still there. The recipe is still wrong. This is the medical version of compensation. It can be effective for a while. If the underlying illness isn't particularly life-threatening, this strategy is very effective. But, if the disease causing the fever is more serious, this strategy could be downright deadly.

To purge the fear, you have to cure the underlying illness and not just treat the symptoms. You have to find the source. You have to find the salt. When a physician evaluates a child with a fever, she is attempting to isolate the source of the disease causing the fever. She can then identify a plan to treat the disease. Eradicating the underlying disease is the best way to treat the fever. Remove it. Erase it. Delete it. Purge it. After treatment, the disease is no longer present and can't continue to affect the child. The child will be fever free. More importantly, the child will be disease free.

MFers don't spend time treating the fever, because they understand this is a form of compensation. They don't just overcome the fever. They attempt to eradicate the illness. MFers don't spend time compensating for their fears. They deal with the cause of them. They eradicate fear, so no remnant lingers. By doing this, they never have to deal with that fear ever again. This leaves them free to pursue unfettered success, without restraint.

What are your fears? Are they limiting your success? Are they slowing your Flywheel? Have you addressed them, or are you just compensating? Are you just treating the fever? Is there too much salt? Are you just adding other ingredients, hoping that no one will taste the difference? Are you searching for the underlying disease and attempting to treat it? Compensated fears still decelerate the Flywheel. Therefore, you have to purge as many of these fears as you can. You must treat the fears that specifically affect your motivation, focus, and execution.

Overcoming fear is a compensatory mechanism that only treats the symptoms. Fearlessly pursue your goals by addressing the underlying cause of your fear. Treat the illness, not the fever. Fear is "nameless, unreasoning, unjustified terror which paralyzes needed efforts to convert retreat into advance." If you fear failing, you will never try. If you fear trying, you will always fail. Fear just doesn't retard the Flywheel. It can obliterate entire phases. It can extinguish motivation or erase execution.

Fear is undoubtedly the most powerful obstacle we can encounter. To remember the effect of fear on your success pursuits, use the acronym for fear: Fear Extinguishes Action Required. *Fear extinguishes* the *action required.* We usually know exactly what we have to do, but fear gets in the way. We know what actions are required, but fear extinguishes them. We know we have to make that shot, but the fear of missing suppresses the urge to take it. When your success pursuit requires action, don't let fear extinguish that action.

I have to confess. When I was considering writing this book, I was fearful. Would people buy my book? Would people like my book? I knew the actions I had to take. I had sufficient motivation. I had a strategy and several goals. I even had begun to execute my plan. Suddenly, my Flywheel came to a screeching halt. It didn't take me long to figure out what was happening and why it was happening. My problem was fear!

Fear was limiting me from performing the necessary actions to complete my book. Not until I accepted my fear and dealt with the underlying issue, was I able to restart my Flywheel. Instead of just adding other ingredients, I had to determine the source of the disease. I had to do more than treat the fever.

When I finally understood my fear, I was able to purge it. I was able to treat the illness and not just the fever. I was able to follow the recipe and not compensate with another ingredient. My Flywheel spun with reckless abandon. Now I could engage in the actions required. If I didn't take it, I would never make it. If I feared failing, I would never try. If I feared trying, I would always fail. "So, let me assert my firm belief that the only thing we have to fear is fear itself—nameless, unreasoning, unjustified terror which paralyzes needed efforts to convert retreat into advance." Fear can't paralyze your efforts. You can't retreat. Advance through your Flywheel and pursue your success fearlessly.

FROM WITHIN
ACCELERATORS
COMES HAPPINESS
WHAT DO YOU FEEL
ASSESSMENT
SUPERSTAR
LUCKY
ACCEPTANCE
ALTERATION
MOTIVATION
MANIACAL
INERTIA
FANATICISM
OBSTACLES
INWARD
HIDDEN
M
SUCCESS
FOUNDATION
R
VALUES
FLYWHEEL
FOCUS
SUCCESS
GOALS
EVIDENCE
BLAME
CAPABILITY
BEYOND
PIVOT
GUTCHECK
FUTILITY
THRESHOLD
SWEAT THE SMALL
SUPER TRUST
HERO
PROMISE
YOUR
FAULT
CHECKMATE
DISCIPLINE
DENIAL
NO EXCUSES
NO EXPLANATIONS
BETTER LUCKY THAN GOOD
PAST PERFORMANCE
FUTURE SUCCESS
CIRCUMSTANCE
PERFECT SITUATION
SUCCESSOLOGY
MANIACAL FANATICISM BEST
POISE

CHAPTER XLIV

HOW TO BE A JANITOR

"I long to accomplish a great and noble task; but it is my chief duty to accomplish small tasks as if they were great and noble."

– HELEN KELLER

Success is about results, but what results you pursue is entirely up to you. In the focus phase, you got to develop your goal matrix. During that process, the Flywheel doesn't define what success is. Maniacal Fanaticism doesn't set the goals. It describes the journey, but you get to decide the destination.

Goal achievement is an internal and individual process. The success of Michael Jordan and Jerry Rice is obvious, but success can also be much more subtle. Most successful people never get their name in lights, but everyday successes may be just as difficult to achieve. The less sexy goals may be the most difficult to achieve.

I learned this lesson during my medical school training. My first year of medical school was very difficult. My parents didn't have much money and could barely afford the yearly tuition. My apartment was tiny, and I missed home. This was a very humbling time, and it made me appreciate all the things I had growing up.

Because I didn't have a television, I would often go to the medical school lounge to watch basketball. Sometimes, the medical school janitors would come in and watch basketball with me. They would talk, joke, play cards, and analyze the management of all the major basketball franchises in the country. One would say, "I wouldn't have traded him." The other would retort, "It won't matter much because they don't stand a chance anyway." They spoke so confidently. You would swear they just got back from dinner with Phil Jackson.

Night after night, I talked to them. I listened to their stories. I listened to their wants and desires. I learned about their families, their histories, their successes, and their failures. They would ask me, "Why would someone who's becoming a doctor spend his time hanging with us?" This shocked me! In my eyes, I was no different from them. They didn't think so. After all, they believed they were just janitors. In their eyes, they weren't successful. Or were they?

These men believed they had nothing to offer me, but they offered me more than they could have ever imagined. During one of our conversations, I asked them how long they had been janitors. They answered in sequence: twenty-four years, thirty years, and thirty-five years. Thirty-five years of cleaning up after people who didn't even realize they existed; thirty-five years of picking up other people's garbage; thirty-five years of mopping floors, cleaning tables, and washing toilets. If you think winning a championship is tough, try scooping poop for thirty-five years.

These three janitors gave me an early lesson in what success looks like. They provided a service that many other people wouldn't even consider. They didn't just do their jobs. They were proud to do their jobs. Incredibly, none of them had missed a day of work in their entire careers. What makes someone who has what most people would consider a menial and thankless job never miss a day of work? What made them never call in sick? What made them think that their "chief duty was to accomplish small tasks as if they were great and noble?"

I didn't realize it then, but I realize now that these janitors were MFers. I made it my business to find out more about them. I wanted to know about their motivation, focus, and execution. I wanted to know what made them tick. I learned how to be a doctor in medical school, but I learned something about work ethic from these janitors. Now, I don't call in sick. I don't miss work. I empty bedpans. I make beds. I mop the floors. I spend every day trying to improve and accomplish small tasks as if they were noble ones.

These janitors had a chip. They felt that they were less important than all the medical school students who were training right under their noses. They turned that chip inward and worked harder than everyone else. To prove their worth, they would never call in sick and never miss a day of work. Just like Jerry Rice, they executed with commitment and discipline. Just like Michael Jordan, they exhibited maniacal motivation. They were successful because of what they did and not who they were. They weren't noble because of their pedigree. They were noble because they accomplished tasks as if they were noble.

My experience with the janitors reinforced my work ethic. From that day forward, I made the decision that I would never be outhustled. I suspect that none of you reading this book would list janitorial services as your ultimate lofty goal, but I doubt that anybody would hesitate to call them successful.

Applying the Flywheel to a lofty goal with a huge reward makes sense. Applying the Flywheel to janitorial services is one heck of a commitment! Spinning the janitorial services Flywheel, for thirty-five years, with no break, maniacally, and fanatically is undesirable and difficult. They didn't win any championships and were mostly ignored by those they served, but wasn't what they did success? Didn't these janitors accomplish small tasks as if they were noble ones? We can learn a lot from studying the greatest basketball player in history, but the janitor Flywheel may teach us more than we think.

Our lives are full of Flywheels. Some of these Flywheels are very small and short. Some are burdensome and transition over a lifetime. Whatever the Flywheel and however long it takes to complete, MFers are consistent. Consistency is the ability to apply fanatical effort to all of your Flywheels. How many mundane tasks do you strive to overachieve in? Consistency allows you to spin every Flywheel you have as fast as possible. If you are consistent, you are able to spin your parent Flywheel, your spouse Flywheel, your career Flywheel, your hobby Flywheel, or whatever Flywheel you put your effort to.

Watching those three janitors work as hard as they did and for as long as they had, reinforced my work ethic, my humility, and my consistency. They made me realize that having the opportunity to work hard is an honor. Whatever I am doing, I should consistently apply that same extreme effort. Although I long for noble tasks, I make an effort to accomplish small tasks as if they were great and noble. Applying that fanatical effort to everything I do trains my body and mind to apply it in all future situations.

Applying fanatical effort to all your Flywheels, even those that are very mundane increases your ability to succeed. Every time you advance a Flywheel, any Flywheel, you create synergy and consistency. Synergy and consistency grease all your Flywheels, making it easier for you to achieve in all areas. Consistency is the ability to apply fanatical effort to every task. Completion of a threshold or phase in one Flywheel can accelerate all your other Flywheels. This is synergy.

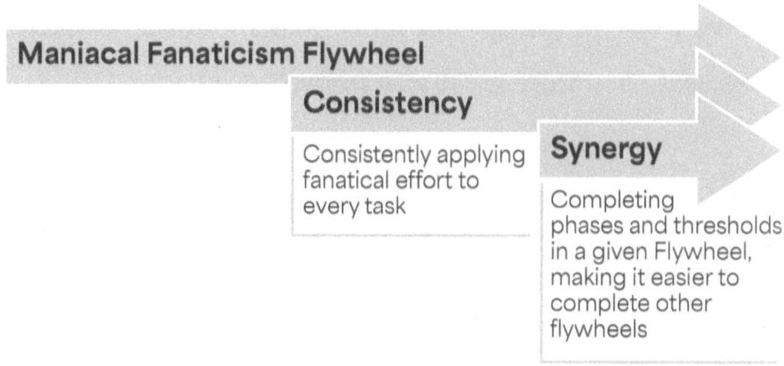

Flywheel accelerators are specific to a given Flywheel. An accelerator for one Flywheel may be a decelerator for another. Decelerating my basketball Flywheel accelerated my medical school Flywheel. Consistency and synergy allow you to accelerate all of your Flywheels. This means that you should apply fanatical energy to even your smallest tasks. The worth of the effort shouldn't be dictated by the value of the reward. If you put your heart and soul into every action, you are training the body and mind for success.

To become an MFer, you don't have to become a millionaire or become the greatest basketball player in history. You are an MFer, because of how you pursue your goals. When I think back, these janitors met all the criteria. They were motivated. They had inertia and an inward chip. They were focused. They developed goals and strategies. They executed through commitment and discipline, never missing a day of work in thirty years. Through blame and variable success, they continued to create opportunities for improvement. Indeed, they were MFers.

To achieve your ultimate goals, you should apply the Flywheel to the very basic of tasks. Goals that aren't as sexy are probably the ones we need to pay the most attention to. Apply your effort diffusely throughout your life. Your fanatical effort should permeate all that you do. Like those janitors, your chief goal should be to accomplish small tasks as if they were great and noble.

CHAPTER XLV

THE PERFECT SITUATION

"It had long since come to my attention that people of accomplishment rarely sat back and let things happen to them. They went out and happened to things."

– LEONARDO DA VINCI

Maniacal Fanaticism outlines the journey necessary to arrive at your success destination. It can identify where you need to go and how to get there. It can't help you overcome the terrain, drive the car, or climb the mountain on your path. You can lead a horse to water, but you know the rest. Maniacal Fanaticism differs from other success theories because participating is considered just as successful as the success itself. In other words, just the completion of the process yields some relative accomplishment.

If you have ever run a marathon, you know exactly what I mean. When you train for your first marathon, you usually pick a time target that you would like to meet or exceed. You set a reasonable goal and create a plan to achieve it. Mike Tyson said, "Everybody has a plan till they get punched in the mouth." Well, everybody has a plan until you run your first marathon. Unfortunately, you can't fully prepare. And, when you finish that inaugural marathon, you hurt in places you never knew you had. You discover places you never knew could hurt.

Preparing for a marathon and running a marathon are two dramatically different things. While running a marathon, you experience sensations you never thought were possible. Even if you don't achieve your time goal, completing one is a relative success. I know what you are thinking. This isn't "everyone gets a medal." This isn't meant to make you feel better about yourself, reward inferior goal performance, or stroke your ego. Going through the process of preparing and running a marathon is, at least in part, success.

The Flywheel is similar, enduring, and completing any Flywheel is considered a success. Completing a Flywheel is exactly like finishing a marathon. You will feel things you have never felt before. You will hurt in places you never knew you had and find places you never knew could hurt. Completing a marathon isn't easy and achieving your goals won't be easy either. My high school basketball coach would tell me, "If something is easy, you aren't going hard enough!"

Whether it's a marathon or your success pursuit, at some point, you will be uncomfortable. Nothing worth accomplishing is easy. If it is easy, you probably aren't going hard enough. MFers overachieve under very arduous circumstances, partly because they are comfortable with discomfort. You should never be too hot, too cold, too hungry, too thirsty or too tired to achieve your goal. You have to push past your previously perceived limits. You have to find comfort in discomfort.

It is human nature to travel on the easier road, but the harder road is more likely to yield rewards. MFers find ways to endure extreme situations to achieve their goals. They thrive on the discomfort of the task at hand. Better put, MFers thrive *in* the discomfort of the task at hand. When the going gets tough, they get tougher. They understand that their motivation, focus, execution, and reinforcement must increase in difficult situations.

On June 13, 1997, the Chicago Bulls suited up for the pivotal game five of the National Basketball Association Championships. Bad news for the Bulls, Jordan was diagnosed with the flu earlier that day. He was dehydrated, dizzy, and barely able to stand. He was so dehydrated that he was near the point of being admitted to the hospital. He lay in bed for the entire day before the game. Nobody expected him to go to the game, much less to play.

On the verge of collapse, Jordan crawled into the gym. After all, he is Michael Jordan. He is an MFer. Astonishing his teammates, opponents, and fans alike, he played. And he didn't just play, he scored thirty-eight points and played almost the entire game. He found comfort in discomfort.

Even though Jordan nearly collapsed, the Chicago Bulls won that game and went on to win the championship. Michael Jordan pushed past his previously perceived limits. I am sure he was too hot, too cold, too tired, too thirsty and too fatigued. However, he was not going to let his discomfort derail his success pursuit. He wasn't going to lay back and let things happen to him. He was going to go out and happen to things.

In December of 1912, Earnest Shackleton embarked on his quest to cross the Antarctic continent. He wanted to accomplish something that hadn't been done before and solidify his place as one of the greatest explorers in history. Unfortunately, he had a huge setback. His ship, the Endurance, was lost to the pack ice in the semi-frozen Antarctic seas. Over the next several months, he would embark on a new quest, survival.

Shackleton had to lead his team through the barely livable Antarctic weather, back to civilization. During his quest, he would endure devastating conditions: pain, hunger, thirst, cold, and disease. He encountered fifty-foot waves. He drank brackish water. He endured frostbite. He ate penguins and washed it down with powdered milk. He didn't sleep for days at a time. He navigated the icy cold seas of the Antarctic. He scaled mountains of sheer ice and rappelled down frozen waterfalls.

After a long, arduous, uncomfortable, and far from perfect journey, he succeeded. He led his entire team to safety after several years of life-threatening discomfort. He was an MFer. Shackleton thrived in discomfort. He was able to push past his previously perceived limits.

Success is uncomfortable. Success is scoring thirty-eight points with the flu, in one of the most important games of your life. Success is enduring life-threatening cold to free your team from an icy grave. Success is finishing medical school on time after surviving burns to twenty percent of your body. Success is performing in spite of your discomfort. Things will happen, but you can't let them happen to you. You have to happen to things.

For Michael Jordan and Earnest Shackleton, success didn't happen when conditions were perfect. Great sailors aren't made on smooth seas. We often wait for that perfect moment, that perfect situation. When the going gets tough, most of us recoil. We let things happen to us. Perfect situations are unpredictable and rare. If we only wait for perfect situations to perform our best, we may be waiting for a very long time.

Although he may argue this point, my golf partner has much better golf mechanics than I do. Of course, I removed his name to protect the innocent. His perfect drives are about ten yards farther than my drives. I think he has much more golf talent than I do. However, he does have one very interesting Achilles heel. He is always in search of the perfect situation.

When he plays on a perfect day, with a clear head, on a perfect lie, with no pressure to perform, his swing is pristine. It's perfect. It's a beautiful thing to watch. He performs his best when conditions are optimal. When conditions aren't so perfect, he's an entirely different golfer. When the pressure to hit a good shot increases, like in a tournament, his performance plummets.

His golf score is indirectly proportional to his discomfort. The more discomfort, the worse he plays. In golf, he is uncomfortable with discomfort. He is very aware of this affliction and even adopted the nickname "Perfect Situation." But there's a catch. He's entirely different in his life endeavors. At work, he's very comfortable with discomfort. When work conditions are at their worst, there isn't anyone else that I would rather work with.

My golf partner's preoccupation with the perfect golf situation gives us insight into why people fail. If we perpetually wait for the perfect day, the perfect conditions, and the perfect shot, we will inevitably fail. If we adopt this mindset, we are doomed to fail. Perfect situations don't exist. Something will always be askew. Situations will always be imperfect. Things will never be just right. The statistical randomness of life doesn't often create periods of perfection.

The second law of thermodynamics, simply put, states that a system will continue to an increasing level of entropy over time.

Entropy is chaos. It is the randomness by which all matter is governed. By rule, our world is constantly increasing its entropy. Perfect situations decrease as entropy increases. If we wait for the perfect situation, the perfect opportunity, the perfect day, and the perfect mix of external factors, we will never be successful.

It is statistically more likely that you will endure an imperfect situation than a perfect one. It is more likely that you will experience increasing levels of entropy, than order. It is more likely that you will experience randomness. It is much more likely that you will experience discomfort. Jerry Rice's training, Michael Jordan's flu game, Earnest Shackleton's journey, all weren't comfortable. And being burned in medical school was painfully uncomfortable. Jerry and Michael and Earnest were comfortable in uncomfortable situations. They found comfort in discomfort. Things didn't happen to them. They happened to things.

If you always have to sleep when you are tired, if you have to eat every time you are hungry, if you have to drink every time you are thirsty, you will find achieving success very difficult. If all of these things are true, then you may not be able to tolerate being uncomfortable. You may not be able to deal with the perpetually increasing amount of entropy. You may not be able to cope with the worsening randomness of life. If you always wait for the perfect moment, you will never take it or make it.

Do you find yourself waiting for the right opportunity or the right moment? Are you always waiting for the perfect situation? MFers seize these moments and accomplish the best they can with what they have. These periods of discomfort give MFers their advantage. They are able to succeed despite their discomfort. Maybe just maybe, they succeed because of discomfort. Their ability to persevere beyond their comfort zone gives them a profound advantage. Their ability to push past their previously perceived limits enhances their success journey.

The story of Amundsen and Scott tells us more about MFers and their refusal to let their environment dictate their outcomes. Roald Amundsen and Robert Scott were both racing to be the first explorers to the South Pole. Amundsen was fanatical, maniacal, relentless, and consistent. Despite the uncomfortable weather, he maintained his approach. Consistently, he traveled twenty miles every day. When the weather was good, he traveled twenty miles. When the weather was bad, he traveled about twenty miles.

Amundsen understood the entropy and the randomness of his environment, but he didn't let that randomness determine his outcomes. He didn't let things determine his success pursuit. Scott, on the other hand, waited for perfect days to try to make up time. He refused to travel on the most uncomfortable days and tried to make it up when the weather was perfect. The belief that tomorrow will be better and that a better situation will allow an improved goal pursuit are hallmarks of failure.

Who do you think reached their goal, Amundsen or Scott? It should be obvious. Amundsen reached the South Pole in record time, attaining his ultimate goal. Scott failed to achieve his goal. That perfect day never came. Unfortunately, Scott and his team lost sight of their goals and paid with their lives. Amundsen followed a blueprint. He followed a road map. He stayed on track, even when it was uncomfortable.

Maniacal Fanaticism is uncomfortable. This book isn't titled *The Seven Simple Secrets to Succeed.* Although I agree, that sounds like an awesome title! Success pursuit hurts. You will have pain in places you didn't know existed. You will discover places that you never knew could have pain. The road to success will always be uncomfortable.

To achieve success, you can't let things happen to you. You have to go out there and happen to things. To achieve your goal, you have to find comfort in what other people find uncomfortable.

As the entropy of your world increases, be sure to stay compulsively consistent. Perfect situations are unpredictable and rare. Waiting for one is fruitless. Inevitably, you will find ultimate success because of your ability to find comfort in discomfort. Don't waste energy looking for that perfect situation. Waiting for it consumes inertia and decelerates your Flywheel.

If you wait for those perfect situations, you are assuming that some outside entity mitigates success and that external factors are responsible for your results. If you have learned anything from reading this book so far, I hope it's this. Successful people always believe that success is an internal process. They create the best possible situation instead of waiting for the perfect one. They don't let things happen to them. They go out and happen to things.

CHAPTER XLVI

CIRCUMSTANCE

"People are always blaming their circumstances for what they are. I don't believe in circumstances. The people who get on in this world are the people who get up and look for the circumstances they want, and if they can't find them, make them."

– GEORGE BERNARD SHAW

Most of us define ourselves by how our environment impacts us. We tend to define ourselves by our hometowns, our schools, and our families. The external environment influences what we do, what we say, and how we act. During the holiday season, we tend to be happy and jovial. We crave the feeling of euphoria that comes from spending time with our family, assuming you like your family. When the weather is gray and rainy, we are sullen and lack motivation. When the sun finally comes out, we are invigorated and ready to take on the world. Nothing is wrong with this mentality unless you want to succeed.

Circumstances are external factors that should never affect your performance. If we analyze the word circumstance, we can gain insight into our relationship with our external environment. Circum, translated from Latin, means to encompass or surround. Circum is the external world that surrounds us. Stance, the second part of the word, describes our general emotional or intellectual attitude.

If we combine the definitions of *circum* and *stance*, circumstance translates to *the general emotional or intellectual attitude that originates from our surroundings*. Understanding words and their meanings can give us insight into what we do and why we do it. Relying on your circumstance is a losing proposition. Your emotion and intellectual attitude should never be dependent on your surroundings. Circumstance should never dictate your ability to succeed.

Instead of living by circumstance, MFers prefer to circumnavigate. Instead of having a general emotional or intellectual attitude (stance) based on the surroundings (circum), MFers direct or manage (navigate) their surroundings (circum). In other words, you should affect your surroundings and not just react to them. MFers create their environment rather than reacting to it. Merely responding to your environment limits your ability to achieve your desired results. You will be limited and very predictable.

Our responses to our environment are within our control. Who your parents are, what your heritage is, and where you are from are only as important as you make them. Some situations require more circumnavigation than others do, but we still have some control. A bad circumstance indicates that you had a negative intellectual attitude to your surroundings. Conversely, good circumstance is a result of a positive intellectual attitude to your surroundings. Don't get me wrong. There are always external factors that we can't control, but success is always within your control. Our demeanor, behavior, reaction, temperament, happiness, and effort are all within our control.

MFers use the Flywheel to circumnavigate themselves to success. They don't accept the conventional or typical reactions to their surroundings. Were Jerry Rice's circumstances better than the fifteen other draft picks chosen before him? Were Michael Jordan's circumstances better than Hakeem Olajuwon's and Sam Bowie's? Was Tom Brady's circumstance better than Drew Bledsoe's?

We view our circumstances retrospectively. We tend to look at our circumstances to determine the success of our results. Marginal results are excused if the circumstance is perceived as poor. For those blessed with good circumstance, a marginal result is considered a failure. Allowing your circumstance to dictate your results is problematic because your results can only be as good as your circumstance.

MFers define their success by the results they achieve and their ability to keep the Flywheel spinning. Results are measured by a consistent standard, not by the circumstance. An A is an A. It doesn't matter how hard the class is. The Flywheel gives you the framework to minimize the effect of the environment on your ability to succeed. It gives you the ability to circumnavigate instead of succumbing to your circumstance. Circumstances may make the road more difficult, and goal acquisition may take a little longer than expected. However, circumstances shouldn't change what goals you choose or decrease your ability to succeed.

We often blame our circumstances for what and who we are. It is easier to blame our circumstances for our results. We seldom blame ourselves. We seldom blame our behavior or performance. If you want to accomplish anything in this world, you must create your circumstances. MFers seek the circumstance necessary for success. They do this by circumnavigating. They don't stop there. If they can't find those circumstances necessary for success, they make them.

You aren't a product of your surroundings. You are a combination of your reactions to your circumstances. You create the environment around you. It doesn't matter where you are from, when you were born or what your current situation is. It doesn't matter what neighborhood you are from, your heritage, or who your parents are. You are in complete control. You determine your success. To get on in this world, look for the circumstances you want and if you can't find them, make them.

CHAPTER XLVII

SUCCESS

"We are what we repeatedly do. Excellence, therefore, is not an act but a habit."
– ARISTOTLE

Traditional models of success view success as a noun. In those models, success is something you get or a place that you go to. For most of us, it is a destination. In this context, success is a result, and most of our time spent trying to attain it. Not surprisingly, MFers interpret the word success in a slightly different way. They treat success as a verb, not a noun. It's something you *do,* not something you get. It's an action, not a result. It's a journey, not a destination. It's a means, not an end. Viewing success in this way completely alters its definition.

As a verb, success allows us to define behaviors and actions. In this way, success isn't a destination. Success defines what we repeatedly do. It becomes habit. Understanding this approach alters the intent of the word. Think of it this way. Let's explore the word marathon. When we use the word marathon as a noun, the action is vague. It is ambiguous, unclear, and not actionable. When I hear the word marathon, I think of several things. I can run a marathon. I can walk a marathon. My last meeting was a marathon. In these examples, marathon doesn't describe the action.

Isn't this obvious? You have already learned this in grade school. Nouns don't describe actions, verbs do. My goal isn't to change the fundamentals of the English language, but to point out that the way we use the language often limits our ability to understand certain concepts. Using marathon as a verb paints an entirely different picture. The action is clearer without changing anything other than its vocabulary designation.

Marathon, as a verb, makes you think of the word in a completely different way. As a verb, the word marathon forces you to consider several different actions. It instantly conjures up a host of actions and behaviors. What words do you think of when you consider marathon as a verb? Words like endure, pace, and persevere come to mind. As a verb, Marathon implies consistent, incremental hard work. It gives a sense of intense performance that occurs over the long haul. It implies that you run hard, for a really, really, really long time.

Now, let's apply this to the theory of success. What would happen if we used success as an action instead of a noun? Success then becomes a way of life. Success becomes habit. It becomes something you repeatedly do, not something you get. In this context, success becomes actionable in markedly different ways. It's no longer the end of a journey. It becomes the journey itself.

Success, the action, is much more powerful than success, the result. Don't get me wrong—the result is important. We need our ends to follow our means. Periodically, you need some result reinforcement. It helps to have a light at the end of the tunnel, but success is more about the journey than the destination. Sure, MFers are motivated by results. But, their true motivation comes from spinning the Flywheel.

When Jerry Rice and Michael Jordan retired, they were both devastated. The tears flowed at their respective press conferences. They were devastated because they were giving up something they loved. They were devastated because they had to stop their success pursuit. Success described what they were doing, not what they achieved. Retirement changed who they were. In part, they defined themselves by the verb success. The actions of their success pursuit were tough to stop because it wasn't just about the results.

Is success a verb for you? Is it what you want or what you want to do? Is it where you want to go or how you get there? Is it your end or your means? Is it your noun or your verb? Most of all, does the pursuit of success excite you? Is the journey more intriguing than the destination? Success is what you do and not what you get. You don't become successful. You *success*!

FROM WITHIN HUMBLE
ACCELERATORS
WHAT DO YOU FEEL
HAPPINESS COMES
ASSESSMENT
SUPERSTAR
LUCKY
ACCEPTANCE
ALTERATION
MOTIVATION
MANIACAL
INERTIA
FANATICISM
OBSTACLES
INWARD
HIDDEN
SUCCESS
FOUNDATION
VALUES
FLYWHEEL
FOCUS
SUCCESS
BLAME
STRATEGY
CAPACIBILITY
GUTCHECK
FUTILITY
THRESHOLD
SWEAT THE SMALL
SUPER TRUST
HERO
PROMISE
YOUR
FAULT
CHECKMATE
NO EXCUSES
NO EXPLANATIONS
BETTER LUCKY THAN GOOD
POISE
PAST PERFORMANCE
FUTURE SUCCESS
CIRCUMSTANCE
PERFECT SITUATION
SUCCESSOLOGY
MANIACAL FANATICISM BEST
PIVOT
DISCIPLINE
GAME DAY
DENIAL
CONSISTENCY

CHAPTER XLVIII

WHEN FAILURE IS SUCCESS AND SUCCESS IS FAILURE

"I failed my way to success."
– THOMAS EDISON

Why doesn't the Flywheel end in success? Isn't success the goal? Isn't success why we do what we do? Shouldn't the Flywheel at least have success as an endpoint? A Flywheel with a single successful endpoint wouldn't truly represent Maniacal Fanaticism. If Michael Jordan's ultimate goal was to win a championship, the process would be a straight line, and the pursuit of success would have stopped there.

If Michael Jordan never achieved that goal, would his success pursuit continue? The answer is yes. Failure isn't the opposite of success. It's a necessary part of it. Failure is inevitable, and success may best be measured one failure at a time. Like Thomas Edison, MFers usually fail their way to success. Those who have succeeded have seen failure many more times than they have seen success. As many shots as Michael Jordan made, he missed many more. He said, "I've missed more than nine thousand shots in my career. I've lost almost three hundred games. Twenty-six times, I've been trusted to take the game-winning shot and missed. I've failed over and over and over again in my life. And that is why I succeed."

Failure is always a possibility, and that makes success pursuit daunting and terrifying. Statistically, you will fail more times than you will succeed. If you are statistically assured of failing, what is the point of trying? Would you try if you knew you were going to fail? MFers ignore the odds. They understand that failure is necessary to succeed. The blame threshold relies on failure or at least suboptimal success to keep the Flywheel spinning. This is the mechanism by which failure may actually accelerate the Flywheel.

For most people, failing decreases energy and limits them from ever trying again. MFers respond to failure very differently than most people. For them, failure increases their success pursuit enthusiasm. Instead of being a hindrance, failure becomes a success necessity. MFers believe failure is more than a result. It is an opportunity.

Failure is the foundation on which future performance is built. In this peculiar way, failure is positive. It creates opportunities for improvement. Failure measures progress and benchmarks our success pursuit. It heightens motivation and inertia. It makes blame and the inward chip easier to accomplish. It heightens the energy towards the next success. In a weird and convoluted way, failure is success.

Failure is humbling and forces us to be introspective. It causes us to analyze and interpret where we went wrong and where we can be better. In the long term, it encourages positive change and creates opportunities for improvement. Does this sound familiar? This is the first step in blame, and it contributes to the inward chip. Failure makes us reevaluate our abilities, goals, and strategies. For these reasons, failure is a necessary detour on the road to success.

Abraham Lincoln was one of America's most successful presidents. As successful as he was, his early political career was riddled with failure. In 1832, he was defeated for state legislature. In 1838, he was defeated for speaker of the house. In 1843, he was defeated for nomination for Congress. In 1848, he lost his renomination after being elected to Congress in 1846. In 1854, he was defeated for United States Senate. In 1856, he was defeated for nomination for Vice President. In 1858, he was defeated for United States Senate again.

In spite of all these failures, Abraham Lincoln was elected the sixteenth president of the United States in 1860. How the heck did someone who failed so much, manage to succeed? It is no coincidence that Lincoln succeeded after so many failures because those failures prepared him for success. Though we may believe that he succeeded despite his failures, it is more likely that he succeeded because of them.

At some point in your life, you will fail. It is a mathematical inevitability. Your success depends on how your failure affects you. Whether you fail or not isn't as important as how you respond to it. Although failure can spin the Flywheel faster, it isn't automatic. Henry Ford, the founder of the Ford Motor Company, said, "Failure is only the opportunity to begin again, only this time more wisely."

The success that follows failure is satisfying, richer, and more fruitful. It allows us to grow. It drives peak performance through the incremental improvement that follows each failure. This is the way that MFers gradually peak their performance. What happens if you have no initial failure? Never failing is potentially worse than never achieving.

Early non-fatal failure can accelerate success pursuit, but what about early success. How could early success possibly be bad? The problem with early success is that those who succeed early assume they have done everything right. Think of an aspiring athlete. If that athlete has exceptional success, without failure in high school or college, the transition to professional sports can be difficult. These people become "sore losers." They become entitled. They expect to win because they have always won. These are the draft busts. They have difficulty meeting their potential established by their early success.

Early successors, or so we will call them, never had to fail and get better. They never had to fail and concede that would never fail in that way again. They never had to introspect, find blame, and deal with the inward chip. Their early success has taught them that they do most things well. They become complacent. Their success entitlement assures them that there is no need to change, and no room for improvement. Soon success becomes an expectation rather than an aspiration. They can't get better, because they feel they are already doing their best.

When success comes too early or too easily, it can handicap future success. MFers seem to time their success. They seem to peak at exactly the right time. Michael Jordan's peak was several years after Sam Bowie's. As a result, Michael Jordan's peak was far greater. More than a dozen athletes peaked before Jerry Rice.

Consider how students transition through school. Those students who breeze through high school often fail to develop the skills necessary for success in college. Many parents hold their kids back to give them a perceived academic or athletic advantage. Unfortunately, that early advantage can prove to be a late disadvantage. The development of the appropriate study habits, work ethic, and self-corrective behavior is more prevalent in those students who have early failures. Often, failure is required to grow and develop. Unfettered early success can limit future opportunities for improvement.

The best baseball players in the world are successful at hitting the ball only thirty percent of the time. That means seventy percent of the time, they miss the ball. Seventy percent of the time, they fail! At best, the world's greatest basketball players hit fifty percent of their shots. That means they miss half of the time. Half of the time, they fail. It's obvious. Failure is inevitable and is necessary for a successful journey. To have long-lasting success, you have to develop a strategy to learn from your mistakes and failures.

Success and failure are separated by the ability to grow, compensate, and self-correct. Remember Abraham Lincoln. Your ultimate goal may require some early pitfalls to spin that Flywheel faster. Take ownership of your failures. Expect that some failure is mathematically inevitable. Own your failures. In the end, your success will be measured one failure at a time.

FROM WITHIN HUMBLE
ACCELERATORS
WHAT DO YOU FEEL
HAPPINESS COMES
ASSESSMENT
SUPERSTAR
LUCKY
ALTERATION
ACCEPTANCE
MOTIVATION
MANIACAL
FANATICISM
INERTIA
OBSTACLES
INWARD
HIDDEN
SUCCESS FOUNDATION
VALUES
FLYWHEEL
FOCUS
BLAME
PIVOT
GOALS
GUTCHECK
FUTILITY
THRESHOLD
DON'T SWEAT THE SMALL
SUPER TRUST
HERO
YOUR
FAULT
CHECKMATE
NO EXCUSES
NO EXPLANATIONS
BETTER LUCKY THAN GOOD
POISE
PAST PERFORMANCE
FUTURE SUCCESS
CIRCUMSTANCE
PERFECT SITUATION
SUCCESSOLOGY
MANIACAL FANATICISM

CHAPTER XLIX

I THINK I CAN'T

"Whether you believe you can or believe you can't, you're probably right."
– HENRY FORD

Didn't your mother teach you about the power of positive thinking? Unfortunately, she was wrong! Positive thinking is often confused with a realistic assessment of skill. Thinking positively and being realistic aren't mutually exclusive. They can coexist because they serve markedly different purposes. Exceptionally successful people understand what they need when they need it and what will affect their performance. Most people believe that if you think it, it can come true.

Remember the *Little Engine* that could? What did we learn from that lesson? We learned to think we can, even if we thought we couldn't. Thinking we can—in theory—appears to give us enhanced ability to accomplish. "I think I can. I think I can." The words of the *Little Engine* are inspirational, but they aren't very instructive. Don't get me wrong. Positive thinking can be a powerful motivational tool, but it isn't very realistic. Thinking you can, doesn't make it so. What is more powerful than saying you can, is saying that you can't. You are probably shocked by this blasphemous comment, in direct opposition to your parenteral nurturing. You were taught that the first step to every action is thinking you can. This is true, but there is a little more to it.

If you think you can, you already have the skills, ability and effort to accomplish a goal. If you knew how to attain success, you should have already attained it. If you already achieved a goal, there isn't much left to do. Thinking you can't is the first step to accomplish any goal. The trick is when to say it. When you say you can't, you have to understand why you are saying it and the purpose that it serves. If you are saying it because you are defeated, this does you no good. If you are saying it because it is a realistic assessment of where you are, then it can be very helpful.

Saying you can't sets the foundation for what you have yet to do. You have to acknowledge what you can't do to determine how you improve. This isn't can't and won't. This is can't and will. It doesn't mean that the task is impossible. It doesn't mean that you are static and have no ability to improve. It simply identifies where you are in the process.

Capacibility lets you know where you are. Saying you "can't," begins the process of determining how you are going to get to your destination. Can't is powerful. It starts your Flywheel. Can't leads to more inward chip. If you can't do something, it should bother you. If it bothers you, it increases your inward chip. More inward chip means a faster Flywheel.

The reason I ran a half-marathon is because I couldn't. Being unable to run, it was a powerful motivator for me. I assessed that I couldn't and then devised a plan that would take my can't to can. More inward chip means more motivation, more focus, better execution, and so on. Saying I can't was necessary. It served as an entry point and an accelerant to the Flywheel.

Making the assessment that you are unable to do something doesn't mean that it is impossible. When you can't do something, you get more motivated, more inward chip, and inertia. When you can't do something, you get more focus, more goal, and strategy development. When you can't do something, you get more execution, more commitment, and discipline. When you can't do something, you get more reinforcement to complete your task, more blame, and variable results. Saying you can't accelerates every phase of the Flywheel and makes achieving thresholds that much easier.

What we mean to say is that we can't—yet. The word yet makes the phrase entirely different. It alludes to an action that must follow. It alludes to the underlying intention. It is an assessment that is followed by a plan. It is the first step in analyzing the gap between can't and can. Thinking you can means you're a cheerleader. Thinking you can't begins the work. It is much more instructive and far more motivational.

At the end of the day, the *Little Engine* was a cheerleader. Cheerleaders play a huge role in trying to motivate a team, but no team builds a strategy that uses cheerleaders to win. That isn't to say cheerleaders don't serve a purpose. But by definition, they aren't responsible for any of the work. Saying you can isn't very instructive, and being a cheerleader isn't very productive.

"Whether you believe you can or believe you can't, you're probably right." Just because you can't doesn't mean you won't. Just because you can doesn't mean you will. Where you are right now isn't where you will end up. You decide where you want to go. The power doesn't lie in saying you can. The power lies in saying you can't—yet!

FROM WITHIN
ACCELERATORS
WHAT DO YOU FEEL
HAPPINESS
COMES
ASSESSMENT
SUPERSTAR
LUCKY
ACCEPTANCE
ALTERATION
MOTIVATION
MANIACAL
INERTIA
FANATICISM
OBSTACLES
INWARD
HIDDEN
M
SUCCESS
FOUNDATION
R
VALUES
FLYWHEEL
FOCUS
SUCCESS
FACTORS
BLAME
GOALS
EVIDENCE
GUTCHECK
FUTILITY
THRESHOLD
DON'T SWEAT THE SMALL
SUPER TRUST
HERO
PROMISE
YOUR
CHECKMATE
NO EXCUSES
NO EXPLANATIONS
BETTER LUCKY THAN GOOD
POISE
PAST PERFORMANCE
FUTURE SUCCESS
CIRCUMSTANCE
PERFECT SITUATION
SUCCESSOLOGY
MANIACAL FANATICISM BEST
PIVOT
PERSISTENCE
DISCIPLINE
DENIAL
CAPACIBILITY
FAILURE

CHAPTER L

LIMIT LESS

"If you always put limits on what you can do, physical or anything else, it'll spread over into the rest of your life. It'll spread into your work, into your morality, into your entire being. There are no limits. There are plateaus, but you must not stay there, you must go beyond them. If it kills you, it kills you. A man must constantly exceed his level."

– BRUCE LEE

If you never try, you will never fail. This is a very safe way to live. The trouble is, if you never risk trying, you will always fail. Even the most ambitious of us tend to limit ourselves. We limit our risk, and in turn, we limit our success. When we say, "we do our best," we are saying we are limited. When you do your best, it means you can't do anymore. You have no more to give. Our best is our peak performance. Our best is our maximum. Our best is our limit. Whether we avoid the endeavor completely, or we do "our best," we are still limiting our ability to succeed.

On May 7, 1995, Indiana Pacer's scoring guard Reggie Miller found his team losing by six points, with only nineteen seconds remaining in the game. This wasn't just any game. It was a playoff game against their archrival. Even in professional basketball, this was a daunting situation. The probability of success was limited, to say the least. Reggie Miller's situation highlights how most of us view our circumstances. We are limited by our situation. We are limited by time. We are limited by what we think is possible. We limit ourselves by our draft pick. We limit ourselves by doing our "best."

Reggie Miller thought differently. After receiving the inbound pass from Mark Jackson, he took and made a three-pointer. Now the Indiana Pacers were down by three. After scoring, Miller stole the inbound pass from Anthony Mason. He scuttled back to the three-point line and scored again. On the ensuing play, he was fouled after corralling a rebound. He went to the free-throw line and made both of his free throws. His team was now up by two. Reggie Miller scored eight points in nine seconds to win the game.

Even professional basketball pundits didn't anticipate this result. Eight points in nine seconds was beyond the limits of almost everybody's imagination. Eight points in nine seconds was beyond the limits of everybody's expectation. Everybody on the Indiana Pacer's team probably assumed that losing was the only possible result. Everyone had done their best; everybody, except Reggie Miller.

Miller wasn't concerned with limits. If he limited, he would have never taken the shot. If he limited, he would have never stolen the ball. If he limited, he would have never grabbed the rebound. If he limited, he would have already done his best. Because he lacked limits, Reggie Miller was able to take the risk necessary to succeed. He pushed past his previously perceived limits. He didn't put a limit on what he could and couldn't do. This lack of limitation fueled one of the greatest scoring feats of all time.

In 1977, a young Canadian athlete was diagnosed with a devastating disease. He was a runner and a basketball player. He was poised to have a very long and promising athletic career. Unfortunately, his career was cut short by osteosarcoma. This promising young athlete had to have his leg amputated because of this malignant bone cancer. These were devastating and very limiting circumstances, but that didn't limit Terry Fox at all.

In 1980, Terry Fox began the Marathon of Hope. To raise awareness and money to fight cancer, he would attempt to run across Canada, from the Atlantic to the Pacific coast. As crazy as it sounds, his goal was to run a marathon every day until he crossed Canada. Yes! His goal was to run a twenty-six-mile marathon every single day! He ran for one hundred forty-three days, covering three-thousand thirty-nine miles. Running on one leg, his maniacal mission to cross Canada eventually was thwarted by his advancing disease.

It was a sad day in Canada when Terry Fox died in 1981. During my childhood and to this day, this story inspires me. Though he was limited physically after his diagnosis, he never limited himself mentally. He accomplished what other able-bodied athletes could never accomplish. Before starting his miraculous trek, he had no idea what his best was. He wasn't going to let physical, mental, or emotional limits alter the pursuit of his goal. He wasn't going to let an amputated leg or cancer stop him from constantly exceeding his level.

Limits only hinder your success pursuit. They only get in the way. Don't do your best. Your best should serve only as a plateau. You must not stay there. You must push beyond it. Your success potential can only be as great as your limits. Terry Fox and Reggie Miller both did what was necessary for ultimate success. They limited less. "If you always put limits on everything you do, physical or anything else, it will spread into your work and your life. There are no limits."

You should never limit your success pursuit. You should never limit your anticipation of victory. You should never limit your execution to what you consider your best because you can always do better. True success isn't about what you can do. Success is about what you will do. Don't limit your success pursuit to what you think is fathomable. You have to believe you can score eight points in nine seconds. You have to believe you can run a marathon every day of your life. For your success to be limitless, you must limit less.

CHAPTER LI

SUCCESSOLOGY

"Always bear in mind that your own resolution to succeed is more important than any one thing."
– ABRAHAM LINCOLN

Successology is the study of success. It starts with a few fundamental questions. What is success? What are its fundamental components? In our search for success, we often attempt to break it down to its components. We study success to determine what is at its core. An appropriate study of success should give us an idea of the building blocks, equations, general principles, and causal relationships that exist.

Why study success? We study success to make success less daunting and more tangible. Like nature, success has predictable and consistent relationships that govern its pursuit. The laws of gravity, conservation of mass, and entropy are notable examples of this. These laws are predictable, measurable, and repeatable. Likewise, the laws of success should be predictable, measurable, and repeatable.

To arrive at his brilliant deduction that $E=mc^2$, Albert Einstein used extensive mathematical and scientific analysis. This distillation of mathematical heuristics changed our understanding of energy, mass, and the relationship between the two. The equation is an elegantly simple distillation of more complex previously misunderstood concepts. The implications of the equation and the underlying science have fundamentally changed the world.

Success is similarly broken down in this book. If *successology* is the study of success, Maniacal Fanaticism is the equation. Once you identify and understand the building blocks, you can then use the equation and apply it to all of your success situations. The following represents the Maniacal Fanaticism equation expressed in words.

Motivation (inertia + inward chip) x
Focus (strategy development + goal development) x
Execution (commitment + discipline) x
Reinforcement (variable success + blame) = Success

Here is the same equation represented mathematically.

$$M\,(m^1+m^2) \times F\,(f^1+f^2) \times E\,(e^1+e^2) \times R\,(r^1+r^2) = S$$

Each variable in this equation increases the amount of success. More motivation increases the amount of success. More focus increases the amount of success, and so on. Each threshold is added together to comprise a phase. The phases are then multiplied by each other, having an exponential impact on success. Increasing any individual component increases the amount of success. An uncompleted phase results in a zero value for that phase. A zero in any phase creates a zero result for the entire equation.

In other words, an inability to complete a phase shuts down the entire Flywheel. The mathematical relationships are clear, but the human factors are more muddled. Science and math are the epitome of logic, until human beings get involved. Human behavior muddies the water because a good portion of what we do isn't mathematical or scientific.

We have studied how the inward chip and inertia come together to create motivation. We have learned how goal and strategy development coalesce to create focus. We have developed an understanding of how commitment and discipline create maniacal execution. Finally, we have determined how successful people are reinforced by blame and variable results. We also now know that Maniacal Fanaticism is a cycle. Each phase feeds the next and repeats itself, spinning faster and faster, churning out success after success.

Math and science aside, we still have an unanswered question. We have a question that is much more difficult to answer. It's a question that is tougher to answer because very little outward objective evidence is available. The question is why. Why do MFers pursue success? Why is it important for them to be successful? Why follow the Flywheel? Mathematics, science, and heuristics won't fully answer these questions. We have discussed Michael Jordan's inward chip and Jerry Rice's commitment, but we haven't discussed their why.

Why did they pursue success so maniacally? Why did they repeatedly spin the Flywheel over and over again? Why did Michael Jordan come out of retirement twice? Why did Terry Fox try to run across Canada? Why did Jerry Rice train so doggedly? Why did Reggie Miller keep shooting, with only nine seconds left? Why motivate? Why focus? Why execute? Why reinforce? Why Maniacal Fanaticism?

Not even Nobel-Prize-worthy mathematics can adequately determine the answer. The answer can't be determined by successological analysis, scientific investigation, or contemporary success theorizing. The answer is obvious and somewhat rudimentary. MFers pursue success because of the pursuit itself.

One of the most profound effects of the Flywheel is the satisfaction received from spinning it. Success isn't the product of the Flywheel. It is the byproduct. Success isn't the end of the equation. Success is the equation. For MFers, success is replaced by success pursuit. MFers gain satisfaction from the pursuit of success, irrespective of success, or failure. The process is *why* they do what they do.

I know you were hoping for some profound analytic calculus. In the end, MFers pursue success for the thrill of the pursuit. If success is the destination, the journey to get there is Maniacal Fanaticism. Think about a cross-country journey from California to New York City. New York is a fantastic destination, but what you see along the journey may be even more breathtaking. Climbing Mount Everest is more about the climb and less about the peak.

As simple as it may sound, MFers pursue success because the pursuit brings them great satisfaction. It's an addiction, where the high is the struggle, and the success causes withdrawal. We all know extraordinarily successful people who are never satisfied and always want to do more. No matter how much they achieve, they never want to give up the pursuit.

Think of your success pursuit. Are you truly addicted to the pursuit of success? Are you more intrigued by the journey or the destination? Do you derive satisfaction plugging each variable into the equation? If you ever hope to have a fraction of the success that those like Michael Jordan, Jerry Rice, and Roald Amundsen had, pursue success as they did. It's fanatical because this pursuit is a compulsion. It should be an irrepressible urge. It should be an irrepressible impulse. It should be an inexhaustible journey. It should be a perpetual pursuit whose side effect happens to be success.

As you endeavor to be great, going through the process will ultimately yield more than the result. Your own resolution to succeed is more important than any one thing. It is more important than any study, equation, or theory. Understanding the mathematics and the science is only the beginning. Your ability to succeed is dependent on your compulsion to pursue success. No goal will be as motivating as your resolution to succeed. That resolution is more important than any one thing. It is more important than any result or accolade. The study of success starts with you. Finding the success equation isn't as important as your willingness to plug yourself in.

FROM WITHIN
ACCELERATORS
WHAT DO YOU FEEL
HAPPINESS COMES
ASSESSMENT
SUPERSTAR
LUCKY
ALTERATION
ACCEPTANCE
MOTIVATION
MANIACAL
FANATICISM
INERTIA
OBSTACLES
INWARD
HIDDEN
SUCCESS
FOUNDATION
VALUES
FLYWHEEL
FOCUS
BLAME
PIVOT
GUTCHECK
FUTILITY
THRESHOLD
DON'T SWEAT THE SMALL STUFF
SUPER TRUST
HERO
PROMISE
YOUR
FAULT
CHECKMATE
NO EXCUSES
NO EXPLANATIONS
BETTER LUCKY THAN GOOD
POISE
PAST PERFORMANCE
FUTURE SUCCESS
CIRCUMSTANCE
PERFECT SITUATION
SUCCESSOLOGY
MANIACAL FANATICISM BEST

CHAPTER LII

SHORTEST DISTANCE BETWEEN TWO POINTS

"Every day you may make progress. Every step may be fruitful. Yet there will stretch out before you an ever-lengthening, ever-ascending, ever-improving path. You know you will never get to the end of the journey. But this, so far from discouraging, only adds to the joy and glory of the climb."

– WINSTON CHURCHILL

Mathematically, a line is the shortest distance between two points. It describes the fastest, most efficient, and most direct way to get from one point to another. Just think about how much quicker it is to fly than drive. Of course, a plane is faster than a car, but it isn't just the plane's speed. An airplane takes a more direct route. For the easiest way to get somewhere quickly, the airplane is the best choice.

Our society attempts to apply this mathematical line to success. Everybody is looking for a direct route. They look for the shortest distance between the lack of success and success. Society reveres and, in many ways, promotes the success straight-line. We look for the quickest, most efficient, fastest, and easiest path. We want get-rich-quick schemes. After all, most of us would rather take the airplane. Unfortunately, it isn't that easy.

Our view of success is retrospective. We are quick to notice the success, but we often don't see all the points that precede it. Our retrospective view of success focuses on the endpoint without the context of the starting point. We look back at those people who are successful and analyze how they got from point A to point B. We assume they took a success airplane from one point to another. We assume that their success pursuit was rapid, efficient, and direct. We assume that they took a straight line.

If we pay closer attention, we will see that straight-line success is rare. If you just won the lottery, you might disagree, but most successes don't happen that way. Success pursuit doesn't consist of traveling from point A to point B. Success pursuit may not even consist of traveling from point A to point B to point C. Success pursuit is convoluted. It doesn't occur with a single brushstroke, a single hit song, or one great game.

Success stories often begin with years of unheralded preparation. Those years are full of futility. Most successful people prepare with a destination in mind and no guarantee that they will get there. For the most part, they don't travel a straight line. They may stop at several points along the way, but that portion isn't always evident. It isn't always visible. Much of what hinders us from succeeding is the anticipation of quick success and the associated let down when we find out it isn't very quick at all.

My sister understands this all too well. After finishing a communications degree, she set her sights on reporting. Reporting is highly competitive. Because of this, many in our family attempted to dissuade her from this pursuit. To many of us, becoming a reporter was like winning the lottery. We thought that the only way she could get there was to take an airplane. We assumed it would require a rapid, efficient, and quick ascent to get her dream job. And that kind of success is so rare. We were concerned that her goal was unachievable.

Like everybody in our family, my sister is stubborn. She refused to take no for an answer. She never found that airplane to take her from point A to point B, but she was determined to pursue her dream. She left her stable, well-paying writing job at a local television station and took a reporting internship in London, Ontario, approximately two hundred miles from her home in Toronto. After finishing that internship, she took a job in Winnipeg, which was thirteen hundred miles from home. After reporting in Winnipeg, she moved to Edmonton, a whopping twenty-one hundred miles from home. After reporting in Edmonton, she moved to Iqaluit, fifteen hundred miles from home, and seventeen hundred miles from Edmonton.

After all that, my sister finally got the opportunity to be an anchor in her hometown. It isn't her dream job, but it's darn close. This is her definition of success. She is a reporter and anchor in her hometown.

Now that's impressive! My sister's success pursuit is more typical than the airplane ascent that most of us envision. She went from point A to point B to point C to point D to get to her successful point E. This transit took years and literally thousands of miles. Anybody watching her on television now may remark at how lucky she is to be an anchor.

Most people aren't privy to all the steps that were required for my sister to get where she is. They see her point B and assume she started at point A. They assume that she took the airplane to success. If we carefully study successful people, it is more likely that they arrived at success in this convoluted way. Success pursuit is complicated. It isn't an airplane ride. It is more like a cross-country car ride, with multiple stops and many changes in direction along the way.

My sister understood that her success pursuit was going to be circuitous. People who expect a rapid commute to their success destination are often let down. When they are forced to make multiple stops, they get discouraged. MFers understand their success journey will have multiple stops along the way. They view each stop as necessary, not as a hindrance. Every stop is filled with growth and education. Every change in direction allows for adjustments, redirection, and opportunities for improvement.

Our misunderstanding of how success happens creates the feeling that it should occur quickly. We want to believe that success should quickly follow our effort. Hard work should summarily be rewarded. When the reward is delayed, the effort wanes. When the reward doesn't come, the work becomes more mundane. In this way, society has brainwashed our understanding of how we should pursue success. We are told that "hard work pays off!" But what we aren't told is that the timing of that payoff is often extremely unpredictable.

If we look closely at successful people, we find a different paradigm. Much of their success is based on their journey. Their successful strategy continues to be refined and redefined. We will discover they didn't go from A to B. The success journey is one step at a time, but it doesn't happen with only one step. Each step serves a purpose, and every day is progress. Every stop is fruitful. There will never be an end. The success pursuit itself is the destination.

Knowing my sister, she will continue to strive for that better job. She will continue to add new stops on the road to success. She understands that success isn't the shortest distance between two points. She understands that there is no quick fix, and that the payoff is unpredictable. I foresee many more miles and many more opportunities in her future. The road may meander, but her ultimate success will come soon enough.

FROM WITHIN
HUMBLE
ACCELERATORS
WHAT DO YOU FEEL
SUPERSTAR
ALTERATION
MOTIVATION
MANIACAL
INERTIA
FANATICISM
OBSTACLES
INWARD
M
SUCCESS
FOUNDATION
R
VALUES
FLYWHEEL
FOCUS
BLAME
GUTCHECK
FUTILITY
THRESHOLD
SWEAT THE
SMALL
SUPER TRUST
HERO
YOUR
CHECKMATE
NO EXPLANATIONS
NO EXCUSES
BETTER LUCKY THAN GOOD
PAST PERFORMANCE
CIRCUMSTANCE
SUCCESSOLOGY
MANIACAL FANATICISM BEST

CHAPTER LIII

BE ACCOUNTABLE?

"Duties are not performed for duty's sake, but because their neglect would make the man uncomfortable. A man performs but one duty–the duty of contenting his spirit, the duty of making himself agreeable to himself."

– MARK TWAIN

I am often asked where accountability fits into the Flywheel. People are often surprised when I tell them that accountability isn't a part of Maniacal Fanaticism. What? How can this be? Almost every model of success, to varying degrees, has accountability as a hallmark. What exactly is accountability? Merriam-Webster defines accountability as "an obligation or willingness to accept responsibility." Accepting responsibility and being accountable is important to an extent, but they are more applicable to team or group situations.

The success Flywheel is a uniquely singular effort. Michael Jordan and Jerry Rice were great teammates. They expected accountability from their teammates, and their teammates expected them to be accountable. That's just it. Accountability is something that occurs between people. Accountability becomes exceedingly important with leadership and team management, but that's a different book. Accountability doesn't apply to the success Flywheel because success isn't a responsibility. It implies that your success pursuit is responsible for someone or something else.

For MFers, the pursuit of success is self-fulfilling. The pursuit of success isn't a responsibility or accountability. If you are pursuing success because you feel responsible or obligated to someone or something, you are probably going to fail. Your duty to succeed shouldn't be performed for duty's sake, but because their neglect would make you uncomfortable.

Responsibility implies that there is an external force driving your behavior. From what we have learned so far, success pursuit comes from within. If you always need external responsibility or obligation to motivate you, then you aren't likely to succeed. In that case, your success pursuit will only be as powerful as the strength of your responsibility or obligation. If you look closely, MFers' success pursuits aren't based on others. Whether Michael Jordan played for the North Carolina Tar Heels, the Chicago Bulls, or the 1992 Olympic Dream Team, his competitive spirit was not fueled by accountability. Whether Jerry Rice was playing with Joe Montana, Steve Young, or with the Oakland Raiders, he pushed himself beyond his responsibility.

At my son's school, they give "accountabilities" to those students who don't follow the rules. After a certain number of these accountabilities, the child receives detention. The school uses this "stick" to negatively reinforce poor behavior. What do you think would happen if the teacher wasn't watching? Would the kids still be accountable for their behavior? If the teacher leaves the room, look out! When the cat is away, you know this cliché. When someone is watching, most of us do the right thing. Discipline is doing the right thing when no one is watching.

Jerry Rice's fanatical training didn't end when the coach wasn't looking. Michael Jordan's competitive spirit didn't end when he played for the Washington Wizards. MFers' behaviors are internal. They don't require anyone or anything else to hold them accountable. Who holds you accountable? To whom are you responsible? Are you able to spin the Flywheel, without being obligated or responsible to someone else? Do you have to wait for someone to be watching to do the right thing?

The Flywheel is comprised of inertia, the inward chip, goal development, strategy development, commitment, discipline, blame, and variable success. Obligation and responsibility aren't a part of the Flywheel. Accountability is much more important when you have a team with a common goal. Accountability is especially important for teams comprised of individuals with different skills. In this respect, each individual has to be accountable for the tasks that they have to accomplish. Without accomplishing each individual task, the overall goal will be harder to achieve. This is the true definition of accountability.

Accountability and discipline often get confused. Jerry Rice's fanatical training was disciplined but not necessarily accountable. Discipline is internal. The external environment should never affect it. The circumstances may change, but discipline is consistent. If the ability to perform is based on the external environment, performance will only be as good as the circumstances. Remember my golf partner?

Think about an elite athlete who only performs with certain coaches. Think about a student who only excels with certain teachers.

You have to be able to excel, no matter the environment, no matter the circumstance and no matter the situation. Internal commitment and discipline are far better than accountability to an external source.

If your success is solely based on your responsibility to someone else, you are bound to fail. Being accountable to your boss, your coach, your team, your spouse, your children, or your teacher can limit your performance. Would you train as hard if the coach didn't tell you to? Would you show up on time, if the boss wasn't looking? Would you work as hard if no one was watching?

Inertia, the inward chip, goal development, strategy development, commitment, discipline, blame, and variable success are all intrinsic processes. Accountability isn't a bad quality. In the "beyond self-interest" chapter, we learned how external factors can inspire us. This is different from accountability. That chapter described inspiration, not responsibility.

"A man performs but one duty, the duty of contenting his spirit." The pursuit of success is the greatest Flywheel accelerator there is. The pursuit itself is much more powerful than accountability will ever be. How can you apply this to your everyday life? Don't use external accountability to replace your fanaticism for success. Pursue excellence in an unwavering fashion. Your coach, teacher, friends, boss, or family can create accountability for you, but they will never create the intrinsic need to pursue excellence.

My wife and I rarely argue. But, when we do, it is usually about something really important. I remember one argument in particular that emphasized this point. I don't remember every detail. But, I distinctly remember feeling that my wife was questioning my performance as a husband and a father. That definitely hit a nerve!

I remember saying, "I'm a good husband and a good father!" Her answer shocked me. She told me, "You don't get credit for that! It's what you are supposed to do!" To be honest, she shouted it. I started to respond, but I stopped. I couldn't say a thing. She forced me to evaluate what I was doing and why I was doing it. What she was saying was this: "Duties are not performed for duty's sake, but because their neglect would make the man uncomfortable." It was clear to her that "a man performs but one duty, the duty of contenting his spirit, the duty of making himself agreeable to himself."

I wanted credit for what I was supposed to do. I wanted credit for what should have been agreeable to me. I wanted credit for duties that aren't performed for duty's sake. I wanted credit for duties that, if neglected, should make me uncomfortable. Being a good father and husband are my duties. I shouldn't do it because I feel obligated. I shouldn't do it because I feel accountable. Being a good father and a good husband should be intrinsic to what I do.

You may feel accountable, but your actions shouldn't solely hinge on your obligations. Your success pursuit should content your spirit. Michael Jordan pursued success because neglecting success would make him uncomfortable. Jerry Rice pursued success because it contented his spirit. Pursuing success for external reasons will limit how fast your Flywheel can spin. It will limit your ability to succeed. The accountability for your success pursuit should come from within. It should be your duty. My wife was right. "It's what you are *supposed* to do."

FROM WITHIN
ACCELERATORS
WHAT DO YOU FEEL
HAPPINESS COMES
ASSESSMENT
LUCKY
SUPERSTAR
ALTERATION
ACCEPTANCE
MOTIVATION
MANIACAL
INERTIA
FANATICISM
OBSTACLES
INWARD
HIDDEN
M
SUCCESS
R
FOUNDATION
VALUES
FLYWHEEL
FOCUS
BLAME
T
PIVOT
CAPABILITY
BEYOND
GOALS
EVIDENCE
GUTCHECK
FUTILITY
THRESHOLD
SWEAT THE SMALL
SUPER TRUST
HERO
PROMISE
YOUR
FAULT
CHECKMATE
NO EXPLANATIONS
NO EXCUSES
DISCIPLINE
MEMORY
BETTER LUCKY THAN GOOD
POISE
PAST PERFORMANCE
FUTURE SUCCESS
CIRCUMSTANCE
PERFECT SITUATION
SUCCESSOLOGY
MANIACAL FANATICISM BEST

CHAPTER LIV

ALL MFERS AREN'T CREATED EQUALLY

"The worst form of inequality is to try to make unequal things equal."
– ARISTOTLE

As there are varying degrees of success, so too are there varying degrees of Maniacal Fanaticism implementation. I indirectly touched on this earlier in the book when I described Flywheel's accelerators and decelerators. Accelerators and decelerators make implementation variable and success stratified. Even within this highly successful subset of people, we find stratification. Alas, not all MFers are created equal. MFers stratify themselves based on how well they adopt the foundation principles, how well they spin the Flywheel, and how they affect those around them. MFers fall into one of four levels.

Level one MFers are the Novices. They understand the Flywheel and its components, but they have a rudimentary ability to meet each threshold and satisfy each phase. They have mastery of at least one of the foundation principles. A typical level one MFer would be the budding high school athlete. Student athletes are just beginning to understand motivation, focus, execution, and reinforcement. They may not fully understand what each phase is, but they intuitively accomplish them.

Level one MFers require tons of help and coaching. They are prone to slipping in and out of the Flywheel, making success accomplishment take much longer. Most commonly, the execution phase is where they falter, because they have limited synergy and consistency. Level one MFers have difficulty managing multiple Flywheels and generating lofty goals. They tend to make goals they can touch and feel, goals that aren't as lofty. This limits their ability to succeed, but it gives them some early wins. Due to these early wins, they can spin the Flywheel a little faster.

Starting at level one isn't required, because the levels aren't necessarily sequential. However, most MFers do start at level one. Their most common mistake is limiting the scope of the inward chip and blame. Some of those doubtful feelings find their way into the execution phase and limit their discipline. Lastly, level one MFers have little or no effect on the people around them. They can achieve individual success, but they have a limited impact on their teams, organizations, and families.

Level two MFers are known as the Vice Presidents. They are much more seasoned than the Novices are. They have a particularly good understanding of the Flywheel and know exactly how to meet each threshold and satisfy each phase. They have mastery of two or three of the foundation principles. This is where most successful people tend to reside. These are people with a high level of individual success.

Level two MFers have an intuitive understanding of the Flywheel. They know what phase they are in. They know where they need to be and how to get there. They rarely fall off the Flywheel, although they are susceptible to a few Flywheel decelerators. They struggle with effectively managing multiple Flywheels, but they do this much better than level one MFers. Although these individuals have powerful chips, they struggle to keep them inward.

Peers identify level two MFers as experts in their fields. Other than their expertise, they rarely have any significant impact on those around them. Level two MFers also require outside reinforcement to achieve lofty goals. In the organizational model, these people tend to fall into middle management jobs and remain there. They are called Vice Presidents because that is where they usually top out.

This is where it starts to get exciting! Level three MFers are the Superstars. They have achieved massive amounts of individual success. Their transitions through the threshold and phases are practically imperceptible. They blur the lines between phases, making transitions from one phase to the other seamless. They also have mastery of at least four foundation principles.

Level three MFers can apply multiple Flywheels in multiple areas. They pause certain Flywheels to conserve energy and pick them right back up where they left off. They have no difficulty setting and accomplishing lofty goals. Level three MFers have a large introspective inward chip, but that chip is limited to the motivation phase. Because of blame, they respond to variable success with even more maniacal discipline.

Level three MFers spend a considerable amount of time in the blame threshold. This creates multiple opportunities for improvement.

Level three MFers have a profound effect on their peers. They generate Flywheels in everybody around them. They make great leaders because they can influence others.

Level four MFers are called Game Changers. These individuals are a lot like level three leaders except for one major difference. They affect almost everything and everyone around them. Level four MFers not only influence individuals around them, but they also influence entire organizations. They can generate and influence Flywheels across an entire team. They even affect entire disciplines and change the way we see the world.

Level four MFers' pursuit of success is so innovative that they literally change the game. They push past limits previously thought to be impossible. They manage their Flywheels perfectly and can even teach the Flywheel. People who encounter level four MFers are forever changed. Steve Jobs changed the entire landscape of personal computing devices. Michael Jordan changed the game of basketball. Jerry Rice changed the wide receiver position and the entire football landscape.

Attaining level four status is possible for all of us. The levels aren't static. There aren't any secrets here. We have learned what they do and how they do it. Our ability to apply what we have learned, to our everyday pursuits, is our only limit. You *can* change the game. You are only limited by how fast you want to spin your Flywheel. We aren't all created equal, but we all have an equal opportunity to succeed. No matter where you started, where you end up is up to you. Will you be a game-changer?

CHAPTER LV

THERE YOU HAVE IT

"This is not the end. It is not even the beginning of the end. But it is, perhaps, the end of the beginning."
– WINSTON CHURCHILL

There you have it! Now, you understand a slightly different perspective on success. As you embark on your success journey, you are better prepared to succeed. You have reviewed the evidence. You understand that success prototypes and pedigrees don't exist. You don't need to be a number one pick. No matter what society tells you, your draft pick isn't as important as you think.

Being the right height, going to the right schools, having the right parents, and being in the right place helps, but none of those things is required for your success. You now know that the hidden evidence is more obvious than you thought. You just have to pay better attention to all the evidence. You now understand the foundation principles.

You understand how these principles can create a solid foundation for success.

You have learned to be an eternal optimist. You have to know it. With hard work, success is always possible. You now know that tolerating the ambiguity of the outcome will allow you to take and make that game-winning shot. You will take that leap of faith because you have contingencies for most outcomes. You will no longer tolerate mediocrity. You will no longer be happy with the status quo.

To be successful, you must be an innovator and think about things slightly differently. You understand success requires immediacy. You must stay in the moment. You must execute in the here and now. You must ground your actions, reactions, and decisions in the present. You now know you can't dwell on the last shot you missed. You can't execute today if you are preoccupied with what may happen tomorrow or what happened yesterday. You have to assess your ability to succeed. No matter what your ability, you know you can always improve your capacity. You can and will.

You understand what it takes to enter the Flywheel. The evidence is clear. You don't have to be a prodigy. You don't have to be a prototype. You don't need the right pedigree. You understand motivation is the "why" of your success. You understand focus is the "what." You understand execution is the "how." You understand the "when" of success, reinforcement.

You understand you need a spark to start the Flywheel. This is your inertia. You understand the chip on your shoulder, and you know it should be turned inward. You know you can always get better. You can always do more. No matter how good you are, you never feel like you are good enough. You know that your motivation should go beyond your self-interest. You know how to focus and refine your motivation to a single point.

To determine your success journey destination, you develop requisite, expected, and lofty goals. You know how to stratify your goals. You know that you should keep your goals in sight and always sweat the small stuff. You understand that you need a strategy to achieve your goals. You know that activity isn't productivity and action isn't production. Goal and strategy development should always precede any action.

For an effective strategy, you know you have to prepare. You know that you must research, use your experience, anticipate an outcome, and be creative. You know that documenting your tactics is your map to success. For your every success action, there is a pre-action. You will need to execute your strategy. You know that obstacles shouldn't limit your success pursuit. For obstacles, you have to create an unrelenting strategy. As you start to think about executing your strategy, you know that you will encounter pivot points. You don't have to make the right decision, but you know you need to make one.

As you continue to move through the Flywheel, you know the hard work is coming. You understand commitment is the promise, and discipline is the delivery on that promise. You know that commitment is composed of belief, promise, and trust. You have to believe in your strategy, your process, and yourself. You know that discipline is difficult. It will require self-denial and sacrifice. You have to adhere to a specific regimen. You are aware that you have to make sacrifices and always give up something.

Unfortunately, you know that success won't be easy. If it were fun, it wouldn't be called work. When times get tough, you get tougher. Nothing can stop you. When your gut check comes, will you know what to do? You accept, assess, alter, and accelerate your way to execution. You are a superhero. If you work long and hard enough, you will always win. You know that when you miss your goal, you should blame yourself. You should take responsibility for your wins and losses. It is always your fault. You know that suboptimal success leads to blame, but you also know that blame leads to opportunities for improvement and a change in strategy.

You are prepared for all possible outcomes and variable successes. Just in case, you have prepared an alternative plan. You know that you have to be crazy to push past the possible. You never make excuses or give explanations. You know that your results are your results. You own your results. Not good, not bad, just is.

You know you will always execute with maximal effort. Even though it may seem futile, you know that you will eventually become a superstar. It is great to be lucky, but you aren't waiting for that. You control your outcomes. You know your results will eventually match your effort.

Because of your preparation, you know that you should have poise. You maximize any luck that you do have. You potentiate luck events. Your success effort is persistent and pervasive. You know you should have short-term memory for failures and success, but long-term memory for your success know-how. The memory of past results can be motivating, but you know that past results don't predict future success. You know chess pieces only move a particular way, but they all have the potential to win the game. You know what skills you have and understand how to apply them.

You are ready for your game day because you have game day primed. On your game day, you purge your inward chip. You maximize your inertia. You anticipate your goal and strategy fulfillment. You envision a successful strategy execution and maximize your belief. You anticipate your lofty goal accomplishment. On game day, you have to know it, take it, and make it. At the time of execution, when your best effort is required, you know you should feel absolutely nothing. When you finally score, you should hand the ball to the ref. You know your happiness comes from within. Success is what you do, not what you get.

No matter how much success you achieve, you know you may need a helping hand. You will need a Scottie Pippen. You will need a Steve Kerr. You will need a Joe Montana. You know what accelerates and decelerates your Flywheel. You know what you can and can't control and the difference between them. You know how to be a janitor and accomplish small tasks as if they were noble ones. Your Flywheels must have synergy and consistency. You apply your process to every task and know that over time they get easier to accomplish.

You now know not to wait for the perfect situation. Things don't happen to you. You should happen to things. You know not to rely on circumstance. You circumnavigate and take control of your surrounding environment. You understand that success is a verb and not a noun. It is something you do and not something you get. Success isn't a person, place, or thing. It is an action.

You know sometimes success is failure and failure can be success. The lessons that you learn from failures are priceless. You know not to relish your successes for too long. You also know you may have to fail your way to success. If you fear failing, you will never try. If you fear trying, you will always fail. You know what you can do. You also know what you can't do yet! Without can't, you can't improve. If you are truly going to succeed, don't do what you can. Do what you can't.

You now know that limits are only plateaus that you must push past. For your success to be limitless, you have to limit less. You know that you have to plug into your success equation. You understand that success isn't always the shortest line between two points. You know the road may be tortuous and arduous.

Success isn't point A to point B. You may have to go from point to point to point. You will be taken out of your comfort zone. You will have to find comfort in discomfort. In the end, you know that you are accountable to yourself. Only you can test the limits of what you can do. You perform your duty not for duty's sake, but because neglecting it would make you even more uncomfortable.

You can push past your previously perceived limits. You can outperform your draft pick. You can outperform your pedigree. Don't settle for superstar. Change the game! You can transcend your talent. You can be more than the sum of your parts. You are ready to leave ordinary for extraordinary. Armed with this knowledge, how can you possibly fail?

You may not have been born in the right place, at the right time, with the right parents. You may not have attended the right schools, attained the right degree, or worked at the right company. If you are willing to work, you can succeed. With maniacal motivation, fanatical focus, extreme execution and relentless reinforcement, you can and will succeed. You know that this isn't the end. This isn't the beginning of the end. It's the end of the beginning. Your success pursuit is just starting. You will now view the world in a slightly different way, from a new perspective. This is the end of the beginning of your life as an MFer. Whether you are twenty-five or sixty-five, your success pursuit starts right now. Go forth and prosper!

CHAPTER LVI

PICTURE PERFECT

"To finish a work? To finish a picture? What nonsense! To finish it means to be through with it, to kill it, to rid it of its soul, to give it its final blow the coup de grâce for the painter as well as for the picture."

– PABLO PICASSO

What was your last major accomplishment? Was it graduation? Was it the purchase of a new car? Did you win an award? Whatever it was, I am sure you memorialized it with a picture. Digital cameras are so readily available now that every major accomplishment in your life has a picture associated with it. When I look back at my pictures, they are particularly revealing. I look at my graduation photo. I have a wry smile, feeling confident and accomplished. My parents are smiling proudly. I remember every moment frozen in that picture.

This is how most of us remember our lives. These intermittent static images are how we remember these moments. When we look back at these photos, we see how different we are now from the static images we took then. At times, we perceive ourselves very differently from the images that memorialize us. This is also how we view success.

Our society takes snapshots. When people succeed, we literally and figuratively snap a picture of them. We picture Michael Jordan flying through the air with his tongue out. We picture Jerry Rice catching touchdowns. We see Barry Sanders handing the ball to the ref, after a thirty-five-yard touchdown. We picture Steve Jobs brooding in front of thousands, revealing the new iPhone. We picture Reggie Miller miraculously scoring eight points in nine seconds. We picture Terry Fox valiantly running a marathon every day on one leg.

We always picture successful people in their success moment. These are success snapshots. We memorialize the moments with picture perfect accuracy. Napoleon said a picture is worth a thousand words. Each of these success snapshots has a thousand words to tell. Unfortunately, it would take millions of words to tell their true success story.

Success isn't a snapshot, as most of us have been trained to believe. It isn't a draft pick. It isn't static. It isn't a picture. Success is more like a portrait. It's constantly being worked on. It's constantly being updated. Layers are added. Colors are mixed in. Errors are reworked. Lines are emphasized, and others are erased.

Your success pursuit is similar. Your success portrait is constantly being worked on. The process is constantly being updated. Layers of learning are added. Experiences are mixed in. Weaknesses are reworked. Strengths are emphasized. Some efforts are erased. Your success portrait is never complete. Improvement can always be made. Your success portrait will never be finished.

The thought that you can finish the picture is nonsense! "To finish it means to be through with it, to kill it, to rid it of its soul." Taking a snapshot is a success killer. It gives the appearance that the work of success is complete. We keep taking snapshots and wonder why success isn't repeatable. Snapshots are pictures at a singular moment in time. We see the snapshot of the ball in the air. We see the snapshot of each of our singular successes. We immortalize those singular moments and spend a lifetime trying to recreate them. Our success pursuits tend to focus on each individual granular detail of each isolated success snapshot. We assume that our successes are completed portraits or finished pictures. If you are looking at the finished picture, that is the final blow, and the coup de grâce for the painter as well as for the picture.

If you are to take away one thing from this book, I hope you take away an understanding of this point. Success isn't static. It isn't based on your draft pick. It isn't based on your snapshot. It's based on what you do from this point on. You can decide how you paint your picture. Success isn't what you get. It's what you do.

In this book, I use the term MFer. This term doesn't describe a particular group of people. It describes a group of people that employ a particular process. They don't have a monopoly on this method. They don't have a patent on this practice. They don't have a stranglehold on success. You have an opportunity to be an MFer. You have an opportunity to be successful. You are a painter, and you are creating your success journey portrait. To think you are finished would be the final blow. It would be the coup de grâce. If you haven't started already, start your portrait today. Start painting, and don't ever stop!

FROM WITHIN
ACCELERATORS
WHAT DO YOU FEEL
SUPERSTAR
ALTERATION
MOTIVATION
MANIACAL
INERTIA
FANATICISM
OBSTACLES
INWARD
HIDDEN
SUCCESS
FOUNDATION
VALUES
FLYWHEEL
FOCUS
BLAME
GUTCHECK
FUTILITY
THRESHOLD
SWEAT THE SMALL
SUPER TRUST
HERO
YOUR
CHECKMATE
NO EXCUSES
NO EXPLANATIONS
BETTER LUCKY THAN GOOD
PAST PERFORMANCE
CIRCUMSTANCE
SUCCESSOLOGY
MANIACAL FANATICISM BEST

EXITUS

I will leave you with this quote.

"It is not the critic who counts; not the man who points out how the strong man stumbles, or where the doer of deeds could have done them better. The credit belongs to the man who is actually in the arena, whose face is marred by dust and sweat and blood, who strives valiantly; who errs and comes short again and again; because there is not effort without error and shortcomings; but who does actually strive to do the deed; who knows the great enthusiasm, the great devotion, who spends himself in a worthy cause, who at the best knows in the end the triumph of high achievement and who at the worst, if he fails, at least he fails while daring greatly. So that his place shall never be with those cold and timid souls who know neither victory nor defeat."

– THEODORE ROOSEVELT

FROM WITHIN
HUMBLE
ACCELERATORS
FEEL
SUPERSTAR
ALTERATION
MOTIVATION
MANIACAL
FANATICISM
INERTIA
OBSTACLES
INWARD
SUCCESS
FOUNDATION
VALUES
FLYWHEEL
FOCUS
BLAME
GUTCHECK
FUTILITY
THRESHOLD
SWEAT THE SMALL
SUPER TRUST
YOUR
CHECKMATE
NO EXPLANATIONS
NO EXCUSES
BETTER LUCKY THAN GOOD
PAST PERFORMANCE
CIRCUMSTANCE
SUCCESSOLOGY
MANIACAL FANATICISM BEST

EPILOGUE

How did you develop the name Maniacal Fanaticism?

The development of the name was based on the way certain people pursue success. The individuals I talk about in the book had an obsession with excellence. The words maniacal and fanatical give an image of how success is pursued by these people. This particular kind of success pursuit isn't for the cavalier. It isn't for the success weekend warrior. This kind of success requires a relative obsession with excellence. It describes a success maniac or a success fanatic. I felt this was the best way to describe the way these people pursue success.

Why do you use so many examples from sports?

Sport is truly a microcosm of life. It truly can transcend socioeconomic class, race, gender, and nationality. Sports play a big part in most of our lives, whether we participate or just watch. In my life, sports have taught me several important lessons. Just think. You learn how to deal with loss. You learn how to work as a team. I chose examples from sports, because of its ability to connect people from all walks of life. Another compelling reason I chose sports analogies is the data.

Our society's obsession with sports has created a vast database of success evidence. Every effort is contained in the data. We keep track of wins and losses. We keep track of points. Every touchdown is documented. This presents a unique opportunity to quantify success more tangibly. The data from the rest of society isn't so clear. Many successful people are broke. Others, who aren't very successful, have millions. Only using money, as a measure of success, wouldn't give us such stark success contrast. Nobody would argue on a basketball level that Michael Jordan was not successful. By using objective data from sports, we can analyze the characteristics of successful people, instead of debating the merits of success.

What roles do science and mathematics play in describing success pursuit?

Math and science give us a great framework for investigation. Unfortunately, human behavior doesn't always lend itself to mathematic and scientific analysis. Science, in particular, gives us a framework to assess human behavior. To the degree we can, we can apply the scientific experimental model to the study of success. Science and math give us the ability to analyze behaviors. We can then collate them into their related subgroups. Like behaviors and unlike behaviors can be observed, their causality can be interpreted.

Science also gives us rules about how to perform a scientific inquiry. We start with a question. That question leads to hypotheses. We can then determine the structure of the experiment and decide what we will measure. We measure results and develop a conclusion. Human behavior isn't that cut and dried, but it's a good starting point. At the end of the day, human beings don't always behave predictably. That said.

We can attempt to codify human behavior. Through observation, we can find patterns and trends that allow a better understanding. Specifically, analysis in this way can help us understand success pursuit.

Lastly, the hallmark of scientific inquiry is reproducibility. If we can find success behaviors that exist amongst a group of successful people, then we can reproduce success. At least that is the theory. The next step of the experiment would be to evaluate those people who read the book and employ its practices. Theoretically, they should have a greater degree of success after employing the Maniacal Fanaticism strategies.

Blame and the inward chip aren't typically considered successful traits. Do you believe they create successful people?

Absolutely! The inward chip and blame create the humility of success. These qualities are the opposite of hubris. What was evident, in all MFers, is the fanatical need to improve. You have to doubt yourself a little bit if you are going to endeavor to get better. The inward chip and blame separate Maniacal Fanaticism from other success pursuits. The inward chip creates the motivation to improve. Blame internally assigns responsibility for all results, even the negative ones.

Michael Jordan's inward chip fueled his competitive fire. It's what spun his Flywheel to get better. These traits have their limits. If they leak out to the other phases of the Flywheel, success is much more difficult. Even the best basketball player in the world was trying to get better. That is how the inward chip and blame create successful people.

What inspired you to write this book?

The inspiration for this book was my family. My wife and two children, my parents, my sister, and my grandparents all inspired me to write this book. Our family principle is that no one can work harder than we do. We still believe that hard work can conquer all. No matter how long it takes, no matter how bumpy the road, we will prevail. My grandmother used to say that it will be long, but not forever. This is the kind of work ethic that I was raised with. Although our lives have been filled with variable success, we are never defeated.

During one summer, my son participated in fourteen basketball camps and had four days off the entire summer. My wife chased her dreams across the country, traveling from California to Ohio. My grandfather would stay up for days at a time sewing suits to make a living. As a family, we believe that socioeconomic status and access to success aren't static. Your only limit is how hard you are willing to work. I remember playing basketball in middle school and showing up for practice at six in the morning. The practice didn't start until eight. The janitor would let me in, and I would shoot and shoot and shoot. I am no Michael Jordan, but I was always taught to maximize the talents I had. This family history is what inspired me to test this hypothesis. It inspired me to develop this theory.

Are you an MFer?

My knee jerk answer is to say no. I believe I've stumbled on something great. I am just starting to get it implemented in my life. I used Maniacal Fanaticism to write this book, trying to recognize where on the Flywheel I was. When I wrote this, I would say I was a level one. I am just starting to understand the nuances of the Flywheel. I am learning how to accelerate it and avoid decelerating it. It's a work in progress. At times, I feel like a golf coach. I know what to teach about the swing and how the swing should look. Executing a perfect swing is an entirely different matter. I spend every day studying, learning, and trying to be an MFer. I am constantly trying to perfect my swing.

How did you develop the term MFer?

MFer stands for Maniacal Fanatic and is pronounced em-eff-er. Truth is. I didn't want to type the entire word every time I referred to this subgroup of people. After using it once or twice, the name stuck. And it stands out.

The novel is divided into three books: Videre, Unum, and Docent. What does that mean, and why did you divide the novel into three books?

In the medical field, these three words describe how we learn. Videre is Latin for see one. Unum is Latin for do one. Docent is Latin for teach one. This is a known scientific procedure for learning. I tried to apply that learning style to the study of success and the study of MFers. See what MFers do. Do what MFers do. Teach what MFers do.

What's next for you?

I can't sit still. The next book in the series is *Maniacal Fanaticism, a Path to Leadership*. If you look at Michael Jordan, Jerry Rice, Barry Sanders, Ernest Shackleton, and the other individuals I pointed out in this book, what you will find is that they are all great leaders. Many of the theories that apply to success also apply to leadership. If you remember the chapter on the levels of Maniacal Fanaticism, you see that level three, and level four MFers have a propensity to lead. They influence people, and that is what leadership is all about. My name, Imamu Osei, is of eastern African origin and means noble leader. Because of that, leadership has always intrigued me. I think it will be interesting to apply the theory to leadership. Once those traits are identified, we can then use them in our own leadership growth and development.

Is there one message that you are trying to convey?

I think Winston Churchill said it best: "Success is not final. Failure is not fatal: it is the courage to continue that counts." If readers take one message from this book, it should be this. No matter who you are, you can succeed. It just requires some courage. Success requires the courage to continue. Success requires the courage to be better than your draft pick.

You can be greater than the sum of your parts. Extraordinary people are extraordinary because of their extraordinary effort. Most of our limits to success are self-inflicted. Success isn't the end, and failure won't kill you. It's all about your courage. It's all about the courage to challenge yourself. Be more than you are. That statement truly embodies the entire theory.

<1%

www.ingramcontent.com/pod-product-compliance
Lightning Source LLC
LaVergne TN
LVHW091546040926
847245LV00002B/10
9798891882676